# Heaven and Earth

# Heaven and Earth

## THE LAST FARMERS OF THE NORTH FORK

Steve Wick

PHOTOGRAPHS BY

Lynn Johnson

ST. MARTIN'S PRESS ❧ NEW YORK

Book design by Gretchen Achilles

Marks originally made on land deeds by the Corchaug Indians were reproduced by
Ron Barrett.

*Endpaper*   Courtesy Map Division, New York Public Library, Astor, Lenox, and
Tilden Foundations

*Frontispiece photo*   Bounty of the potato fields: Andrew Dzenkowski, Sr., September 20, 1935. Photograph by Charles Meredith. Courtesy of the Southold Historical
Society.

Library of Congress Cataloging-in-Publication Data

Wick, Steve.
    Heaven and earth : the last farmers of the North Fork / by Steve Wick ;
    photographs by Lynn Johnson.—1st ed.
        p.     cm.
    ISBN 0-312-14352-4
    1. Farm life—New York (State)—Cutchogue Region.   2. Farms, Small—New
York (State)—Cutchogue Region.   3. Farmers—New York (State)—Cutchogue
Region.   4. Wickham, John, 1908–1994.   5. Cutchogue Region (N.Y.)—History.
I. Title.
S521.5.N7W53   1996
974.7'25—dc20                                                             96-4328
                                                                         CIP

FIRST EDITION: June 1996

10  9  8  7  6  5  4  3  2  1

ALSO BY STEVE WICK

*Bad Company: Drugs, Hollywood, and the Cotton Club Murder*

To Larisa, Kathryne, and Andrew
and to Chris Sidor

And to the memory of
WILLIAM TUTHILL
1950–1972

EDWARD TUTHILL
1954–1973

WILLIAM S. WICKHAM
1955–1966

And to the memory of
JOHN WICKHAM
1908–1994
Truly, he was a good man.

# CONTENTS

# ACKNOWLEDGMENTS

In the winter of 1987, I began talking to John Wickham about the history of his family and the land they have farmed since the late 1600s. I am grateful for the long hours he gave me, the many family letters, papers, and other documents he shared with me, and for his encouragement to write about the history of the farm families whose roots go all the way back to the seventeenth century.

My thanks also go to many people who helped with research and the finding of key documents, including: James Axtell, David Cressy, Ken Homan, David Kerkhof, Karen Kupperman, Kevin McBride, Dale Moyer, Wendy Reeve, Michaeleen St. John, Parnel Wickham-Searl, Gaynell Stone, John Strong, Virginia Wells, Anne Wickham, and William Wickham.

This is a book about a small pocket of farmers on the North Fork of Long Island. The book's emphasis on the remaining farmers in Mattituck and Cutchogue excluded many other farmers in the region. I hope by telling the stories of a few that I have captured the heart and soul of a much larger story. My apologies to those farmers whose names do not appear in this book.

*If this land be not rich,*
*then is the whole world poore.*

— THOMAS MORTON

*The potato harvest the hard way, October 1935. Photograph by Charles Meredith. Courtesy of the Southold Historical Society.*

# Preface

JULY 1994. ALL month it is hot. Late in the day most afternoons, a dry wind blows across the land as thunderstorms roar past the saltwater sides of the North Fork. Over the ocean, great white thunderclouds sweep across the sky like mountaintops uncoupled from the earth.

But there is no rain, only distant rumblings that herald nothing. On dark nights near the end of the month, there is fire from heaven as far-off electrical storms sweep out to sea like great armies fleeing an uncertain battlefield. The sky spits nothing toward earth.

On his farm between the salt creeks, Tom Wickham is up early starting irrigation pumps. His neighbors, David Steele and John Tuthill, also get up early, David to start his pumps and John to cut hay. The Tuthill farm and the Wickham farm are not far apart, maybe a mile and a half across flat, rich farmland. Wickham is a fruit farmer, and he is selling more than two dozen varieties at his Cutchogue, Long Island, farm stand. But he must wet down the land all day, moving pipes from orchard to orchard, stopping for dinner, shutting off the pumps late at night.

David is principally a potato farmer. He farms land that has been in the Tuthill family for generations. Once, there were so many Tuthills they had a community of their own: Tuthill Town. But the residents are mostly gone today, their community's existence a wisp of history kept alive in the memories of some old men. This family goes all the way back to an Englishman who arrived in a shallow-draft boat from the Connecticut mainland in the 1640s.

There is a green checkerboard of farmland east and north of where David has his potatoes. North is the good ground once owned by the bachelor Tuthill brothers, Stanley and Leslie. Best potato land anywhere, people say. East and south of David's home, connected by a dirt road, David has potatoes planted on Sigmund "Ziggy" Kurkoski's farm, where a deep kettle-hole pond sits lushly along an edge of trees. East and south of the Kurkoski farm, there are potatoes on the old Horton farm, a low spot of trees and brush anchoring one corner of it.

East of Horton land, there's hay on Bill Wickham's farm. Since a group of Englishmen led by a minister arrived on the North Fork in 1640, only two families have held title to this Wickham land, the Hortons and the Wickhams—two families in three and a half centuries.

Mornings and afternoons on hot summer days, David rides the edges of his potato land in his pickup, sometimes alone, sometimes with his sons or his daughter along for the ride.

For years, since he was a young boy without a father at home, David worked for John Tuthill. Now, Tuthill, a man of few words, eighty years old and slow in his legs, works for David. The cold hand of fate has changed their destinies, reversed their roles.

This summer, as it has been for so many summers, John Tuthill is the last Tuthill to farm this fertile North Fork land. Tuthill Town is now only a place in his heart.

Working with David is a black man named Eddie Clark. He is from Arkansas, and he came to Cutchogue two decades ago to work on farms. He lives alone, away from the labor camps where other black men live.

This is a bad summer for him. The only kidney he's got is failing. Most mornings, his fingers are swollen, the backs of his hands puffy. He has utterly no expectations of getting much past fifty.

I'm okay if I sweat, he says.

Still, he works all day—plowing, moving irrigation pipes, cutting hay in hot fields where the purple martins fill the air, stacking bales in quiet barns.

The dry summer is now the worst on record—that's what the government keeps saying. Worst anyone can remember. It causes tensions to rise, bills to go up. Irrigation pumps blow up; tractors break down. The heat hates mechanical equipment.

Prices are good when Frank McBride, grandson of an Irishman who came to Cutchogue a few days after the battle of Gettysburg, begins to dig up his potatoes. And they are still good when Martin Sidor, the grandson of a Polish man who walked nearly the entire length of Long Island to find his good ground, begins to dig up his potatoes. It is early to dig, but they like the good prices, pushed up by the heat.

As he bags his potatoes in his barn near a supermarket, Marty thinks: If my grandfather had had a few more good years, he'd have built another barn or bought more land; if my father had had a few more good years, he'd have bought a tractor; if I had a few more good years, I could pay my bills.

At the labor camp alongside the Cutchogue railroad tracks, a small group of black men and a raw-gummed white man begin their mornings waiting in the heat for the potato trucks to rumble in. Some of these men, their roots in the rural South, have known little else but labor-camp lives, rotgut liquor, and sleeping it off until the next workday. Some gamble too much. On any given day, there isn't three dollars' worth of change in their pockets.

But soon they will begin to sort and bag potatoes in the noisy, dusty-hot barn that sits alongside the tracks like a museum to the fading away Long Island potato industry.

Somebody ought to close up this building and leave it just as it is as a reminder of what went on here.

This was the second summer of drought. This one was worse.

The dry spell had broken in 1993 in mid-September with nightlong deluges. After a night of rain, the mornings would be still, and then late in the afternoon a wall of blue rain would come out of the western sky.

Early one September morning that year when the land north of the big Wickham house was wet, I drove down the lane to find John Wickham. The morning light gathered on the creek behind the house, then flowed outward through the orchards and the open land. Vaporous clouds of mist rose from the damp land as the soul of the earth breathed life into the morning.

John Wickham was waiting for me behind the house. Well over six feet tall, with angular and lean features, John was standing near his barn. His face was brown from weeks of working in the hot sun. Inside the house, Jim Barr, a retired Presbyterian minister, was sipping coffee at the kitchen table. Tom, John's son, had just walked in, having pushed stumps into piles since sunup. We shook hands, and he said, "We'll get our coffee later."

John and I drove north from the house along the lane toward his family's farm stand.

I knew that John Wickham, Tom, other family members, and employees who worked the

Wickhams' 250-acre Cutchogue farm had been running crazy the last three months, trying to keep water flowing. From the east side of Wickham Creek, near where I live, I had heard the pumps humming late at night and early in the morning.

Looking at the rainwater pooled along the road, he said, "That was a good rain last night—more than an inch. I think the dry spell might be over. I'm quite surprised it lasted this long."

I had been talking to John Wickham, eighty-four years of age this September morning, and writing down his thoughts about his family's farm and his history on a stretch of remarkably productive farmland on the North Fork of Long Island, two hours east of New York City.

Along with a small number of other farmers in Cutchogue and elsewhere on the North Fork, a peninsula of rich topsoil that sticks like a bony finger into the Atlantic Ocean, Wickham can trace his history back to the Englishmen who arrived in the fall of 1640 with the purpose of setting up a religious colony, a heaven on earth, where God's rules would apply to religious as well as civil life. They named their town Southold, after the farming and fishing community of Southwold, England, the town from which their minister had fled three years earlier. This stretch of ground was to be their Kingdom of God, away from the religious bickering in the churches around Boston.

Led by their minister, the Englishmen crossed Long Island Sound—"the North Sea," they called it—and landed on the sandy bayside of the North Fork. An island lay to the south and east, close to them; past it, in the green distance, shimmering above the water like a vision, another island. Directly south, another peninsula, another deep, mysterious forest. John Winthrop's explorers had been in these waters in 1633, in the bark *Blessing of the Bay.* They presumably knew how far the bay ran to the west, that another island, small and wooded, was tucked in between points of land, and that it ended in a bog of freshwater surrounded by pine trees.

Where the minister's group landed on the North Fork, the forest ran to the salt grass, thick and green. They were the sole white people for miles. The Dutch were on the island of Manhattan, one hundred miles to the west, but out here there was but one other Englishman, an engineer named Lion Gardiner, who for a black dog and enough rum to do the job had coaxed from the native Algonquins the island to the east of them. The Indians called it the Island of Death; the English called it the Isle of Wight before Gardiner, now the lord of his own manor, blessed it with his family name.

On the North Fork, the land was flat and rich, fertile, and almost free of rocks, the way it wasn't farther north along the New England coastline. To their endless joy, the English found large tracts of open meadows that had been cleared by the Indians for use as cropland. They also found the native population low, the result of such factors as diseases brought to New England by the English and spread to the North Fork by other Indians. This was the way God wanted it, surely—one people leaves and another people arrives. God had cleared title to this newfound land for His people. They built a church, made their own rules, and proclaimed God the ruler of their lives.

The native people, whom the English, in their fumbling attempts to understand Algonquin, called Corchaugs, were smooth-talked out of their land and given throwaway trinkets and rum to induce them to scratch odd-looking symbols on pieces of parchment rich in English phrases. The land was no longer theirs; their history was over. The new landowners divided up the soil into large tracts, cleared dense stands of oak and maple trees, and established farms they would carefully maintain through the generations.

Today, more than 350 years later, their descendants are among the oldest farm families in the United States.

In the mid-nineteenth century, English farmers were followed to the North Fork by Irish farmers—men like Owen McBride—who bought land along the wooded bluffs overlooking Long Island Sound. By the turn of this century, Polish farmers—men like Peter Kurkoski—began to arrive as farmworkers. Quickly, they bought up the Irish farms, along with many farms of old English families.

By the mid-1980s, after years of fluctuating potato prices coupled with a sharp rise in land values, many of the second- and third-generation Poles gave up on farming. Some sold to sod companies, speculators or home builders, or to businessmen who planted grapes for a nascent wine industry.

There are scarcely a dozen traditional farmers remaining in Cutchogue and nearby Mattituck, and perhaps a total of three dozen on the North Fork. Where there were some fifty thousand acres of potatoes three decades ago, today there are fewer than seven thousand. In Cutchogue, the very heart of the North Fork, there were seventy working farms at one time; today, a handful of men still work this land.

Yet the sturdiness of these farmers, along with the productivity of their land, is attested to by the simple fact that this small region produces more food than any other area of New York State. The outwash soil is the finest in the state, and among the finest in the country.

This book is witness to the lives of these farmers. These are stubborn men who do not give up easily. They seek to hold on to their land, to pass it on to their children, and to continue their history for as long as they can.

On this September morning, John Wickham and I sat and talked in the car. In an hour or so, the farm stand would open, and peaches and cherries, apples, tomatoes, and corn would be brought out and displayed.

"This is considered the home farm, and part of it is in what was called the Broadfields, the area the English found had been cleared by the Indians," he said, his words flowing like a clear river. He held up his long arms, his large hands opened wide, to draw boundaries in the humid air.

Just west of the John Wickham farm is his cousin Bill's farm. They are both very old farms, steeped in the long history of the family. Yet each tract of land has its own flesh-and-blood story.

"This is the farm my father farmed, and the farm my brother Parker was farming at the time of his death. It is the land from the main road, back to the salt water, and along the west edge of the creek."

Parker Wickham, the oldest of James Wickham's three boys, died in a car accident as he and his brother raced to a fire in April 1930. A newspaper account, published a few days after the accident, read: "John, a brother of James, was driving the car, and it is believed that brakes applied too suddenly caused the car to turn over." This morning, I did not ask him about Parker's death, because we had discussed it before and he had reacted emotionally. That day, we had talked about fate and his faith, the mysteries of God's will, and how it was possible that a single family had stayed on the same piece of farmland for so long.

John Wickham's ancestors were Congregationalists. His faith was simple, unadorned. He believed absolutely in God. Few things were as clear as that. He believed in his family, deeply so, and in his land, this old family land. He felt a spiritual kinship with the first Wickham to arrive in Cutchogue, a man named Joseph, who bought a house and a farm a few hundred yards to the west. Joseph's house sat in a low spot in the road, woods to the north, cleared land to the south and west.

Love of this land entered John's bloodstream through his mother's milk. History was taken on faith. He was firmly, completely anchored into the flesh and blood of his history. He was utterly free of self-doubt. He believed this: Fate is a winding road you travel in the dark with an open heart.

His family's past built up behind him like a great wave, bringing with it all who had lived here, all who had farmed here. First the Indians, who left so much of their history in the soil; then Wells, Booth, Reeve, Albertson, James Wickham, William Wickham, another James Wickham, Parker Wickham, John Wickham, and Tom Wickham.

"William Wickham, my grandfather, died young. And my father, James . . . well, you know I was very young when he died. I remember my mother taking her three sons by our hands to the front of the church. We were stunned with grief. But our mother said we had to say good-bye to him. That's just how she put it—'You have to say good-bye to your father.'"

James Wickham was buried in the Cutchogue Cemetery, and on this morning, John and I drove there to stand in the shade of a row of stately trees. A tall granite obelisk marked the Wickham plot. We had talked about James's death from blood poisoning ("I remember so much crying in the house"), and William's, too, also from blood poisoning. I mentioned his grandfather's front-page obituary, which described him "as the best known man in Suffolk County." There was this line in it: "Truly, he was a good man. . . ."

Tall, erect, John stood in silence, reflective, pulled deep within himself, swept up in the river of his history. The words "Truly, he was a good man" caused the smile to run away from his face. As we stood there, the church bells atop the Methodist church on the south edge of the cemetery began to toll, the sweet music flowing across the land like angels' wings. I don't think he heard it, though; he was not listening.

Finally, he said, "It has occurred to me that I am living out my father's life, the life he didn't have, even as I have lived my own. I believe I am the farmer he wanted to be."

The farm stand was open when we returned. The pale sun was over the cupola of the barn, sweeping away the mist and the drops of moisture in the humid air. We sat in the car and watched his workers unloading baskets brimming with peaches. It looked this morning as if the world could come to this spot and eat its fill.

"Parker's dying made me a farmer. That was his fate; this farm was my fate. The afternoon he died, I walked behind a team of horses and plowed the field north of the house. There was an expression my mother had: 'Let the horses run.' Over the years, it grew to mean you had to let your feelings go; you had to get on with it. Life goes on—that's the eternal mystery of it.

"Years later, my brother Henry—and he was successful and had not lived on this farm since he was a boy—said to me, 'John, if anything happens to you, I'll come home.' He was ready to take *my* place."

These were just nine words, but they had summed up the family's history over all the generations that Wickhams had farmed in Cutchogue.

All July 1994, there is heat. There is fire but no rain. By month's end and into August, the hay is cut and stacked in the big barns. On a warm morning, the sun floating above the tree line east of Ziggy Kurkoski's farm, David Steele begins to dig up his potatoes.

John Tuthill is there at first light, the sky milky with clouds and humidity. He is standing behind the digger, leaning against it to support his old legs. He is a courtly man, a farmer all his life. He stands there silently, drawn inward, like a man saying good-bye.

It begins again now—it goes on—another harvest from this good ground. The clanky digger lurches forward, ripping at the earth, pulling up the potatoes, sending them into the truck. Two and a half passes up and down the field and the truck is so full, it can barely move, lurching side to side as it moves up the dirt road, over the railroad tracks, toward the barn where the black men are waiting.

Inside the potato grader, the workers from the labor camp are getting back into the routine: loud morning voices; broken voices; the dusty, wet smell of potatoes moving up the ramp; the noise of the machinery. Trucks fat with potatoes are lining up outside.

# PART ONE

# Newfound Land

*This question they oft put to me:*
*Why come the Englishmen hither?*

—ROGER WILLIAMS

# ONE

# Contact

IN THE LATE fifteenth century, English fishermen began pushing farther and farther west across

the mysterious vastness of the Atlantic Ocean. Sometimes it was the pursuit of fish to fill their nets

that sent them farther than they had gone before. Other times, it was wind that pushed them,

pushed them so far that rocky outcroppings appeared before them, rising up from the horizon like

the gates to the promised land.

This newfound land, as they called it, was a place of wonder to these men, who knew only crowded cities and poor countrysides. Rivers filled with fish flowed into the sea. Islands covered with dark forests sat along the edges of coastlines with deep, clear harbors, beckoning these Europeans to drop anchor and come ashore.

Badly in need of new fishing grounds, Bristol fishermen had become experts fishing in the distant waters off Iceland. Soon they were moving to the west, striking the rocky islands north of what today is Cape Cod. Their voyages may have begun in the 1480s, a decade before Columbus made his historic voyages. A book published in London in 1622, *The History of the Reign of King Henrie the Seventh,* states:

> And there had been before that time [1492] a discovery of some lands, which they took to be islands, and were indeed the continent of America, towards the Northwest. And it may be that some relation of this nature coming afterwards to the knowledge of Columbus, and by him suppressed, (desirous rather to make his Enterprise the Child of his Science and Fortune, than the follower of a former discovery) did give him better assurance, that all was not sea, from the west of Europe and Africa unto Asia.

Following the fishermen, explorers intent on staking claims to the newfound land appeared on the horizon. John Cabot lived in Bristol, a port where the spirit of discovery and exploration ran high. Under a patent from the Crown, Cabot sailed from Bristol in 1497, striking the North American coastline near Cape Breton Island. Members of his crew went ashore and found snares set by the Indians to catch deer and other animals, along with a fire pit. He returned the following year, but little is known of this voyage.

Cabot's son, Sebastian, passed along the American coastline in 1509, marveling at its great beauty. He was deeply impressed by the immense quantities of fish, more fish than any European country could ever consume. Somewhere on the northern coastline, he dropped anchor and went ashore to meet the Indians, who he said were "clothed in skins and not anywhere devoid of intelligence." Contact had now been made between Europeans and the Algonquins, who had lived along the coastline for thousands of years.

In 1524, Giovanni da Verrazano, an Italian-born navigator in the service of France, explored the coastline near present-day North Carolina. He proceeded north, hugging the shoreline as close as he could, slipping past the sandy coast of New Jersey and entering New York Bay, possibly the first European to do so. He was struck by the wooded island at the top of the bay: ". . . a very agreeable place between two small but prominent hills; between them a very wide river, deep at its mouth, flowed out into the sea." As his ship entered the Hudson River, Indians appeared from the shoreline.

> . . . we took the boat and entering the river we found the country on the banks well peopled, the inhabitants not differing much from the others, being dressed out with the feath-

ers of birds of various colors. They came towards us with evident delight, raising loud shouts of admiration and showing us where we could most securely land our boat. We passed up this river about half a league, where we found it formed a most beautiful lake, upon which they were rowing thirty or more of their small boats filled with multitudes who came to see us.

After leaving the Hudson River, he moved east along the coast of Long Island, past the high green moraine at the tip of the South Fork, and close to Block Island. Everywhere, he saw Indians in great numbers plying the waters in their dugout canoes. In Newport Harbor, those who ventured close to his ship were given trinkets in exchange for maize and other food. His sailors noticed that some of the native people wore copper ornaments. So taken was he by the harbor and the islands around it that he stayed for fifteen days.

Sir Humphrey Gilbert, a veteran of the English campaigns in Ireland, proposed the theory that a ship could sail around the new continent by way of a northwest passage. In 1578, under the authority of Queen Elizabeth I, Gilbert set out for North America. His first voyage failed, but on a subsequent voyage he entered what is now St. John's Harbor, Newfoundland, where a group of fishermen had earlier set up a base, and took possession of the land in the name of his queen.

English efforts to secure a hold on this continent were now in full swing. It had been an accident of wind and tide that had brought them here, but soon they began arriving with greater and greater frequency, staking ownership to land they claimed to have discovered, even though it had been populated for thousands of years.

Looking for homelands, two ships owned by Sir Walter Raleigh, Gilbert's half brother, explored the sandy isles off the North Carolina coastline in 1584. Contact was made with the Indians, who took the English to their villages on Roanoke Island. Late in the summer, one of the ships set sail for England, carrying two Indians, who were put on display after the ship reached home. The site looked good for a future colony, which Raleigh believed he could fill by advertising its potential in England's poor rural countryside, where farmers were economically depressed and where wood was in short supply.

In July 1587, a large group of colonists returned to the island, but this time something happened. When Raleigh returned for them later, they were gone, presumably murdered by the Indians.

Up and down the Northeast coastline, explorers set foot on land, claiming it for England. In some cases, the explorers pushed deep up rivers like the Penobscot, in Maine, where one English vessel sailed twenty-seven miles to raid an Abenaki village and steal moose hides.

The Indians, whom the English regarded as poor users of the land and therefore not its legal owners, were not a consideration in terms of English law. They were more of a curiosity—they were in the way. Verrazano seems to have taken at least one Indian back to France, and the year after his trip, in 1525, a Spanish explorer named Estevao Gomes, traveling the shores of Cape Cod and Maine, grabbed a large number of Indians; fifty-eight were alive when his ship docked in Spain.

By the late 1590s and early 1600s, kidnapped Algonquins began appearing in London as sideshow attractions. On an afternoon in September 1603, a group of Algonquins gave a demonstration of their canoe skills on the Thames River. David Beers Quinn, in his *England and the Discovery of America, 1481–1620*, writes of this curious incident. "What we can reconstruct of the story would seem to be that on 2 or 3 September a Thames boat . . . came upstream from some distance down the river, having in tow or on board an American Indian canoe . . . and also two or more Amerindians, whose description as 'Virginians' could mean at this time that they came from anywhere between Cape Fear and Maine."

They may have come from the area well south of Maine, as three well-known explorers—Bartholomew Gosnold, Bartholomew Gilbert, and Gabriel Archer—had the year before ventured along the coasts of Maine and Massachusetts. Gosnold landed at an island now called Cuttyhunk, where he cut sassafras to take back to England. Another explorer, Martin Pring, was on Cape Cod in the spring of 1603, the same year Richard Hakluyt set up a camp on the site of the future Plymouth Colony.

Well before 1600, reports circulated in England describing the "new" England across the Atlantic as a lush and promising place. Pamphlets were published trumpeting the land as fertile, the sea filled with fish. One account described the region as "like England in certain basic ways . . . though a warmer and less rainy England." Companies were formed to raise funds to support colonies and business enterprises. One major enterprise, the Virginia Company, was granted a charter in April 1606. That summer, a number of vessels left England, some with Indians returning to their homeland as guides.

As a group of Englishmen settled on rich farmland in Virginia, Henry Hudson, an English explorer hired by the Dutch, staked claim to the island at the head of New York Bay. In September 1609, Hudson sailed his *Half Moon* into the bay. One of his men, John Coleman, went ashore and was killed by Indians—the first fatality in a war that would not end for nearly three centuries. Hudson retaliated, killing scores of Indians near Manhattan Island.

After Hudson returned to exploring for the English, Adriaen Block, a Dutchman, arrived in the region claimed by Hudson for the Dutch, to begin trade with the Indians. Like Hudson, Block sailed up the Hudson River almost to where Albany sits today, then turned around. Near the southern tip of Manhattan, Block's boat caught fire. Ashore somewhere, his men cut timber and built another boat, a monumental achievement.

Aboard their new ship, they slipped through a narrow passage they named Hellegat and on into Long Island Sound. They discovered the Connecticut River, a huge flow of clear water running out of the northern forest, and sailed into Narragansett Bay. It is likely they explored the waters off eastern Long Island and set foot on land.

After their rescue by another Dutch ship, a map was drawn that showed the details of the southern New England coast. On the map was a long island poking into the Atlantic east of Manhattan Island. At its eastern end, it was split into two forks, one north and one south.

TWO

# The Migration

WHEN THE PILGRIMS left England in 1620, they thought they were traveling to Virginia, to the

black-soil region near the colony at Jamestown. Their ship, the *Mayflower*, traversed the Atlantic

Ocean to the north, sighting the eastern tip of Cape Cod, far to the north of their destination. They

were within the wide boundaries of the area the English who supported colonization called Vir-

ginia, but as far as they knew, they had made landfall in an undiscovered country.

To the contrary, groups of explorers had been landing on the northern coast, traveling inland on freshwater rivers, for a long time. In some instances, coastal Algonquins, the true discoverers of the area, spoke French, English, and even Basque when they approached explorers. By 1620, the area from the mouth of the Connecticut River, south toward the two forks at the eastern end of Long Island and the heavily wooded islands near where the forks opened their arms to the sea, and on to the northern reaches of Maine and into Canada was known to explorers.

The Pilgrims, having left England to live in Holland for a number of years, were likely sheltered from the abundance of reports of exploration in the newfound land. Shortly after landing on Cape Cod, however, they found how little they knew of who had preceded them. Near where the *Mayflower* dropped anchor off Cape Cod, the Pilgrims found "a place like a grave" that was covered with boards. "Digging it up, they found layer upon layer of household goods, the personal possessions that Indians ordinarily buried with their dead: mats, bowls, trays, dishes, a bow, and two bundles," writes William Cronon in his book *Changes in the Land*. The account continues:

> In the smaller of the two bundles was a quantity of sweet-smelling red powder in which were the bones of a young child, wrapped in beads and accompanied by an undersized bow. Still, what troubled the graverobbers were not these Indian things, many of which they took, but the contents of the larger bundle. There, in the same red powder, were the remnants of a man: some of the flesh remained on the bones, and they realized with a shock that the "skull had fine yellow haire still on it." With the bones, "bound up in a saylers canvas Casacke, and a payre of cloth breeches," were a knife, a needle, and "two or three old iron things," evidently the dead man's most personal belongings. A blond European sailor, shipwrecked or abandoned on the Massachusetts coast, had lived as an Indian, had perhaps fathered an Indian child, and had been buried in an Indian grave.

Who was this blond man? He was probably a Frenchman whose ship had wrecked in the area near Plymouth several years earlier. Most of the crew had probably been killed; it is possible a number of them survived and then lived like Indians. He could also have been an Englishman, perhaps from one of John Smith's ships. According to historian James Axtell, in 1614, one of Smith's captains kidnapped perhaps as many as twenty Algonquins, selling them into slavery in Spain. One was an Indian who would use the anglicized name Squanto. Somehow, Squanto traveled from Spain to England, where he boarded a ship and returned to Cape Cod. There, in 1620, he greeted the Pilgrims, speaking English.

The area of salt water, islands, and sandy points of land from Long Island north to Maine represented an earthly paradise to the English. To many Englishmen pigeonholed by the class system, England was a worn-out country. By the early seventeenth century, the great forests were cleared, the exception being the royal preserves. But these were off limits to ordinary men, and England was largely a country of ordinary men.

By 1602, Englishmen in even the smallest villages knew that a new land had been discovered on the far side of the Atlantic. It was a land described glowingly. In the summer of 1602, two Englishmen lived on Martha's Vineyard. It would seem likely they picked the island to stay on after exploring the surrounding waters, perhaps even the waters between the two forks at the eastern end of Long Island. They would not have come directly to Martha's Vineyard; they would have looked around, walked on other islands, then picked a location where they could spend the summer.

Upon their return, one of the men, John Brereton, published a pamphlet. In it, he described a place of great beauty and rich potential. He could have been describing Long Island, which had a similar geological history dating back to the last great grinding push across this region by a wall of ice.

His description of the farmland they found on Martha's Vineyard could have applied to the outwash soil of much of the region. Of this soil, he wrote: ". . . in comparison whereof the most fertile part of England is but barren." The land was "full of high timbered oaks . . . cedars straight and tall, beech, elm, holly, walnut trees in abundance." Of their summer on the island, Brereton could hardly find the words to describe it: "We stood a while like men ravished at the beauty and delicacy of this sweet soil."

There are explorers who walked on this land whose names and deeds were never recorded. But the history of New England, as well as that of the fertile fingers of Long Island, was not written by explorers. It was written by men who wanted to create their heavenly kingdom out of wilderness, far from the agents of the Crown, and far from the agents of the Church of England.

By 1580, separatism had emerged noisily in England. People who did not like the customs and practices of the official church, seeing in them the rituals of the Roman Catholic Pope in Rome, set up their own places of worship. Even earlier, English Catholics had had to pay a fine for refusing to recognize the Church of England. And by the mid-1580s, the archbishop of Canterbury had begun expelling separatists.

As the seventeenth century dawned in England, the split between separatist Protestants and mainstream Anglicans widened, but probably the split was never as wide as it has been described by many early historians. It is also certainly true that those thousands of people who left their homeland for New England prior to 1640 were more motivated by economic conditions, by the prospect of land without landlords and lives away from what the historian David Cressy calls the "social slavery" of the English manor system.

This is not to say religious squabbles did not play a factor in the migration. What fueled this dispute was the drive toward conformity orchestrated for the most part by an Anglican priest named William Laud, appointed to the post of bishop of London in 1628. Ordained in 1601, he loathed the philosophy of the separatists and demanded strict following of Anglican rituals. With the blessing of Charles I, Laud pushed separatists out of important positions in the church. He was a stern opponent of Calvinism, a philosophy that lay at the heart of the separatist movement.

While Laud is often singled out in the early histories of New England as the reason for the migration, the movement of ordinary men and women across the Atlantic began well before he took up his post in London. He was one reason for the migration, but he was not the only reason. Laud's man in Norwich, in the eastern part of the country, where thousands of emigrants would pack their bags, was Mathew Wren. Wren was considered strict, but when he came to power, East Anglia was experiencing severe economic strife due to, among other things, the collapse of the woolen industry. One community experiencing hardships was Southwold, located on the coast. There were years of bad harvests, the numbers of poor were burgeoning, and in the mid-1630s the plague reappeared like a message from God.

East Anglia was locked in this economic hardship when John Winthrop, a man of no particular stature in his own country and a lawyer, began promoting New England as a place that was "exceedingly good," with "as good land as I have seen." Food could be grown, wood could be cut, and homes for the common man could be carved out of wilderness. There were no classes in the wilderness. Winthrop saw New England as the home for the Englishmen who opposed the Church of England. It was to be a "Protestant showcase," David Cressy writes in his book *Coming Over,* and a "light to the world, a place of godly discipline and spiritual cleansing."

Even as Winthrop was touring eastern England to promote migrations, so was a clergyman named John Wilson, who lived in Suffolk, where the collapse of the woolen industry was keenly felt. Later an early settler in New England and a believer in this "Protestant showcase," he returned to sing its glories and to set in his countrymen's minds the romantic notion that those who wanted to escape the nosy bureaucrats of the Church of England should get on ships and leave.

By the time Laud was named archbishop of Canterbury in 1633, the great migration was in full swing. There was probably little he could do to stop it even after he became the leader of the church, and although regulations imposed by the king to control this exodus through licenses and permits may have made it more difficult to leave, they did not staunch the flow. By 1640, more than twenty thousand men, women, and children had left; in the spring, near the mouths of rivers and harbors, ships waiting for the tide and wind would line up as if waiting for a starting gun to be fired.

While there were great numbers of emigrants, ministers such as Wilson represented a tiny minority of them. Contrary to the commonly held belief that Protestant clergymen in England suffered in great numbers at the hands of Laud's henchmen, there were very few who had had trouble with episcopal authorities and sought to leave. According to Cressy, "Only 76 of the 10,000 ordained ministers in England joined the migration to New England, and of these only 47 had run into trouble with their episcopal superiors."

One of these ministers may have been a young man named John Youngs, who lived in Suffolk, near the village of Southwold. As an American descendant would write nearly three centuries later, John Youngs was a man of sobriety, with a strong religious conviction. Youngs's father was the Reverend Christopher Youngs, or Younges, as it was often spelled. The parish register also listed the family name as Yong, Yonge, Yonges, Younge, and Younges. Christopher Youngs was a man of position and authority who served as the vicar of Southwold and Reydon. From what can be learned of this man, he was an establishment minister, neither a radical nor one to throw his fist in the face of convention.

Southwold is on the east coast of England, twenty miles south of the port of Yarmouth. Reydon is two miles inland from Southwold. St. Edmund, the church at Southwold of which Christopher Youngs was the vicar, was built in 1460. In the early 1630s, as the great migration was under way, two thousand people lived in and around Southwold; many residents of this region crammed onto converted fishing boats and ships used to transport wine and headed west across the Atlantic Ocean.

Records at St. Edmund show that John Youngs had a sister, Elizabeth, who drowned in a boat accident. These records also list, in July 1622, the marriage of John Yonge and Joan Harrington. The couple's son, John, was baptized in 1625, on the tenth day of April; a second son, Thomas, was baptized in May. On the sixteenth of June the following year, Christopher Youngs, the vicar, was buried.

It would appear that John Youngs's brother Joseph was master of a ship named the *Love.* In July 1635, Joseph, his sister Mary, and her husband left for New England. Almost two years later, on the eleventh or twelfth of May, 1637, John Youngs, his wife, Joan, and their six children—John, Thomas, Anne, Rachel, Mary, and Joseph—applied for permission to leave from the port at Yarmouth, aboard the *Mary Anne.* The ship was packed with emigrants who were destined for Boston. Dozens of ships lay at anchor in the harbor, awaiting a favorable tide to carry them toward the Channel and out into the open ocean.

On board the *Mary Anne,* the commissioners who regulated emigration for the Crown evidently decided they did not like Youngs, for records show he was refused permission to leave the country. More than likely, though, his rejection had nothing to do with his being a minister; instead, it was probably because he was carrying incomplete paperwork.

In 1630, the Crown had ordered that no passenger could leave without first obtaining a license. Like any government, this one wished to raise money any way it could. It was, as Cressy points out, politically practical for the authorities to wish to regulate the emigration of thousands of subjects. The authorities might also have wished to note the emigrants' names and status for bookkeeping purposes. But within a few years, and certainly by the time John Youngs was applying for permission to board the *Mary Anne,* the government had begun to impose restrictions based on religious grounds.

One way to exert authority over a group of people who seemed determined to leave for a distant country was to require the passengers on board ships at anchor to recite their allegiances to the Crown and the official church. Even after ships were free to depart, captains were required to hold shipboard services using the Book of Common Prayer. By his actions, Laud manifested his concern that those who were willing to risk their lives on three-month voyages would be beyond the church's authority. But these procedures were easy to circumvent; port authorities were corrupt, and many ship captains refused to hold church services of any kind once their vessels began the westward journey.

As for John Youngs, who had supposedly been refused passage, he must have eventually met the paperwork requirements and boarded a ship bound for America. Three months later, on the fourteenth of August, Youngs was received as a new resident of Salem, Massachusetts. He was given an acre of rocky land on the edge of the settlement on which he was to begin his new American life.

*An undated photograph of John Wickham, taken, most likely, when he was a college student at Cornell University.*

# THREE

# God's Will

LATE ON A spring afternoon, John Wickham was alone in his farm stand in Cutchogue. Earlier in the day, a light rain had fallen, and now the sky was clear and dark blue, the air cool. The tops of trees and the roof of the old barn near the creek held the sunlight; by the farm stand, we stood in long shadows.

The rain had pushed away the crowds and he was preparing to close up, a southwest breeze shivering the pools of rainwater in the lane that ran to the house.

Quiet and dignified, John had the worldly air of a college professor retired from his teaching post and now home running the family farm. On Sunday afternoons, dressed in a suit, he reminded me of a Presbyterian minister. For a quarter century or more, he had been a Sunday school teacher at the Cutchogue Presbyterian Church, just west of the farm stand, across the street from the village green. His father's funeral had been held in this church. His father's father, William Wickham, had been an official of the church, but after siding with the minister in a dispute among church members over the minister's abolitionist sermons, he had led a stormy walkout. Across the street at the edge of the green, just north of the house that had been purchased by a distant ancestor, Joseph Wickham, William had erected a church for members who backed the minister. John never knew William Wickham. What he knew of this incident he picked up from old Cutchogue residents, from his aunt, Julia Wickham, and from a church history written by a neighbor named Ralph Tuthill. Not knowing the man did not stop John from respecting him, from loving him from a distance.

Like many educated men of his generation, John could recite passages from the Bible from memory. Seated in a quiet room in his house, he could lift his spirits reading from the New Testament. His college training was that of an engineer, like his brother Henry, with whom he had roomed at Cornell. But his mind was so steeped in history, and he was so well read, that he was a historian by avocation. His keen interest in history suited his farming life, and it always seemed when I talked to him that he was the voice of all the Wickhams before him. He was their spokesman, their advocate, living on this land of theirs more as a steward of their collective history than as a landowner.

As he put away baskets of apples, I asked him why the farm stand was not open on Sundays, a heavy tourist day. Wasn't there money to be made? He looked at me for a long moment and said, "Yes, we could do that. But tell me, which of the other of God's commandments would you want me to violate?" I never asked again.

After a moment, he said, "Can you smell the creek? The tide was out when I came up the lane a few minutes ago. Some days I can smell that mud all the way up here; other days I can't pick it up. Do you like that smell? When I was a child there was a boat at the top of the creek that had been my father's. It had such beautiful fittings. It was a wonderful playground for his sons. That salt creek has always meant a great deal to me."

John viewed his history in America as beginning with the arrival of the Pilgrims, whom he talked about often. He admired their bravery in crossing the ocean to live on a rocky shoreline with uncertain neighbors. In his mind, his farm, bracketed by two salt creeks, Wickham Creek and West Creek, was part of the same landscape the Pilgrims found in New England. This was his view because, as he looked backward toward the seventeenth century, he could see the men from whom he was descended, could follow their lives from England to Massachusetts and to the New Haven Colony in Connecticut and from there to the North Fork, and in their lives he could see his own. He lived out their lives as—and this was an article of faith with him—he lived out his father's and grandfather's lives, three men together in one life. But it was also true that he lived his brother Parker's life, a young man dead at twenty-three.

"There is so much in the Pilgrims' story that I admire," he had said one afternoon, adding quickly that he did not think they were the stiff-necked, humorless people they were often portrayed as. "They loved music, they loved books. They read history and followed politics and every-day events. They were Englishmen in their hearts, even when they were living on the Massachusetts coast far from home. I don't think they left that behind, and you know they wrote to England many times, and it's also quite obvious that the more affluent among them returned to their homes as often as they could. It would not surprise me if some of these Pilgrims returned once a year to take care of family business in the old country. As small and insular as their religious community was in New England, they remained connected to the world around them. They were not hermits by any means."

A woman drove up and bought a basket of apples and they chatted for a minute or two about the morning's rainfall. When she left, he closed up the farm stand and we stood by his station wagon. It was a bit darker now; the yellow light had fled the treetops.

"I've often thought just what it took to leave their own country, to set sail in small boats, most of them no longer than one hundred feet and no wider than perhaps twenty-five feet. Can you imagine how they felt as England faded over the horizon? They prayed the whole way, you can be certain of that."

They saw God in the journey itself, in the wind, the sea, he said.

"But what I've spent perhaps the most time thinking about is how they reacted when they first arrived at the very spot on which they would build Plymouth. That first day, that first night. It was fall, you must remember, and whatever food was on the ship was no doubt gone soon after their arrival. So they were looking at fear. Without the Indians showing them how to live on that land, they would have died off that first winter and that experiment might have died with them. Then what would have changed in our history?"

He looked south toward the house. "An Englishman named John Booth lived right here, where we are standing. From what I have learned of him, he was a well-to-do sugar trader, with interests in the Caribbean. Why he came to *this* spot, I would like to know. Would other Englishmen like Booth have come up this bay and found this land?"

South of the Massachusetts Bay Colony where the Reverend John Youngs first made his home lay a wilderness that to the English seemed unimaginably vast. Only its shoreline and the off-shore islands had been explored, with excursions up freshwater rivers toward the green interior. Most likely every freshwater stream was explored, if only to see where it went and if it led west. Maps generated by explorers showed rivers poking well north from the coast, but these were placed there mostly by guesswork and to show any potential competitors that the land was claimed. Indian tribal names were often included on maps, although very little was known of these interior Indians, except those who traveled to the seacoast to collect shells from which to make wampum.

Beginning in the early 1630s, Englishmen put off by religious squabbles among the churches in the Massachusetts Bay Colony, as well as by shortages of good farmland, began probing south along Indian trails that followed the coastline. In and around Boston, there was turmoil. There were strong feelings among some Puritans that the old colony had lost its way, had wandered away from the one true path. Groups were beginning to splinter off. In London, where pamphlets by critics of the colony appeared, rumors spread that the New England colony would soon fail.

In New England, some argued that a stricter religious colony was needed, and there were many people who longed to fill it. For them, there was only one direction to go—south, to where they knew freshwater ran into salt. Along riverbanks and where the Indians had cleared away forests by fire, small settlements were soon constructed and trading posts set up.

There were at this time explorers plying the waters between Connecticut and Long Island, moving north and south and into the great river between the north and south forks of Long Island. One explorer whose name has been recorded was John Oldham, and he appears to have been a wanderer in search of new lands, trading with the Indians as he went.

On July 4, 1631, a bark named *Blessing of the Bay* was launched at "Mistick," a port on the Connecticut shoreline. Documents do not reflect where it was for the next two years, but the journal of Governor John Winthrop of Connecticut shows that on October 3, 1633, it returned. He wrote: "The bark *Blessing,* which was sent to the Southward, returned. She had been at an island over against Connecticut, called Long Island, because it is near fifty leagues long, the east part about ten leagues from the main, but the west end not a mile. There they had stores of the best wampampeak, both white and blue. The Indians there are a very treacherous people. They have many canoes so great as one will carry eighty men."

At no time in the next two decades would anyone else—at least anyone whose writings have been found—argue that the eastern Long Island Indians were treacherous. It is possible, then, that Winthrop, who did not record the name of the captain of the *Blessing* nor exactly where on Long Island he had visited, was referring to the Pequots, who lived on the Connecticut mainland and who considered these lands surrounding the "Great River" between the two forks part of their domain. They were the dominant group, and these islands of Long Island produced the best wampum in all of New England. If for no other reason, this one fact made these lands valuable to outsiders.

From the English point of view, what stood in the way of further colonization away from Boston were the Pequots. By the mid-1630s, the Pequots had had contact with Europeans since Adriaen Block had visited twenty years before. They also appear to have had contact with individual traders and businessmen. The English did not like them, perhaps because other native groups, like the Narragansetts, filled them with stories that these were savage people, prone to killing and torturing their captives.

This area along the southern New England coast was critical territory. Once secured from the Indians, it would open access to the twin forks at the eastern end of Long Island, which the Dutch had explored and mapped. It was also important because the bays and the islands between the two forks were an early American mint. Here, more than anywhere in the region, were the shells that, cut and polished, counted as money. Indians from as far west as the Ohio River Valley possessed this wampum. New England Indians coveted the shells for what they bought, and it was the Long Island Indians on both forks who controlled the mint itself. To the Dutch as well as the English, it was wampum that opened up the interior rivers and lakes to fur trading. Therefore, securing these lands became a goal of John Winthrop, Jr., and other Puritan leaders as a newer group of colonists moved into Connecticut.

To keep the natives from blocking expansion—and, secondarily, to keep the Dutch from expanding up the New England coastline from their base in New York—an Englishman living in Holland, Lion Gardiner, an engineer by trade, was summoned to erect a fort at Saybrook. He was a mercenary who thought stirring up the Indians like angry wasps was a foolish policy that would lead to bloodshed. He was also a man with a keen eye toward his own future, and, upon seeing the waters and lands of eastern Long Island, he realized he could establish a manor like those of rural England.

There was another mercenary who was in New England prior to Gardiner's arrival. His name was John Underhill, and later he would live on the North Fork. People who have studied local history regard him as an unsavory character. Born in England, Underhill had accompanied John Winthrop to Massachusets. There, Underhill had a checkered history, flouting the Puritans' strict community rules and siding with people who were opposed by the church leadership, such as Anne Hutchinson. She was a brilliant woman who had a different view of the covenant of grace and was punished for it. In spite of their critical view of Underhill, church leaders would find him useful.

As a mercenary, Underhill had a view of the Indians that could be considered extreme, even for the times. Like many men of his time and place, Underhill saw the hand of God in the slaughter of the Indians whose land the English coveted. He also saw his place in history, which he attempted to secure in a lengthy manuscript, published in London in 1638, entitled *News from America*. In it, he wrote of "that insolent and barbarous Nation, called the Pequeats, whom by the sword of the Lord, and a few feeble instruments, soldiers not accustomed to war, were drove out of their Country, and slain by the sword, to the number of fifteen hundred souls in the space of two months and less: so as their Country is fully subdued and fallen into the hands of the English: And to the end that God's name might have the glory, and his people see his power. . . ."

Even before the English pushed into the area along the Connecticut coastline north of Long Island's East End, John Oldham was exploring the area, trading with Indians. His murder on Block

Island—he was "martyred most barbarously," Underhill wrote—was the excuse that the English needed to go after the Pequots.

"The blood of the innocent called for vengeance," Underhill wrote. Along with a force of men, Underhill landed on the island and, not finding the Pequots but, instead, a "most eminent plantation" rich in corn, burned wigwams, cut down the corn, and shot dogs.

On his boat near the mainland, Underhill's unit met with a Pequot "ambassador," telling him that it was "not the custom of the English to suffer murderers to live" and that if he and his people wanted peace, they would turn over "the heads of the murderers." In response, the Pequot ambassador talked of meeting a Dutch sailing vessel, "before the coming of these English," whose crew kidnapped a sachem and demanded a bushel of wampum as ransom. The Pequots paid the white men, but instead of releasing the sachem, the Dutch killed him. It was the deaths of Oldham and others that avenged the murder of the sachem. The ambassador asked, "Could ye blame us for revenging so cruel a murder: for we distinguish not between the Dutch and the English. . . ."

Underhill did not accept the excuse, and he told the ambassador to tell the Indians that the heads of the murderers must be turned over. When the ambassador returned, he said he could not get an answer because the tribe's sachems "were gone to Long Island." Several hours later, the English were told the Pequot sachem Mommenoteck would speak to them, but hours went by and he did not come. In response, Underhill's men attacked, "gave fire to as many as we could come near, firing their wigwams, spoiling their corn and many other necessaries that they had buried in the ground . . . which the soldiers had for booty."

Afterward, Underhill fled the country, and in retaliation the Pequots killed white men and approached the Saybrook fort built by Lion Gardiner, daring the English to come out from behind its wall and fight. Dressed in Englishmen's clothes, the Pequots taunted Gardiner's troops: ". . . come out and fight if you dare; you dare not fight, you are all like women, we have one amongst us that if he could kill but one of you more, he would be equal with God." The English soldiers found the religious reference blasphemous, but they stayed in the fort.

The plantation of Connecticut, small and undermanned, sent Capt. John Mason and a contingent of soldiers to relieve the fort. The colony in Massachusetts was asked to send supplies to strengthen the fort, and Underhill and twenty armed soldiers were dispatched. With the fort heavily armed, the Pequots moved out into the countryside, attacking the tiny settlement at Wethersfield, where an Englishman named Thomas Wickham had erected a house. Nine men, women, and children were killed and two women taken prisoner. To taunt the soldiers at Saybrook, the Indians hung shirts and other items of clothing they had taken at Wethersfield from poles in their canoes, then paddled by the fort. In one canoe, the soldiers saw the two English women, but they were without boats to rescue them.

The fort sat at the mouth of the Connecticut River and was surrounded by "good timber . . . a variety of fish of several kinds, geese, ducks . . . deer, squirrels, which are as good as our English rabbits." Underhill knew the country to the north and south, and across the waters to Long Island; he characterized the area as "the garden of New England." In his manuscript, Underhill wrote that he hoped to encourage more settlers to come to the region along Long Island Sound.

What stood in the way of English expansion throughout the "garden" were the Pequots, who, unlike the other Indians the English had encountered, seemed resolute in their opposition to accommodation. Like Gardiner, Underhill knew of the fabulous lands and islands to the south; and he knew, if only because Winthrop's reports were widely circulated, of the two forks at the East End of Long Island, where there were large areas of woodlands cleared by fire, revealing rich brown earth. New settlements breaking off from the Puritan effort on the New England mainland could be set up here. With the sheltered Great River in the saltwater valley between the two forks filled with fish, an easy life could be established.

The cover of his manuscript makes clear that his work was about new settlements rather than being simply a glorified account of his war against the Pequots. He lists eleven possible new plantations, including Long Island, and says of them they "yet have very few or no inhabitants." Surely, Underhill and Gardiner, different in their views of the new world but both military men, knew the English could not settle there permanently until the Pequots, who had dominion over the Indians of eastern Long Island, were put in their place.

But he was also telling a story, one about the demise of the Pequots, and he did not intend to leave out any details.

While Gardiner and his troops were holed up in the Saybrook fort, an Englishman named Tillie, evidently from Massachusetts, sailed into the Connecticut River aboard a shallow-draft vessel. Unaware of events that had preceded him, he and another man went ashore, where they were fallen upon by Indians. One of the men was killed, the other taken prisoner. The prisoner was tied to a stake and his skin peeled off by inserting hot embers underneath the skin. His fingers and toes were cut off and "hatbands" made of them.

Hoping to crush the Pequots, the English enlisted Mohegans, whom the Pequots had displaced from their land. Even as they brought them into their company, the English feared the Mohegans would turn against them and join the Pequots. To prove their fidelity, the Mohegans went out and brought back five Pequot heads, along with a prisoner. Underhill was encouraged, believing now that God had truly answered the prayers of the English that a way be found to slay the Pequots.

Meanwhile, a Dutch vessel from Manhattan Island approached the mouth of the river, seeking to trade with the Pequots. The English blocked them, and the Dutch, hearing of the two captive white women, volunteered to help retrieve them from the Indians. The captain of the Dutch vessel lured seven Pequot men to his boat and held them. "One of the Dutch called to them on the shore, and told them they must bring the two captive maides, if they would have the seven Indians, and therefore briefly if you will bring them, tell us, if not we set sail, and will turn all your Indians overboard in the maine ocean, so soon as ever we come out. . . ." There was no response, and the Dutch boat set sail down the river, toward open water.

This tactic worked, Underhill wrote, and the two girls, the elder only fifteen years of age, were turned over to the Dutch. They were brought to the fort at Saybrook, where the elder child spoke of praying fervently that they would not to be harmed by the Indians.

On his ship, Underhill and his soldiers left the Saybrook fort and sailed for Narragansett Bay, where they made landfall and "marched overland about two days journey before we came to Pe-queat, quartering the last nights march within two miles of the place, we set forth about one o'clock in the morning, having sufficient intelligence that they knew nothing of our coming."

Near the Pequots' main encampment, a log fort had been built on an acre of ground, with trees sunk in the ground like a wall. Capt. John Mason took a contingent of soldiers and passed to the west of the fort, where a cut in the trees opened up like a gate; Underhill marched to the south side. In a ring about the fort, the soldiers opened fire, and "we could not but admire as the Provi-dence of God in it, that soldiers so unexpert in the use of their arms should give so complete a vol-ley, as though the finger of God had touched both match and flint." It was near dawn, and with the first shots, the Pequots began to cry out, but the soldiers were without pity, "considering the blood they had shed of our native Country-men, and how barbarously they had dealt with them, and slain first and last about thirty persons."

The soldiers pushed past logs and branches over the opening and attacked the wigwams in-side. Then Mason and Underhill, their armor saving them from a sky filled with arrows, set the fort on fire. The flames "meeting in the center of the fort blazed most terribly, and burnt all in the space of half an hour . . . mercy they did not deserve for their valour. . . . Many were burnt in the fort, both men, women and children, others forced out . . . twenty, thirty at a time, which our sol-diers received and entertained with the point of a sword; down fell men, women and children, those that escaped us fell into the hands of the Indians, that were in the rear of us; it is reported by themselves, that there were about four hundred souls in this fort, and not above five of them es-caped out of our hands. . . . Sometimes the scripture declareth women and children must perish with their parents." More Pequots, perhaps more than one hundred, were killed or wounded as the soldiers retreated from the burning fort toward the Pequot River.

Nearly destroyed as a tribal body, the Pequots had nowhere to go. Their sachem Sassacus saw there was no way to fight back. Underhill quoted Sassacus:

> . . . we are a people bereaved of courage, our hearts are saddened with the death of so many of our dear friends; we see upon what advantage the English lye, what sudden and deadly blows they strike. what advantage they have of their pieces to us which are not able to reach them with our arrows at distance; they are supplied with everything necessary; they are . . . heartened in their victory; to what end shall we stand it out with them? we are not able, therefore let us rather save some than lose all.

The survivors gathered all that they could carry, spoiled any food they could not take, pushed down their wigwams, and took flight. Many who were taken prisoner were turned over to the Narragansetts, their enemies, and to other Massachusetts Indians. Winthrop writes that one captured in a canoe near Block Island was sent as a slave to England. Mason, emboldened by the slaughter at the Pequot fort, went searching through the forests for the sachems. Two who were captured were beheaded, including Sassacus; others, Winthrop wrote, fled toward Mohawk country. Some escaped to the North Fork to live among the Corchaug people.

# PART TWO

# Good Ground

*Potatoes is the crop that irrigation got started on around here, because potatoes was the bread-and-butter crop. The major crop here for as long as I can remember was potatoes. All around my house was Tuthill potatoes. South was my father's potatoes, west of that was Ralph and Clarence's potatoes. But at that time, they also raised cabbage seed, so sometimes a field would be designated for cabbage seed instead of for potatoes. Some farmers even raised strawberries. Another crop was brussels sprouts. When I got out of the army, Ralph was growing brussels sprouts, and we'd pack them, his wife would pack them, and the next day I would take his pickup and go down to the auction with his brussels sprouts.*

*A man had his money in his farm. He didn't have anything else. If he lost it, he lost what money he put into the farm. So he hung on to it, good times or bad. He stuck it out. There used to be quite a number of farm auctions, two or three, maybe five one winter. Some years were worse than others. It's economics, but it's also who has he got to take over, you know. If the boy doesn't want to take over, he can get out.*

—JOHN TUTHILL

# FOUR

# Water Like Milk

THE NORTH FORK is a peninsula of sand, woods, and topsoil poking out from the main body of

Long Island. In places, it is little more than a road wide, salt water on both sides. It pokes north

and east in a jagged fashion and arcs slightly toward the south near its eastern tip, like a tired fin-

ger bending over. On its north side are high sandy bluffs; wide necks jut out into the bay on its

southern side.

From the wooded north side of Frank McBride's family farm on Oregon Road in

Cutchogue, the land is a plain that runs downhill to the bay. Before houses were built, the plain was heavily wooded, and the creeks that pushed up from the bay reached nearly to the middle of the peninsula. The English, not long after their arrival in 1640, ran their east-west road perpendicular to these creeks and erected windmills at the tops of most of them, noting their whereabouts on maps with small *x*'s.

North of the McBride home, north of the land bought by Owen McBride in 1863, boulders stick up out of the ground like intruders from a lower world. They have been heaved up by the forces of thawing and freezing from the rock pile that sits beneath the soil covering—slowly, incredibly slowly, pushed up as if they were seeking oxygen on the surface. But large rocks are not the norm in this section of the North Fork, and the land toward the south is nearly free of them. Because of this, and because huge swaths of land had been cleared by the Algonquins with fire, the English could plant their crops immediately. It was all perfect for them, as if they had been invited to a place that had been arranged with their well-being in mind.

In several places, there are knuckles of land that stick oddly out of the flat landscape. Manor Hill, west of the hamlet of Cutchogue, is one of them. Along one side of Manor Hill is a freshwater pond, and north of this pond is a second pond, both of which were carved out by shards of glacial ice. There are places with poor topsoil (John Tuthill calls them "gravelly spots"), and there are places—like those along the spine that runs down the middle of the North Fork—where the topsoil is heavy and deep, perfect farm soil. In Orient, at the very eastern tip of the fork, the soil on the Latham farm is among the very best found anywhere.

More than sixty thousand years ago, warm air moving north along a proto–Gulf Stream struck cold air over the landmass now called Labrador. The air was quick-chilled, the moisture wrung out. Because of the deep cold, the precipitation that fell was in the form of snow. After endless days and nights of snowfall, thick layers of ice formed on the ground.

It took extraordinary amounts of moisture to form vast archipelagoes of ice in the northern hemisphere, perhaps enough moisture to drop ocean levels by several feet worldwide. As moist air poured north from the tropics, more snow fell, and the ice sheets on the ground grew thicker and thicker. At a certain point of thickness, gravity began to move the ice outward from its center. Picture pancake batter poured onto a grill and flowing outward from the middle. As the middle piles up with batter, the outside edges move farther and farther out. It was this way with a new continental glacier that would flow south, grinding rock and gravel, sending out from its outer edge milky water filled with rock flour. When this process ended twenty thousand years ago, the North Fork, the islands of Peconic Bay, and the mass of the South Fork were formed as they now exist, with rich layers of brown topsoil sitting atop them like icing on a grand cake.

The evidence of glacial advances earlier than sixty thousand years ago is obscure, but tantalizing signs occasionally stick out like probes from another time and place. During a brief window in 1992, sudden erosion on Shelter Island exposed boulders that may have been the end product of an ice action that predates the sixty-thousand-year mark. Shelter Island, the second island in the Peconic Bay system, sits like a cork between the necks of the two forks. It is east of Robins Island, which is much smaller, and west of Gardiners Island, the island that Lion Gardiner finagled from the Indians who lived on the islands and the South Fork after the mass slaughter of the Pequots.

Sixty thousand years ago, the beginning of the beginning, is a period of ice movement called the early Wisconsinan. During this period, a movement called the Ronkonkoma Advance created Montauk, the eastern high tip of the South Fork, as well as the ridge that forms the spine of Long Island itself. This ridge was nothing more than rock debris scooped up by the ice and deposited at the terminus of the glacier as if by a conveyor belt. The landmass formed at the end of a glacier, at its most distal point, is a terminal moraine. It is built up when a glacier stops moving.

As glaciers retreat, they continue to grind the land, passing back over their own path, and the result of this is called a recessional moraine. When ice advances over a moraine formed earlier, a composite moraine is formed. The South Fork of Long Island is in all likelihood a composite moraine; the North Fork, therefore, would be a recessional moraine, formed as the ice recrossed its earlier path.

It is astonishing to people like Steven Englebright, an expert on glaciers who teaches at the State University of New York at Stony Brook, that the ice could advance from its center near Labrador to the South Fork of Long Island, retreat during a period of warming, and then advance to almost exactly the same southern point.

"It reflects a remarkable similarity of conditions—different sheets of ice advancing to almost the very same position. And these sheets would not have a uniform edge because, as the ice passed through southern New England, some of it would get hung up on ridges, allowing lobes of ice to proceed south ahead of others."

Englebright believes the ocean side of the South Fork, with its own rich cover of topsoil, was created at a different time from the northern, or Peconic Bay, side. "The only thing I can say with certainty is that there is a strong likelihood that the southern portion of the South Fork is early Wisconsinan, and the north side is late Wisconsinan, which represents a progression in the time line that begins at sixty thousand years ago and ends at twenty thousand years ago. Ask this question: Why did the ice sheets—different ones at different times—end here? Because the rate of melting equaled the rate of advance, stopping it in its tracks."

But ice sheets that appear to be dead, or no longer moving, are not dead at all. Ice that is standing still continues to form the moraine, the land at the end, spitting rock and gravel debris out in front. The moraine, then, is the result of the stopping of the ice.

That is one moraine, though, the first of several. The process of land and soil formation is not over. If it had ended in the early Wisconsinan, eastern Long Island might look *similar* to what it does today, but colder and with a severely reduced growing season and poor topsoil. Hemlock forests would cover the land.

To arrive at the conditions we have today, another ice advance was needed, the late Wisconsinan period of twenty thousand years ago, which, when it arrived at the very same spot where it had earlier stopped its forward progress, plowed into the sediments of its earlier advance, welding itself to the terminal moraine it had left before.

"Over thousands of years," Englebright says, "thick layers of alluvial deposits were laid down in layers, stacked one upon the other. Standing on a Long Island Sound beach in Cutchogue, looking south toward the bay, you can see the alluvial beds in the bluffs—the most coarse debris is at the bottom, above that is gravel and sand, then a material called till, or morainal rock fragments. These are ice-contact products—that's how we explain them. Above that are the bird holes, swallows and such nesting in the upper cliff just below the roots. On top is the loess, which is not an ice-contact product. This is the topsoil. It's the secret of these North Fork farms."

The topsoil: the rich brown loess that sits majestically on top of it all; the cap on the alluvial fan; the ground we walk on. Maybe the expression "I worship the ground you walk on" refers to the soil, not to the person doing the walking. How does the loess get there?

As the late Wisconsinan glacier edged south across Connecticut more than twenty thousand years ago, it was melting prodigiously, sending outward, toward the Long Island landmass to the south, a shallow lake milky in color because of the silt, the rock flour.

Streams of this milk ran in all directions, drying up in some places as part of the ice lobes broke off or were slowed by obstacles. As the streams dried up, wind caused by the warm air from the south colliding with the cold air over the glacier sent the dry rock flour in all directions. A puffy white cloud of fine earth covered the land and filled the sky.

This was the loess, and as it fell to the earth it formed topsoil. On the North Fork it is thicker in some places than others, almost sand in some spots. The bachelor Tuthill brothers, Stanley and Leslie, raised potatoes on land where the loess was thick and dark brown, as if right there the wind had blessed the land with a heavier coating. Everyone has said for years their potato crops were the best.

It's thick on Ziggy Kurkoski's farm, too, where David Steele now farms, and he is helped by the glacial kettle hole behind the house—out of which he can pump water to irrigate his potatoes. The Latham farm in Orient is blessed with soil that seems incapable of wearing out, of dying like the ice that made it.

"The glacier left very few big rocks on the North Fork," says Englebright, who has almost a worshipful view of the ice that was here. There are exceptions, of course. Where Frank McBride farms his potatoes north of Oregon Road, there is a field in which the rounded tip of a huge boulder sticks up like the bow of a sunken ship.

Frank, who is called "Mick" by his friends and his wife, says it is far too big to push out and into the woods along his hedgerows with a bucket loader. He wonders if it was visible when his grandfather arrived from Ireland. Mick and his sons plow around it.

"The topsoil itself is almost free of rocks because it is just silt," Englebright says. "That's all it is. Where you see small rocks, many of them are round because the ice ground off the corners."

But it is the topsoil that means everything.

"This glacial loess that makes the North Fork farms what they are is a gift of Aeolus, the god of wind."

FIVE

# The Dead People

SOON AFTER THE slaughter of the Pequots, the English arrived on the North Fork and began

bartering with the Indians for their land. Deeds were drawn up, which the Corchaugs could not

read. The church built by Youngs was the centerpiece of the new community. Fine homes were

built east and west of it. Indian land was the wooded landscape west of the church. Carts could

pass by this land on a sandy road, going around the lip of a shallow pond that would soon be called

Corchaug Pond. Indian land lay to the south of this pond, along wooded creek edges, with broad,

.eadows used as planting fields. There the Indians lived in their traditional stick homes, col-
.g shellfish in the creeks and along the edge of the bay.

Generally, local historians have skirted the question of what happened to the Corchaugs after
.ey scratched their marks on deeds that transferred their land to the English. Historians of the
nineteenth century lauded the English as persecuted peoples who carved homes out of the wilderness. One prominent Long Island historian, B. F. Thompson, called John Underhill a "wonderful
man." To C. B. Moore, a Southold historian and writer in the late nineteenth century, who hailed
the town's founders as saints, the Indians who had lived on the North Fork "sold" their land and
"disappeared." In Moore's view, the Indians engaged in a fair and equitable land transaction before
moving away.

Early one morning, I drove along a narrow road near the south edge of the Wickham farm.
Here, John had found scores of artifacts; a tiny carved ceremonial fish had once been found, as
well. John said history told him the Corchaugs had not been treated well.

"It's fair to say the Corchaugs were cheated," he said, "but I would say that it was no worse here
than anywhere else."

His own writings are filled with references to the native people. I pictured John as a man who
recognized that he was an inheritor of their history. He once wrote: "I was plowing today by Shell
Bank (a section of low dark soil along the western edge of Wickham Creek) and my thoughts
turned to the Indians who farmed here before we ever set foot on this peninsula."

Like so many farmers, he collected Indian artifacts his plow unearthed, finding some more
than a foot deep. These were the oldest ones, left by the people who had arrived here soon after
the ice wall had retreated north, back to where it had been created in Canada. Holding on to something of the Indians was a reminder that they had farmed this same land—it kept Wickham thinking of them as a people of substance, not a wisp of a civilization that would have died off anyway
had no Europeans arrived in search of new lives.

Many times, Wickham spoke about his father's interest in history, saying he had helped a historian named Peter Ross research a history of Long Island that was published soon after the turn
of this century. In reading Ross's work, what struck me was his dramatic break with the historians
of the past on the key question of what had happened to the Indians. According to Ross, they had
been "beaten in the struggle for existence, cheated, wronged and cozened at every turn. . . ." He
wrote that the few Indians remaining by 1903 were "facing the inevitable end, of total annihila-
tion. . . . It is a sad story, a painful story, but it must be told."

As for Underhill, Ross detailed a mass slaughter of Indians in western Long Island orchestrated by Underhill, in which he "piled the bodies in a heap on the brow of a hill, and then sat down
to breakfast." Referring to the deeds for land sales on eastern Long Island, Ross said they were
"strange at best," noting the Indians were given "a few tools and trinkets, and then (were supposed
to be) glad as a matter of charity to be permitted to live on and cultivate a few of the poorest acres."

But Ross seemed to single out local historians who had glossed over land transactions such as that between Lion Gardiner and the Montauks. He wrote: ". . . the most objectionable feature to readers nowadays is the sanctimonious manner in which the transactions were sweetly glossed over by the historians of the island and held up for our admiration. The natives were, as it were, given sugar coated pills, and were asked to consider the sugar and forget the gall and wormwood. . . ."

The Indians, he argued, "had to be crushed. . . . But why, in this twentieth century, continue to treat the matter hypocritically, shed crocodile tears over the various incidents . . . and assert that a few beads, a gun or two, some cheap, often cast-off clothes and tools—to say nothing, now and then, of a modicum of rum—sanctified the proceedings attendant upon the despoliation of the Indian?"

When the Reverend John Youngs arrived on the North Fork in the early fall of 1640, the Corchaugs may have been a people in transition. History shows us that the native groups to the north, near the Englishmen's first settlements, were rapidly dying off because of diseases, and it is likely these diseases spread south as Indians traveled to the two eastern forks to collect wampum shells. Some groups in the north experienced a 90 percent death rate. Indians were dropping dead like "rotten sheep," one Puritan wrote. In the Puritan view, God had swept the land clean of Indians to make room for His people.

"God hath hereby cleared our title to this place," John Winthrop wrote.

It is believed by some that Youngs's group, before their arrival in 1640, had made arrangements to buy the land called Yennicott (or Yennicock) from the sachems of the North Fork. (Years later, when linguists tried to make sense of a long-dead language, they said that Yennicott meant "extended country.") If this occurred, no deeds have been found. It is most likely that the Corchaugs were told in advance that a group was coming and that an advance party of that group had arrived on the North Fork to pick out a location on which to construct a church, as well as to plant crops that could be harvested in the fall. Houses would also have been built so the minister and his flock would have places to live. Much later, deeds validating English ownership could be secured through an appointed sachem.

From the English point of view, the Indians did not actually own this land because they did not live on it as a settled community. They were idle wanderers who held title to nothing. Historians like John Strong at Long Island University, and Karen Kupperman and Kevin McBride at the University of Connecticut, argue that the Indians' ownership of the land was symbolic, that rights were sovereign, not individual.

"The major question is, Why did these native groups sell their land?" Kupperman says. "You have to read yourselves into the minds of these people. They were wealthy and important because of the wampum trade. They had a middleman role. Because they controlled the wampum lands, they had a client relationship with other Indians. When the Pequots were gone—with the help of

Lion Gardiner—the English were suddenly thrust into the role of overseers of the eastern Long Island Indians. As for these sales, these were not straight capitalist transactions. The Indians may have seen these transactions as making Gardiner a client of theirs. By giving him what he wanted, the natives on the East End now had a powerful advocate among the English. They were forging alliances. In terms of some of the sales—on the North Fork in 1640 and Gardiners Island before that—the Indians might have asked themselves, Which of the English should we give this land to? But I don't think they thought the end result would be that they would have nothing."

McBride says, "It is my guess the natives thought they were allowing their new friends to use this land, not possess it in such a way that it was no longer theirs. It would seem obvious that the English were taking advantage of the fact that the Pequots were beaten to make private real estate deals on Long Island. The Pequot War changed everything. It was total warfare for the first time here. It had a major psychological impact on the natives of Long Island. Now these natives had to pay tribute to the English, the way they had to the Pequots.

"There is this whole debate on just what the natives thought they were conveying. Maybe in the first couple of transactions they could see they got nailed. But I do believe they were adaptable people; they learned quickly. You can see in later deeds they put in caveats about collecting ground nuts and fishing and hunting."

If caveats played any role at all, they were short-lived, because soon the Corchaugs found themselves strangers on the North Fork. By the logic of the English system—that the Crown owned the land and could sell it off through patents—the Corchaugs would have had to buy the land from the English in order to live on it. In 1648, the town fathers began collecting deeds from the Corchaugs—deeds that said the Indians were the true owners of the land and had the full power and permission of their people to convey everything to the new residents.

If we know very little about these Algonquin people, we do know some of their names. We can see them on the deeds, written down by the English. After their names, the Indians scratched X's, then were given their gifts. One deed was written in March 1648 but not recorded until 1660. The Corchaug named Paucumpt, "an Indyan of about eighty years old . . . descended from the House of the Sachem at the end of the Island," said he was the owner of land at the western end of Peconic Bay, near five salt creeks. This was Occabaucke, now Aquebogue, near the west end of the North Fork, where it attaches to the main body of Long Island. He said the previous sachem to possess this woodland was Ockenmungan, dead by 1648, an Indian who possibly never knew white men.

A prominent town resident named William Wells, soon to make the first purchase of land in present-day Cutchogue, took the testimony of Paucumpt, carefully noting, even if the man did not tell him this, that the earlier sachem did fully approve of selling the land to the jurisdiction of the New Haven Colony, which had sponsored Youngs's religious expedition to the North Fork. At the bottom, next to his own ornate signature, he wrote down the names of four Indians—two of whom,

Paucumpt and Ambusco, were father and son—and then handed them his quill to put down their own marks.

The names and marks look like this:

Paucumpt

Ambusco

Nippacommucks

Nenoneges

A second March 1648 deed covered land from Aquebogue east to Mattituck. John Youngs and two other men, Thomas Moore and Richard Terry, witnessed the Indians' marks on this instrument. Two of the four names on this deed match the first deed, although in one case the spelling is different. The marks for the two Indians who signed both documents are different, which might be an indication that they had no idea of the true meaning of the transaction.

The deed begins by saying that a native woman named Mahahamucks, now dead, was the legal proprietor of this land and that she had earlier sold the land to Youngs, with payment to her, "and all the four sachems then living knew of her sale" and did not object to it.

The Indian names and marks are on the right side of the page, followed by squiggly lines unlike the others, even in the case of Nippacommucks.

Nonannege

Paumatux

Nippacommucks

Squant

A document rife with legalese is an instrument dated May 16, 1648, and witnessed by Youngs, his son, John Youngs, Jr., Henry Whitney, and four Indians—Occomboomaguus, Mahahamucks, Muckoomash, and Saggamaug. The deed covers the same land as the preceding deeds, but it is more particular in saying the English were protected against legal action brought by Occomboomaguus, Mahahamucks, "their heirs and assignes and all or any other person or persons claiming any title or interest. . . ."

No Indian could have understood the concept that they were barred from seeking legal redress to get their land back. Picture the Englishmen sitting around a table with Indians dressed in deerskins and bird feathers, saying, 'Now once you sign this, don't try to come after us in court.'

A note by Wells at the bottom of the deed shows why the English selected Mahahamucks to make his mark on the paper: ". . . there was an Indyan squaw of the Sachem blood that was the wife of Mahahamuck, who to their knowledge was true Proprietor of a Tract of Land commonly called Ocquebanck. . . ." Another deed, dated May 6, 1648, covers all of what is today Orient, at the tip of the fork, and Plum Island, east of Orient Point.

This time, the buyers picked a Corchaug named Mamawetough, whose name is spelled differently on almost every document where it appears. He made a mark after his name that looks like a pitchfork with a circle at the end of the handle. His name would appear later on a deed in East Hampton, which could mean he had moved to the South Fork or, perhaps, that he was pliable enough to sign anything the English asked him to. The deed describes Mamawetough as the "sachem of Corchaug," which was convenient for the English but probably not true among the Corchaugs.

In June 1686, "Ambosco, ye sonne of Paucompt," signed a deed for the sale of Hashamomock. The deed says Paucumpt, "the Last Sachem of Hashamomoke," signed over the land "about forty years agoe. . . ." (The year before, the town fathers had set aside a reserved tract of land west of the settlement for all the Indians to live on, so the signing of deeds at this point would seem to have been merely a legal formality.) In the earlier documents, Paucumpt and Ambusco together signed for the sale of Aquebogue, at the far western end of the town. The English no doubt played a game of finding Indians who would say they "owned" a piece of land the English wanted, then getting them to scribble lines on a paper selling it.

The most Algonquin names appear on a deed recorded in March 1667. This deed backdated the white ownership of the entire North Fork, from Wading River at the west end east to Plum Island in what the colonists continued to call the North Sea. The deed suggests that there was no earlier, all-encompassing purchase of the North Fork before Youngs's arrival. It covers all land, creeks, small brooks, and ponds "and all necks of land, meadows, islands, or broken pieces of meadows, rivers, creeks with timber, woods and wood lands, fishing, fowling, hunting and all other commodities whatsoever. . . ."

Referring to the large group of native signers, the deed says they are the "true successors of the lawful and true Indyan owners and proprietors of all the aforesaid tract of land and island." For signing it away, the Indians were given forty yards of cloth "or the worth of same," the receipt of which forever ended any ownership of land or any claim in the future to this land.

The three English names on the deed were John Youngs, Jr., Barnabas Horton, and Thomas Mapes, on behalf of all residents of Southold, and they carefully noted that the colonists would be protected against any action questioning the legality of the deed. It was signed December 7, 1665, "in the 17th yeare of the reign of our Sovereign Lord, Charles, by the grace of God, of England, Scotland, France and Ireland, King, Defender of the faith."

The only things we know about these people are their names and their strange markings, which serve to remind us that they were here.

Their names, a memorial to a dead people, are in three long columns at the bottom of the deed.

Samson

Poquassuck

Wegotaquak

Immonox

Webinaug

Luaksco

Winheytem

Quamaccusso

Cautusquam

Aquapino

Chukiason

Mauqussack

Tawones

Yaughus

Ambusco

Pammatuks

Tucksquon (smeared)

Kekeuminash

Tonnannons

Ounsoonquat

Tuscam

Paucamp

Matnackom

Pimshame

Ninebonch

Wagauchu

Wautackquessin

Wambyam

Nonunneg

Washam

Yontonish

Ahambautanack

Hatchchedow

Hassequohock

Passacoquia

Luaquaton

Patoquam

Sequannat

Mecksamp (no mark)

Upscott

Paumanton

Koepcomb

Adsay

*Jeanne Tuthill holding a photograph, taken in the early 1920s, of the three Tuthill brothers. From right to left: Quintin, John, and Hallock. Only John Tuthill farms today. He is the last Tuthill to farm in Tuthill Town.*

# SIX

# Corchaug and Tuthill Town

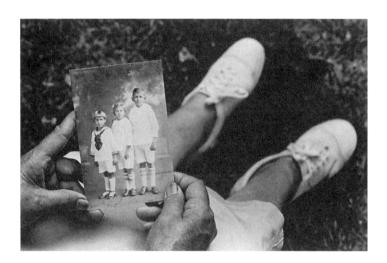

THE DUTCH, encamped on the lower tip of Manhattan Island, then a thick forest between rivers, were keenly interested in the English living at the far eastern end of Long Island. Their maps show Lion Gardiner living on his island, and a count done by the Dutch in 1650 shows there were thirty houses in Southold. If there were three persons to a house, along with a small number of slaves who began arriving on the North Fork after Youngs's arrival, then perhaps the population was one hundred. But it was probably far less, perhaps no more than fifty.

By 1658, eighteen years after Youngs's arrival, there were thirty-six names listed as heads of households in the town. A 1687 census, which lists each resident by name, plus the number of people living at each household, shows 113 whites were living here, along with 27 slaves, some of whom may have been Corchaugs but the majority of whom were Africans.

"My understanding of the numbers back then was that it remained very low until well into the eighteenth century," John Wickham told me. "Heads of households, as they were called, were here, but many family members may have stayed on the Connecticut mainland until a certain time arrived when enough land had been cleared and enough crops planted to feed everyone with a certain measure of certainty.

"Considering how hard it was to clear land, you can say that it was a slow process. It would have taken years to clear large areas for farming. And, of course, the population would not have experienced a sharp increase until the English felt entirely safe from the Indians. If you study enough of the history, it would seem clear the Narragansetts in Rhode Island remained a threat to the North Fork well into the 1650s, when they were still raiding Indian villages on the South Fork and on the islands. And there were the Dutch, too, who didn't want us here in the first place. With the community so tiny, they could have sailed out here, put soldiers on land, and Southold would have ended in one day."

The year the Dutch did their survey, Youngs was living like an English lord on seven acres at the top of a salt creek. Surely very few people lived as grandly in his old hometown of Southwold. And here there were no church bureaucrats, no nosy meddlers from the Crown to bother him about his religious practices. He could be the man he wanted to be.

To his east was the cart path to the creek and south of that was the bay. To the west, the narrow sandy road poked inquisitively into the deep woods. And beyond that lay the land the English called Corchaug.

Prodded by William Wells, who seems to have seen his role in his new North Fork home as that of a real estate baron, the colonists began pushing west toward the large cleared area they called the Broadfields, an area of more than two hundred acres that formed the center of what is today Cutchogue. The land was open and wide, the salt grass they needed for their livestock thick and plentiful. It was a better place than where they had first landed. Between the original settlement and Corchaug was the Indian land, south of Corchaug Pond. As they looked toward the Broadfields as their second settlement, the colonists seemed more than willing simply to go around the native villages. What they wanted were the wooded necks of land farther west, and the Broadfields, which could be declared common land and where crops could be planted immediately.

Wells, though, appears to have been eager to broker a private deal with the Corchaugs to buy the land for himself. This failed when his actions were reported to the town's sponsors in New Haven. But the momentum to spread west had begun, and soon the Southold settlement began drawing up lists of residents who would be given "dividends" in Corchaug and in lands farther west, at present-day Mattituck and Aquebogue. The land at Corchaug began at a fixed place, a "fresh meadow" near the top of a saltwater creek. The first neck of land in Corchaug was called Pequash Neck, and it was wide and heavily wooded.

Twenty-one residents were given forty-four lots in Corchaug, which ran from the fresh meadows west to the inlet at Mattituck where the natives carried their dugout canoes between the Sound and the bay. The lots were huge, more than one hundred acres, and ran from the cart path north to the Sound. Nineteen men, including many who had also acquired land in Corchaug, were given land in the Aquebogue dividend. Wells managed to get himself in both groups. There were Hortons in both groups, and a John Tuthill had three lots in Aquebogue. Both the Tuthills and the Hortons would end up farming in Mattituck and Cutchogue, their farms almost back-to-back.

As I read the town's early records, it would seem that the John Wickham farm is just inside the original eastern boundary of Corchaug. West of where the Wickham farm stand is today was the Broadfields, which ran all the way to the rounded knuckle of high ground at Manor Hill, the little pond on one side of it, another pond just to the north of it.

"Look at the map of Cutchogue. Duck Pond Point is a little knob that sticks into the Sound," John Wickham wrote in his diary. "It's small, but the beach and the bluffs sort of bend back from it on either side. Go down from there in a straight line and you hit the top of Wickham Creek. That was one melt water stream. The other melt water stream dug out West Creek, or Tuthill's Creek on the old maps. It is these two salt creeks, on either side of this very old farm, that make it unique."

Wells would have seen in his day what John saw three centuries later—open land free of rocks, bounded by salt creeks deep enough for shallow-draft boats, and lined with grass for livestock.

John wrote: "It is remarkable, I have always thought, that the soil is so uniform, and except for some boulders left at the south end of the farm the topsoil is almost rock free. In fact, any black stone might be an artifact. Soil scientists tell us the topsoil is created at the rate of about an inch in a thousand years. Therefore it is not surprising that the deepest Indian arrowheads found on the farm are uniformly found at 14 inches."

Born in the big white house at the top of Wickham Creek, John and his two brothers, Parker and Henry, were raised by their mother, Cora, who was ably assisted by their father's sister, Aunt Julia. Julia Wickham was the family historian, and in time John took up the history, reading old family records, searching the town archives, and talking to other local historians. When he got older, he wrote down what he knew in chapters, had them typed, and put them in a brown leather briefcase—a book, he called it, for his grandchildren. The seventeenth century in Southold intrigued him, and he learned about the owners of his Cutchogue farm between the salt creeks

"In 1640, when the first Europeans arrived on the North Fork," he wrote, "they found the Indians' Broadfields—two hundred and forty acres in corn and other crops. It is apparent that this was not a slash and burn type of agriculture because it had apparently existed long enough to earn the name we call 'Cutchogue,' meaning 'The principal place.' It seems the first old village of

Southold founded by Reverend Youngs was begun on the 'Old Field' of about sixty acres; the 'Indian Field' in Peconic, between the original Southold settlement and the 'principal place' at Cutchogue, was smaller. The first colonists here were practical and accepted what they found without writing about it, so we know very little."

The North Fork was not the frontier. It was remote from England, from all that England was in the seventeenth century, but it was not virgin land, not with Indians living there since the ice had retreated.

"It is tempting to believe that when the Europeans arrived in the New World," writes William Cronon in *Changes in the Land*, "they confronted Virgin Land, the Forest Primeval, a wilderness that had existed for eons uninfluenced by human hands. Nothing could be further from the truth. In Francis Jenning's telling phrase, the land was less virgin than it was widowed."

On the North Fork, the land was especially plentiful, the soil heavy and brown. In places, the land was heavily forested, particularly along the high bluffs overlooking Long Island Sound. The presence of unlimited (or so it seemed in the beginning) amounts of wood was stunning to the English. Here they could live like noblemen. Since at least the time of Columbus, England had been experiencing a wood crisis, Cronon writes, and what wood was available to people without great wealth was costly. In the winter, warmth was a luxury. Parliament set restrictions on the cutting of wood as early as 1543; by 1620, when the exodus began, coal was being burned, and English cities were choked in gray smoke.

It was not just the abundance of wood that overwhelmed the English; it was everything. In New England, nothing prepared the English for the bounty they encountered. "The abundance of sea fish are almost beyond believing, and I should scarce have believed it except I had seen it with mine own eyes," wrote a minister named Higginson in 1630. In the creeks along the bays, streams became so thick with alewives and other small fish, the water itself seemed to disappear. Birds were everywhere, along with game animals. Unlike in England, where hunting was mostly restricted to the wealthier classes on lands owned by the Crown, here anyone could hunt, anywhere one wanted, all year long.

In the forests, the English found spruce trees twenty feet around. Connecticut and Rhode Island were filled with oak trees, along with chestnut and hickory. Around swampy areas, white cedar seemed to abound. After he plowed along his creek, John Wickham was bewildered when birch trees appeared. He wrote: ". . . if you dredge up soil from any salt creek around Peconic Bay immediately birch trees will spring up from that soil. Where did the seed come from? Was it from long ago birch forests preserved for all these years by the salt? Did the seed come from the Connecticut River and across the Sound . . . ?"

Old burn stands of white pine, Cronon writes, so impressed the settlers that they could hardly believe they existed. They were among the tallest trees in New England—one hundred feet tall, five feet in diameter. In some forests, white pine as tall as 250 feet were found. These trees, vital for shipbuilding, were highly sought after.

In the bays, lobsters were so thick they could be scooped out with long nets, and oyster beds a mile in width were not uncommon. Here, a man could not only be warm like a nobleman, but he could eat like one, too.

But it was the "good ground" that impressed the English so deeply—"fat black earth" in the words of one observer—and the longer growing season. To their surprise, they discovered that on eastern Long Island the growing season was more than 220 days, meaning crops could be managed late into the fall. North of Boston, and in most interior areas, the growing season shrank to 150 days.

Youngs no doubt knew, well before he set sail from Connecticut for the North Fork, that this fertile soil was available to them for immediate planting. The Indians grew crops, but their lives on the land were transitory, while the English were looking for a fixed place to plant their crops year after year. The English sought lives in permanent communities, while the Indians lived in small settlements connected by kinship networks. These Indians grew corn and other crops, and because agriculture fixed them to a specific location, they were more stable than the Indians on the New England mainland. But their numbers were low. A history written at the turn of this century by a Youngs descendant says there were three hundred Indians on the North Fork when the English arrived.

What Youngs knew about the Indians he would have learned while living in Massachusetts. The Corchaugs began their calendar year in April, when corn was planted. The ensuing months marked their activities and the seasonal changes—the weeding of corn, the hilling of corn, the ripening of corn, the coming of frost, the middle of winter, the thawing of ice, the catching of fish. They probably also raised beans and pumpkins, and perhaps tobacco. The women did the farmwork—one woman could raise twenty-five to sixty bushels of corn on a single acre of land. In the creeks, like Wickham Creek, West Creek, and Downs Creek—where, in a wooded tract along the shoreline, the English found a stockaded fort built by the Indians—the men set fish traps.

In his book, Cronon says it is unlikely the natives used alewives to fertilize their fields, the practice the Pilgrims supposedly learned from Squanto, who had lived as a captive in Europe. John Wickham did not believe that this practice of fertilization came from England. "Some authorities have suggested that the Indians learned the trick of fertilizing their corn with fish from Squanto's visit to Europe," he wrote. "This doesn't set well with what we know about fish. In England, most of the coast gets very deep too quickly for fish to be plentiful—even in the low countries, fish is not plentiful. They've gone as far as Iceland for cod, even in those years. They also eat herring which is here a 'trash' fish. On the other hand, here on eastern Long Island, the Bunker or Menhaden was and often still is so plentiful that they can be netted and speared in quantity, the schools are densely packed and past numbering in Peconic Bay. Not only that, but in some years they had a form of apoplexy and swam in aimless circles, eventually dying and coming up on the shore. There is also nowadays oxygen depletion when chased into these narrow creeks by the bluefish—the Indians could not help noticing how luxuriously plants along the shore grew when there were dead fish."

The Indians also collected nuts in the fall, burying them along with any surplus crops in pits. As winter came, villages would move away from the edges of creeks and into deep woods near springs. No matter where they moved on the North Fork, they were close to salt water.

Once the English had planted their crops and built their new homes, they appear to have done well for themselves. If there was suffering and hardship, it was not recorded. "That they immediately prospered is evident," Wickham wrote. "By 1647 John Budd had built a two and a half story house for his daughter in the English style with leaded glass windows. . . . This was a planned enterprise and there is no record of hardship, nor should it have been expected with their base in Connecticut only twelve or fifteen miles away across the Sound. In later years, the lighthouse keeper off the mouth of the Connecticut River used to row across the Sound to spend some weekends with his family."

On the western edge of the original Cutchogue division, west of the Broadfields, the English began clearing land north of the cart path. A number of Tuthills would settle here, and within a few generations there were so many of them they called their stretch of farmland Tuthill Town. Early town records and maps show a remarkable number of Tuthills farming along the Main Road, the main east-west thoroughfare, Elijah's Lane, and north toward Long Island Sound. There were Tuthill potato and vegetable farmers, and Tuthills who raised cows for milk.

John Tuthill lives near the top of Elijah's Lane, south of the railroad tracks, in a house that dates back to the eighteenth century. A portion of the house was moved to the site from the Main Road. His father was Ernest Tuthill, who lived to be almost a century old and who kept a diary for much of his life, recording the weather, farm chores, and family news. As a young man, Ernest Tuthill built a house north of the tracks, almost directly south of the farm where Stanley and Leslie Tuthill, the bachelor Tuthill brothers, grew up and still live. Stan, who was called "Sparky," and Les are John Tuthill's cousins.

Looking at Tuthill land closely, you can see that a meltwater stream caused the land to dip just to the east of the Tuthill brothers' farmhouse. The land on the north side of the road that separates the two Tuthill farms rises slightly and is then flat all the way to a thick stand of woods that separates farmland from a narrow piece of property on which a small church sits.

A slight low dip runs south from Oregon Road, on the east side of the Tuthill brothers' farmhouse, east of Ernest's old house, and, if you follow it directly south, crosses a pond on the west side of Ziggy Kurkoski's farm. This narrow ravine continues to run south, where it connects like beads on a necklace to another small pond (the one by Manor Hill), across the Main Road, and then leads to the top of a narrow tidal creek that empties into the bay.

A map John Tuthill drew shows how his immediate family set up farms in Tuthill Town. G. B. Tuthill's farm, which includes the house and farm where John and his wife now live, ran north of

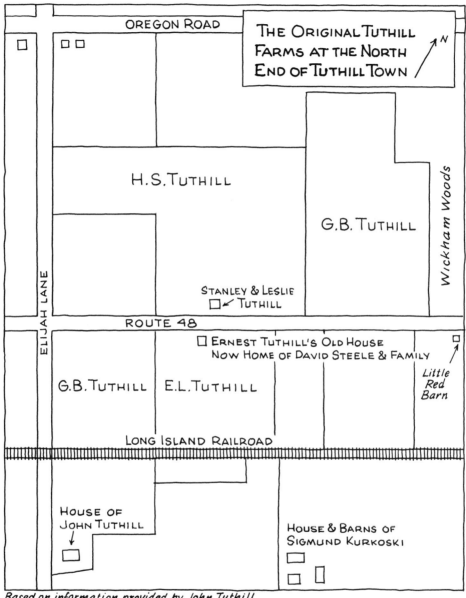

The Original Tuthill Farms at the North End of Tuthill Town

N

OREGON ROAD

ELIJAH LANE

H.S. TUTHILL

G.B. TUTHILL

Wickham Woods

STANLEY & LESLIE TUTHILL

ROUTE 48

ERNEST TUTHILL'S OLD HOUSE Now Home of David Steele & Family

Little Red Barn

G.B. TUTHILL | E.L. TUTHILL

LONG ISLAND RAILROAD

HOUSE OF JOHN TUTHILL

HOUSE & BARNS OF SIGMUND KURKOSKI

*Based on information provided by John Tuthill*

the tracks and across the Middle Road (on maps, this road officially is called Route 48), which was put in later and which cut the farm in half. To the north was H. S. Tuthill's farm; on the southern edge of this farm is Stanley and Leslie Tuthill's house. Ernest Tuthill's farm was south of theirs and east of G. B. Tuthill's. The initials G. B. stand for George Bryden, who was Ernest's father.

East of the old Ernest Tuthill farm is the Kurkoski farm, and south and east of that is the former Horton farm, another very old farm begun by a family who, like the Tuthills, arrived either in the first boat that came across Long Island Sound from Connecticut or soon after. (No one in this town knows who came first, because most town records earlier than 1652 are missing.) North of the Horton farm was another large tract of flat land owned by G. B. Tuthill; east of that, and running south all the way to the Main Road, is the land of William Wickham, John Wickham's cousin. Bill Wickham lives in a large house on the Main Road and practices law. The summer of 1994, his farm was leased to David Steele. David and his young family live in Ernest Tuthill's old house on the hill.

"What I know about my family," John Tuthill explains, "is what I was told or read. I can make a list of the line before me."

He does, and he lists, working backward from his father: Ernest, G.B., Elijah, Jesse, another Jesse, Samuel, Joshua, John ("Chalker John"), another John, Henry, and another Henry. The family may have started farming at the eastern end of the North Fork, in Orient, and then gradually moved westward, settling in what later would be called Tuthill Town.

Southold town records show a "John Touttle" on the North Fork in April 1642. Silas Wood, who published a history in 1828 entitled *A Sketch of the First Settlement of the Several Towns on Long Island,* states that "William Wells, Barnabas Horton, Thomas Mapes, John Tuthill, and Mathias Corwin were the leading men who formed the first settlement of South Old." A Thomas Tuttle (his name often appears as John) was, in the spring of 1642, named Yennicott's first constable, which suggests that he was a prominent member of the new plantation.

"I have always thought of the Tuthills [he pronounces his family name as if it was spelled Tuttle] as being here from the beginning," John told me. "But I was more interested in how we got here to this spot. All the fuss over the years about this family being in the first group, or that family, that was all nonsense. We were never like that. Perhaps because there were so many Tuthills in Cutchogue, New Suffolk, and Mattituck. Tuthills were everywhere. At one time, you look at the old maps, it looks like most residents of New Suffolk were named Tuthill. There was Tuthill Creek, which is now called West Creek.

"My mother was Leila Hallock. She and Pop got married in 1911. Now everyone round here says the Hallocks were here first, too. I don't know anything about that, but it is interesting to me that my mother's father was Jacob Hallock. Jacob was married to Mary Wells, and Wells is another one of those old names. So, you can see, I have three old names in me. For curious reasons, Jacob and his wife left Cutchogue and in the 1880s went homesteading in Nebraska. The story is that Jacob went crazy there for some reason, and they came back on a train, my mother being just a baby. They returned to Cutchogue, where they farmed, but Jacob was never much good at it. I don't think he got any better once he was back here."

# SEVEN

# The Hollow
# by the Road

AT THE EASTERN edge of the Broadfields, a man named Joseph Wickham bought a wide neck of land and a house that had earlier been moved there. The house sat in a hollow south of the cart path. It was 1698, and the town of Southold was barely sixty years old.

Born in Wethersfield, Connecticut, of English parents, Joseph moved to Southampton, the English colony on the ocean on the South Fork, in the 1680s and started a tanning business near Sagg Pond. He prospered and that year left Southampton and bought the land in Cutchogue.

North of his new home, opposite the sandy cart path, stretched a forest laced with hunter's trails. To the south lay creeks, salt marshes, and the bay.

If he sailed a boat directly south from his new farm, Wickham would pass Robins Island. The island, the westernmost of the three bay islands, was heavily wooded, with high bluffs created by the retreating ice flow. Considerably smaller than Shelter Island and Gardiners Island, it was a dreamscape, resplendent in its natural beauty. South of the green mass of the island, which was shaped like a teardrop because of a narrow line of sand that protruded like a tail on its north end, lay the South Fork.

Standing on the beach south of Wickham's new farm, a man could see the universe the English had come to covet—bays and creeks, the island itself, and more land and woods than any of them had ever known in England.

The year he bought the house, the census in Cutchogue showed that the new community had become the centerpiece of the colony, its richest area in terms of farmland, woods, and shellfish. What the Corchaugs had always known, the English now found out for themselves. The prosperity of the colony could be seen in the house Wickham bought. It was the house of an English gentleman. John Budd had built the house closer to the center of the colony. It was moved to the hollow in Cutchogue when Budd's daughter, Anna, married Benjamin Horton.

Other Hortons were farming around him, and Benjamin purchased land from his father that he tacked on to his purchase. He also bought from John Booth, who owned, and presumably lived on, a broad neck of land immediately to the east. Anna Horton died in 1683, and soon Benjamin remarried and moved to the South Fork. He died in 1690, and his brother, Joseph Horton, sold the farm to Wickham, which on its east side stretched to the creek at what was then called Booth's Neck, and on its west side to the creek opposite Fort Neck. Could the Indian fort have still been standing in a jungle of briars and vines on the edge of the creek? History does not tell us the answer.

In 1715, Joseph Wickham bought Robins Island, and even more land was to come into the family. Through his marriage to Abigail Parker, the younger Joseph Wickham acquired a huge tract along the freshwater stream that fed into the Peconic River twenty miles east of his home farm. With these additions, the Wickham family became one of the largest landowners on eastern Long Island. Presently, money was collected from the Wickhams, Hortons, Tuthills, and other farmers in Cutchogue and a church was built along the high edge of the hollow just north of the Wickham house. Southold was now two distinct communities—one built around the original church; the second in Cutchogue.

On a warm afternoon, John Wickham and I drove along the dirt path south of his barn, toward the west side of Wickham Creek. The wind came up and black clouds suddenly appeared. A hard rain fell, but only briefly, and when it was over, John drove along the far western edge of his farm, which is wooded and low-lying. We were just east by a few hundred yards of the house Joseph

Wickham bought. Part of the land on which we were standing had been farmed by Joseph Wickham. It tickled John that he farmed this same land.

We talked as we drove over a section Jonathan Wickham, John's grandson, would later show me on a map he drew. The family called this section Shell Bank, which it had been called for generations, and here, near the edge of the creek, a slave named Lymas Reeve had been given his freedom, a cabin—the remains of which were still there when John, Parker, and Henry were young boys—and an acre of land.

It was a brilliant afternoon, the tide beginning to fill the black, grassy edges of the creek.

"William Wells first bought this land, in a deal he made with the Indians," John told me. "It gets murky, because the records are so slim on these points. But my guess is that Wells was the first white owner and John Booth was the second. That's how this land becomes Booth's Neck, and that"—he pointed to the wide expanse of Wickham Creek—"was first called Booth's Creek. I believe that Booth's family owned it for two or three generations. Then, part of the farm passed to the Tuthill family and part to the Reeve family. It was Betty Reeve who freed Lymas and gave him that acre of land at Shell Bank. Somewhere along the line, the Albertsons come into this, because it is from an Albertson that my grandfather's brother, James Wickham, bought the house and the farm we have today."

Town records show that the road that proceeded south from the cart path that ran directly in front of Joseph Wickham's house passed over Dam Meadow on its way to the beach overlooking Robins Island. This split Booth land from Tuthill and Wickham property. Today, the Wickhams farm around Dam Meadow.

While the Booths were still on their neck, the Wickhams were living in the house bought from Horton and in other houses along the east-west road. Each generation was large, and it would seem the land produced enough bounty for several families to prosper. Others left to farm in various parts of the colony or, in some cases, to pursue business interests in the port of New York.

On the North Fork, the Wickham who was to bring his family a measure of notoriety was Parker, Joseph's grandson. Parker inherited the house in the hollow and farmed the same land, including Robins Island, as his father had. On maps, their land between the creeks was called Wickham Neck. Parker served in town politics as a justice of the peace and town supervisor. He was politically active, wealthy, at least in terms of the land he owned, and had powerful enemies.

By the time the third generation of Wickhams was living in Cutchogue, anti-British sentiments were rising among a noisy minority. In small towns across the region, loyalties were tested as the notion of breaking away from England took hold. In Cutchogue, families divided along political lines. Members of some families fled, and others were kidnapped by patriot forces.

"The way I see it," John said as we drove back to the house, "Joseph bought his farm, and he passed it on to his grandson Parker. The line breaks there, but even as it did, another line of Wickhams was farming where my cousin Bill is today, and then in another generation they are on the land Tom and I farm now. Bill and I are on either side of Joseph Wickham's first purchase. So right here, within a half-mile circle, there have been three centuries of Wickhams farming. I just can't get over that."

Parker Wickham was one of nine children. In addition to his four brothers and four sisters, he had scores of nephews and nieces on the North Fork. Active in the town's public life, Parker personified the sort of man Thomas Jefferson would speak of in his writings—a country gentlemen, well-off and intelligent, a man who would temporarily leave his farm duties and enter politics to help manage his community.

His father, Joseph Wickham, Jr., who lived on Wickham Neck all his life, had been active in politics in Southold. He was town assessor, commissioner of roads—one of the most influential jobs of the day—and a judge in the criminal courts.

Parker was twenty-two years of age when his father died in the spring of 1749. The funeral was held in the church across the road from the Wickham home. After the funeral a wagon carried the casket to a tiny knob of land east of the village, where a cemetery had been established. The gravestones in the cemetery, made from slabs of slate brought over from Connecticut in the holds of ships, were elegant in their simplicity; some had small skulls etched on the top, the names of the dead carved below the skulls. Joseph was buried near the north side of the cemetery, a few feet from the roadway, next to his father and grandmother.

Funerals were a weekly occurrence, records of the day show, and a family named Salmon had begun making an index of deaths. The entries at the time of Joseph's death read:

MAR. 13  Limos . . . negro aged . . . about 40 years.
       17  or 18 Elesabeth Brown
       26  Wm Alboson
            Mary Babcoks son Infa . . .
APRIL 26  Thom Whites wife Hannah
   MAY 6  Stephen Leech wife Rebecka
       15  Jn Budd wife Jeminah. Midnight.
       17  Edward Pennies wife Bathsheba
MAY 21  Justice Joseph Wickham

After his father's death, Parker ran the neck farm, and he grew in stature. Cutchogue was an English village; these were English men. Social standing came with land and education. Standing carried with it political duties, and Parker sought these out, too. First, though, in 1752, three years after his father's death, he married Mary Goldsmith, the daughter of another prominent farmer. They named their first son Joseph Parker Wickham, the middle name being in honor of Parker's mother's family, who at this time lived in a grand home on the south side of the Peconic River, near the spot where carriages could cross from one fork to another. Everyone coming from the South Fork—Southampton and East Hampton—to the North Fork for business, or to the courts on the north side of the river, passed their home. (Years later, a writer would find this home overgrown with weeds, the windows caved in, and lost in a patch of overgrowth and trash behind an abandoned church.)

The couple's family grew quickly. There were three sons—Joseph P., John, and Thomas—and three daughters—Parnel, Sarah, and Mary. Like other well-off families, the Wickhams had slaves to work their land. The names of three field hands—James, York, and Osbons—have survived the passage of time. They were either bought at the slave market in New York or, more likely, from other farmers on the North Fork. It is also possible they were brought directly from Africa on a ship that landed in Sag Harbor, which was at this time a busier port than New York. Sag Harbor was a long day's journey by carriage from the North Fork.

As far as one can tell today, the couple's life was quiet throughout the first two decades of their marriage. He worked in several town positions, including justice and town supervisor. He served in the latter post nine times. As justice, he would be asked to assist an attorney sent to Cutchogue by New York's colonial governor. The attorney's task was to inquire about the miserable state of the Indians on the North Fork. The Indians had written the governor an anguished letter asking for help, and the governor, who would later write that he was moved by their plight, had sent a lawyer to inquire as to land set aside for their use. Parker Wickham was asked to take statements from older town residents who recalled where the native villages had been, and his signature is affixed to the statements that have survived.

But nothing he did as a public servant prepared him for the events that would unfold as the revolutionary spirit that had begun in the early 1770s swept into Southold. Wickham surely knew, as so many others did, of the events in Boston Harbor on the night of December 16, 1773, when a group of indignant colonists, led by Samuel Adams and Paul Revere, disguised themselves as Indians, sneaked aboard a ship, and threw crates of tea into the water. The action, widely reported throughout the colonies, had been staged as a protest against the tea tax, part of a broader category of taxes called the Townshend Acts, which had been repealed by Parliament. The tea tax had been retained, however, partly to show the colonists who their masters were and partly to prop up the ailing East India Company.

While support for England on the East End was strong, there were a growing number of revolutionaries who favored ousting the British. By the spring of 1775, a number of residents of Southold began forming a committee that would link up with other committees in the colony favoring independence. If families were divided before on the issue of loyalty to England, they were now ruptured. Records show that some individuals who favored rebellion fled the town. Soon an exodus of sorts would begin; between 1776 and 1778, the town's population would drop from 755 to 506—249 moved away, most of them probably to Connecticut. The British, intent on knowing who opposed them, collected the names of those they called "refugees"; soon, those who sided with the patriot cause began taking names, too.

In the summer of 1776, shortly after the Declaration of Independence was signed in Philadelphia, New York's provincial government declared that anyone who sided with the British would now be considered a traitor. Any belief by men like Parker Wickham that revolution would pass them by was now dashed. That fall, the Crown's agents in Southold went door-to-door administering oaths of loyalty to King George III.

By the following spring, New York's new constitution had been adopted. By then, for reasons that surely included Parker Wickham's political history as a Crown-appointed official, as well as his having powerful enemies who may have coveted his magnificent farm, Wickham's name had been forwarded to the provincial Congress. How he earned a place on a list of enemies of the people is unclear, but when associations of revolutionaries had been drawn up at the town level, Wickham had not placed his signature on the document. Thus he had declared himself a Loyalist—and a Loyalist with several hundred acres of land.

Dwight Holbrook, the author of a book entitled *The Wickham Claim*, states that the naming of Wickham to the Congress as much as condemned him. "History would condemn him without having heard him," Holbrook writes.

On the cold night of December 13, 1777, Americans from Connecticut raided the Southold shoreline, looking for supporters of the British. They found four men, two of whom were living in Cutchogue—Parker Wickham, the Crown's supervisor for the town, and his neighbor Matthew Wells. Wickham was taken from his home in the hollow, escorted to a waiting boat—presumably lying at anchor off Goldsmith's Inlet—on Long Island Sound, and from there shipped to Connecticut. He was given a house in which to live under armed guard, separated from his family.

Nearly two years later, in late October 1779, New York's legislature enacted a law for the forfeiture of property "of persons who have adhered to the enemies of this state." The law accused and convicted, sight unseen, fifty-nine offenders, their names having been drawn up by their enemies, and sentenced them to banishment. Parker was prominent on the list. And since these offenders would no longer be living on their land, their properties were to be turned over to a commissioner of forfeiture, who would sell them at auction.

In his book, Holbrook points out the obvious problem with the law as it related to the North Fork. "New York was divided into two areas, one controlled by the patriots and the other, which was all of Long Island, by the British. In other words, British law was in force on Long Island. This law was meaningless to Wickham. The state could, and this is obvious, not seize property outside its jurisdiction and bring it into its own."

Since British troops occupied the North Fork, Wickham Neck was out of the reach of the commissioners. Parker seems to have stayed in Connecticut for at least part of the war, his son Joseph living in the house in the hollow and farming the land. While the war was still going on, Parker conveyed ownership of the farm and Robins Island to Joseph, no doubt in an effort to prevent the loss of the land bought by his grandfather. So now it was not owned by Parker and thus was legally not within the grasp of the commissioners; therefore, on the surface, Parker's actions would seem to have nullified the effects of the law. Meanwhile, Parker's mother, Abigail, held title to the massive tract of land at the head of the river.

According to Holbrook, further events were to take place that, on paper at least, should have kept the farm and island in Wickham's hands. A new constitution was adopted in the spring of 1777, which said that no citizen could be deprived of his rights except by the "law of the land" and the judgment of his peers. It also stated that the rights of heirs would override a forfeiture action. "Their blood would not be deemed corrupted just because of the alleged wrongdoing of the parent," Holbrook writes.

If Parker Wickham read about the constitution, he had to have been relieved. Surely these words were meant for him. He could not be deprived of his land except by the judgment of his peers, and, in any event, his son's rights of ownership were now paramount.

Perhaps the law lulled him into returning to Cutchogue, which Holbrook shows that he did, at least for brief visits. Mary Wickham, his wife, died on March 25, 1780, and it seems likely he was at the funeral in the church across from his house; one month later, he was witness to the signing of a neighbor's deed. On January 11, Parker's brother Joseph had died at his home in the eastern part of the town. Between his death and Mary's death, the Salmon records list six others:

| | | |
|---|---|---|
| JAN. | 20 | Joseph Booth Negro Josep. |
| FEB. | 13 | Zabullon Hallock Wife Marther. 79 |
| | 19 | William Bennit 80. |
| MARCH | 4 | Wid mary Horton Ralick Jonat. 93 |
| | 14 | Garshom Tarrey Juner Child. |
| | 17 | Joshua Horton Shot by C Boot old. 25. |

As the war neared its end in 1783, Parker was living on the North Fork. On November 1, he was in New York City conducting business. Surely he followed the drafting of the Treaty of Paris, which, to his relief, specifically made it illegal to seize the property of wartime Tories. After his visit to New York City, he made his way back to his neck farm in Cutchogue. To Holbrook's mind, Parker was a broken man, having been so long separated from the place he loved, and he continued to be fearful of retribution, following, as he did, stories in the newspapers of Tories being run off their land, their homes looted.

Late in the month of November, Parker and his family traveled to New London, on the Connecticut coastline, and it may be that Parker toyed with the idea of following thousands of other

Tories to the safety of Canada. But he didn't go, perhaps because he was too ill, or too stubborn. He found a home on the Niantic River, and his son Joseph stayed with him for a few days before boarding a ship for Antigua. He never saw his father again.

In the late summer of 1784, while Parker was in Connecticut, his lands were appraised and sold by the commissioners of forfeiture, in violation of the terms of the Treaty of Paris. The buyer of the neck farm at an auction was Jared Landon, the son of a local judge named Samuel Landon, with whom Parker had publicly feuded and whom he had once sued in a court of law.

On May 22, 1785, Parker's death was noted in the Salmon records. His body was not brought over to Cutchogue to be buried in the tiny cemetery where his wife, parents, and grandparents were buried. He had been banished, even in death.

In the Caribbean, his son Joseph supported himself as a merchant. In 1788, he was in North Carolina, and in October of that year he sailed to London to present the case before a claims board that his father's land had been seized from the family in violation of the terms of the treaty recognizing American independence. In December of 1789, the board awarded Wickham 2,800 pounds sterling for property loss.

Joseph appears to have remained too bitter to hurry back to Cutchogue. In October 1790, he was in Dublin, where he wrote a friend: "I never more expect to see my Native Country. In short the suffering of our family have been so Great in it that I don't want to see it. I am a Single Man and the World is before me."

But the following year, he did return, finding Jared Landon living in the house, and Robins Island owned by a man named Ezra L'Hommedieu. Joseph bought a farm in Cutchogue, and when he died, it was passed on to members of his family.

# EIGHT

# Uncle James

CUTCHOGUE IN THE early 1800s was a community of fewer than two hundred residents, most of whom lived on farms or along the Main Road. Some lived in grand homes that no longer stand to-day, their front porches overlooking the east-west road, their back doors looking north across open farmland to green patches of woods.

On the western edge of Cutchogue, west of Manor Hill, was Tuthill Town. A number of Tuthills lived here, including Elijah Tuthill, the great-grandfather of John Tuthill. There were perhaps a dozen farms that stretched south of the road, bounded by salt creeks, and north nearly all the way to Long Island Sound, now no longer called the North Sea. The British were gone, and so were their place names.

East and west of the Cutchogue Presbyterian Church were Wickhams, Hortons, and Wellses. By the early part of the century, though, the Wells family had run out of male descendants in Cutchogue; there were a number of Wellses farming to the west at Aquebogue, but in Cutchogue, the very land originally bought by William Wells, the male line had ended and the female members of the family, at least those in one line, married into a family named Fleet, who were from up the island. Soon, the Fleets were well-to-do and living in a big home on the south side of the roadway in the center of Cutchogue. Theirs was the first farm to the east of a farm owned by the Albertson family.

The Albertsons were living on what had been called Booth's Neck and was now Robins Island Neck. The Booths, like the Wellses, had produced more daughters than sons, and the west half of Booth's Neck passed into a line of the Tuthill family, who lived in homes north of Dam Meadow, along the road laid out by Joseph Wickham, Parker's father; the eastern half of the neck passed into the Reeve family. The Albertson family followed in turn, and they moved into a big two-story home at the top of the creek, just south of the roadway and reachable down a long lane. It was a beautiful home, one of the grandest in Cutchogue, the kind of home on the kind of farm that was the very image of the North Fork—fertile land bounded by salt water.

The farm on the western edge of the Albertson farm was, of course, the very land lost by Parker Wickham. And to the west of that farm, along the north side of the road and east of Tuthill Town, sat the home and farm of Parker's brother John, who at nearly the same time as the confiscation of his brother's property had bought the land from a member of the Horton family. It is not an exaggeration to think that these Wickhams resented what had happened to Parker; surely they knew he had died a broken man in Connecticut. But they had lives to live and farms to manage, and by all accounts, they lived well.

Perhaps the wealthiest of these Wickhams did not live here. Parker's nephew John, his brother's son, left Cutchogue as a young man and moved to Virginia. By the early 1800s, he was a wealthy Richmond lawyer, a darling of society in that city, and a man who counted among his clients Aaron Burr. It was said that he knew Thomas Jefferson, although from a respectful distance, considering this Wickham's Loyalist sentiments during the Revolution. He had married a Fanning, whose family was also from the North Fork, but there is no record that he ever returned home. Among his large collection of letters and manuscripts in Richmond, there is not a single letter addressed to Cutchogue. It is as if he forgot where he was from, or, perhaps, refused to associate with people who had seized his uncle's property.

In the early part of the century, Parker's sister Elizabeth married a man named James Reeve. They may have inherited some of her brother's slaves, although three of them—York, Osbons, and

# The Family Tree from Thomas Wickham to John Wickman

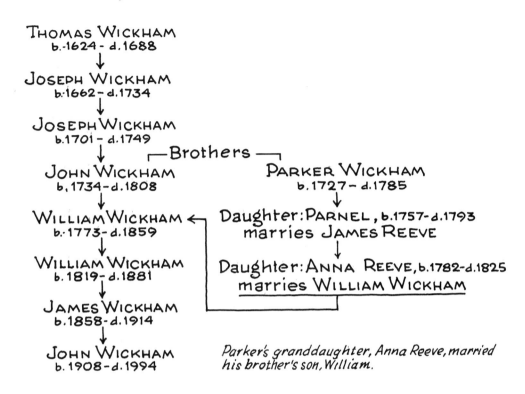

THOMAS WICKHAM
b.-1624 - d.1688
↓
JOSEPH WICKHAM
b.1662 - d.1734
↓
JOSEPH WICKHAM
b.1701 - d.1749
↓

─ Brothers ─

JOHN WICKHAM
b.1734 - d.1808

PARKER WICKHAM
b.1727 - d.1785
↓

WILLIAM WICKHAM ←
b.-1773 - d.1859
↓

Daughter: PARNEL, b.1757 - d.1793
marries JAMES REEVE
↓

WILLIAM WICKHAM
b.1819 - d.1881
↓

Daughter: ANNA REEVE, b.1782 - d.1825
marries WILLIAM WICKHAM

JAMES WICKHAM
b.1858 - d.1914
↓

JOHN WICKHAM
b.1908 - d.1994

*Parker's granddaughter, Anna Reeve, married his brother's son, William.*

Catury, along with a child named Joseph—had drowned on June 6, 1781. There is no record today of where the accident happened or whether the bodies were recovered where they were buried. The shimmering mirror of history often reflects back very little.

The Reeves owned land south of the Albertson farmhouse, along the western edge of the creek where the shells were piled up. Their land stretched west to the north-south road that ran alongside Dam Meadow. One of Parker's daughters, a pretty, dark-haired woman named Parnel, also married a man named James Reeve, who might have been her first cousin, although there were so many Reeves in the area he could have been no relation at all. They, too, seem to have lived near Parker's old homestead.

Parnel and James had a daughter named Anna, who, on November 30, 1802, married a farmer named William Wickham, another of Parker's nephews. William lived on his father's farm on the western edge of Cutchogue, near Fort Neck. The farm ran from the road all the way north to the Sound. The land was heavily wooded except for a large cleared area north of the house that was used to raise crops. This farm had been bought in 1669 by Caleb Horton; it was sold to John Wickham in 1784. For a time, Caleb also owned Fort Neck, including the odd-looking tract of ridged land where the Indian fort stood.

Anna and William's children lived in homes all along the roadway. Their son Henry lived at the foot of Alvah's Lane, surrounded by members of the Horton family. His sister Nancy married a man named Case, and they eventually bought the house and land that had been confiscated from Parker. Another son, William, an attorney of prominence, practiced law and served several terms as Suffolk County's district attorney. (This William was the grandfather of John Wickham and his cousin Bill Wickham.)

Anna and William's son James moved early in his life to Brooklyn, where he owned and operated a profitable grocery store called Wickham and Corwin. Well-off financially, James Wickham returned to Cutchogue in 1850 to buy a farm that sat between two salt creeks.

I do not know what James Wickham looked like. No drawing of him was ever made, as far as I have been able to find. And very little description of him exists, except this: He was of modest build, with dark hair and dark eyes. He was considered a good businessman and had accumulated considerable wealth by his early forties. While he left Cutchogue in his twenties to work in Brooklyn, his birthplace was not far from his mind. It seems he longed to return home, and eventually he did.

What brought him back to Cutchogue was word, in all likelihood relayed to him by his brother William, that the farm of Josiah Albertson, along with his stately home at the top of the salt creek, was to be sold at auction. It was a farm of eighty acres; to its east lay the land of the Fleet family, to the west was Tuthill land, and beyond that was the former Parker Wickham farm.

"What I would say is that James had a desire to come back to Cutchogue, and his brother William was looking out for a farm for him," William Wickham told me. Bill Wickham lives on the farm on the western edge of Cutchogue first bought by John Wickham in 1784 and passed all the way down to Bill. The lawyer William Wickham, James's brother, was Bill's grandfather. "What I believe is that the Albertsons were in some sort of financial distress and the farm was to be auctioned off. James was told of this, and he came out and bought it."

Bill Wickham, unlike his cousin John, is of modest build. John Wickham is tall enough to have to duck through most doors. Both men were well educated—John graduated from Cornell with an engineering degree before he came home to farm the family's land; William is an attorney, like his grandfather. Their fathers were brothers who both died young. Throughout their lives, John's and Bill's memories of their fathers were wisps of pale smoke.

At his farm between the salt creeks, John Wickham has spent years of his life trying to piece together the patchwork history of the land. What can be said is that a portion of the farm on the west side of the creek, a big piece that straddled the broad middle of the farm south of the big house, was owned by Elizabeth Reeve in the very early 1800s. We know this because of a thin, worn document in the John Wickham home that shows that late in her life Elizabeth turned over a portion of the Shell Bank land to her slave Lymas Reeve.

This flimsy piece of paper shows that on June 25, 1812, Elizabeth Reeve freed Lymas and a slave named Jenny and gave to them an acre of land and a house of some sort at Shell Bank. It was probably not much more than a shack built on sandy soil near the south edge of the farm.

Elizabeth wrote: ". . . I give to my two negroes Limas and Jenny liberty and freedom." In addition, she gave them "an acre of land lying at a place called Shell Bank . . . also one hundred and fifty dollars" owed to her by the Albertsons. Elizabeth also provided them with beds and other furnishings, including a dining table. There is no history of Lymas and no record of his ancestry other than a small item published in the local *Suffolk Times* in April 1870, shortly after his death. It states that he was born in Southold in 1784 and that he learned to read the Bible through the efforts of a blind slave named Betty, who was owned by the Tuthill family.

In 1841, eight members of the Tuthill family sold twenty acres of Shell Bank to Josiah Albertson, who owned the land immediately to the north. Nine years later, on October 14, 1850, at one o'clock in the afternoon, James Wickham bought from Josiah Albertson, at an auction in the home of Henry Jennings, eighty acres of farmland, bounded by the road on the north, by the land of Augustine Fleet and the creek on the east, by the land of Benjamin Wells on the south, and by the north-south road and the land of David Tuthill on the west. The price was $7,500.

David Tuthill's family lived in a home several hundred yards to the west of the home James bought at the auction. His descendants would remain in this house, the last being Fred Tuthill, a man who loved to play the violin after farmwork. When Tuthill died in the 1970s, he left the house and farm to John Wickham, allowing John to expand his farm all the way over to the edge of Parker Wickham's old land. John's son Jack and his family own the house today.

Back in Cutchogue, James Wickham and his wife hired servants and field-workers, and, on occasion, they returned to Brooklyn to visit friends. He had been managing his farm for only four years when he got into a bitter argument with one of his field hands. On June 3, 1854, this story appeared in the *New York Daily Times:*

> A horrid murder was committed at Cutchogue last night about midnight at the house of James Wickham, Esq. a retired merchant from your City. The servant girls who lodged in the garret were aroused by screams of "murder," "help," and in the voice of Mrs. Wickham, "Spare our lives!" Rushing to the foot of the upper stairs, they crept out through an upper window upon the roof of the kitchen, thence sliding down to a shed, and thence jumping to the ground, ran to alarm the neighbors. The ones first hearing the alarm were JOSEPH CORWIN, WILLIAM BETTS and DR. BENJAMIN D. CARPENTER, who instantly returned with them to the house. The murderer had fled. Tracks of blood showed the passage he had taken to escape from the house. A hat was found, too, which is recog-

nized as that of an Irishman, NICHOLAS DANE. In the sleeping room, Mr. Wickham was found covered with blood, his head frightfully gashed, clots covering his features and the wounds still bleeding. There was not a square inch upon his face but on which there was not a wound. Yet life was not quite extinct. At the hour of the leaving of the cars (nine o'clock) he was still breathing, though unconscious, and with but the feeblest chance for life. By his side lay the mangled but not quite lifeless body of his wife, MRS. FRANCES WICKHAM, her brains dashed about the floor, and her blood lying in pools upon the bed and carpet. A few moments more and she had ceased to breathe. A colored boy STEPHEN, aged 14 years, who was a great favorite in the family, was also horribly mutilated. He, too, was alive when the house was entered, and continued so when my informant left.

A few days before the attack, an Irish field hand named Nicholas Behan had been fired by Wickham for hustling one of the house servants, Ellen Holland ("He had proposed marriage, but was rejected," reads a portion of the above story), and for stealing from her room. He came back on the evening of June 2, picked up a post ax ("which was found yesterday morning upon the premises, with blood and hair upon it") in a shed, and killed Wickham and his wife in their upstairs bedroom.

More from the same story:

JAMES WICKHAM, Esq. formerly of the firm of Wickham and Corwin, and long a resident in this City (New York City), was married but two or three years since to MISS FRANCES POST, of Quogue, Long Island, and soon after bought the spacious mansion house in Cutchogue, known as the property formerly of JOSIAH ALBERTSON, Esq. The house is very large, modern-built, and beautifully situated on a branch of Peconic Bay, with a deep lawn extended some forty rods in front of the post-road. The village of Cutchogue itself is one of the most quiet and rural on the east end of Long Island. It is a portion of the old town of Southold, wherein the last murder that was committed dates back at least thirty years. The railroad passes some half a mile north of the village, which is about twelve miles from Greenport. The house, standing back from the road, and at a distance of a quarter of a mile from any neighbors, facilitated by its seclusion the designs of the fiend. MR. WICKHAM had purchased a large farm, and employed of course many men upon it. Doubtless it is one of these who has dealt such terrible vengeance for his fancied grievances. Mr. and Mrs. W. were both highly esteemed wherever known, and enjoyed in this City a large circle of friends. Mr. W.'s father, mother, brother and sisters reside within a mile of the scene of this bloody murder. One brother, whose farm lies on the north side, is reputed the largest farmer in Suffolk County. Another, residing in Patchogue, is, and has been for many years, the District Attorney of Suffolk County. It was an uncle of the murdered man, a Virginia lawyer who took an honorable part in the trial of AARON BURR for treason. The greatest excitement prevails throughout the town, and a more monstrous case in all its details, may it never be our duty to record.

THE FUNERAL PROCESSION — IMMENSE ATTENDANCE

Monday afternoon was a time of solemnity and sorrow in the quiet village of Cutchogue, on the occasion of the funeral of the victims. The bodies were placed in coffins with silver plates, bearing the following inscriptions:

JAMES WICKHAM

*Died June 4, 1854 — Aged 53 years and 4 days.*

FRANCES WICKHAM

*Died June 3, 1854 — Aged 33 years and 3 days.*

The burial service was performed by Rev. Mr. Younges and Rev. Mr. Sinclair, of Cutchogue, in presence of a vast number of persons, some of whom came from a distance of 40 miles. The church bells tolled, and when the procession was formed it reached nearly two miles in length, and upwards of two hundred vehicles were in it. The corpses were conveyed to the Presbyterian graveyard in Mattituck, and both were buried in the same grave. Nearly every man, woman and child in Cutchogue was at the funeral, and the town presented a most gloomy appearance.

The morning of the funeral, Behan was found lying under "thick brush" in a "gloomy swamp" east of Cutchogue. He was surrounded by an armed crowd of more than one thousand men and boys, bound, and taken to the county jail in Riverhead. A special prosecutor was named, since William, the district attorney, could hardly try the case, and in October the trial was held.

In late October, Behan was convicted. On December 15, he was hanged in a courtyard behind the jail, and then his body was taken in a wooden coffin to the south side of the Peconic River, a place called Egypt, and buried without a marker of any kind.

*The three Wickham boys, John, Henry, and James Parker, walking down the farm road south of the farmhouse, pasture land to their right and beyond that the salt creek. The exact date of the photograph, or who took it, is unknown. It appears to have been taken a few years after the death of their father, James, who died of blood poisoning in 1914. The oldest son, Parker, as James was called, died in a car wreck near the family farm in the spring of 1930, which transferred management of the farm to John. "We were as tight as three brothers could be," John Wickham once said. "My father's death made Parker a farmer; Parker's death made me a farmer." As for his father, he said, "I don't have an image in my mind of my father. I can see the farm, but I can't see him. But I've always believed I'm the farmer he wanted to be."*

NINE

# "Truly, He Was a Good Man"

IN THE LATE summer of 1993 the weather cooled, and it held cool for a long string of days. I ran

into David Steele several times, and he looked fit and happy. Soon our sons would both be playing

soccer, and we would meet at games and practices and talk about his farming. Hard outdoor work

pleased him, and it showed. There was in him the same kind of honesty about life that I saw in John

Tuthill.

One afternoon I saw John, and he looked tired, as if his body hurt. He is a reserved man, a man of few words, and I wanted to talk with him, but I held back. He was still working with David, who was selling truckloads of potatoes out of his fields, grading them at the barn alongside the Cutchogue railroad tracks. They were cutting cauliflower, too. But prices were not good—California cauliflower had cut into the market, hurting David badly, pushing a number of North Fork growers into thinking that next year they would not do this anymore. Martin Sidor on Oregon Road in Mattituck was in this same position, sitting back wondering how cauliflower could be grown in California, shipped to New York, and sold so cheaply.

Maybe just stick with potatoes—an unthinkable thought, really, considering that a couple of bad years strung together would mean it would be over. The potato industry was so fragile, so on the edge, just teetering back and forth. Everyone remembered 1985, the two-dollar year. Think about that, someone said, and the skin on your neck crawled. You lay in bed at night thinking: I'll never farm again, it's over.

"It's always a seesaw," David said during one game. "It can go one way; it can go another way. Cauliflower used to be a great money crop; now that's disappearing. Cauliflower always kept us busy after potatoes. I'm thinking, What will I do if I don't have cauliflower? How can you make up that loss?"

A few weeks later, I went to the Wickham house to talk to John. The nights were cooler now, but the days were warm, and the apple-picking crowds at the farm stand were heavy. Busy was good, considering the farm stand would be shut down for the winter.

On this morning, I wanted John to talk about William Wickham, his grandfather, who moved into this house after his brother and sister-in-law were murdered. I had found the newspaper clips of the day and I wanted to show them to John, but when I mentioned it, he waved me off.

"You know," he said, "I didn't even hear about that until I was well into my teens. A family friend told me, and I ran and asked my aunt Julia, and she said yes, it had happened. But I never dug into it; I never studied just what had happened."

"But those murders," I said, "those are the reason you are here on this farm. Right?"

"Well, yes," he said. "Had my great-uncle died first, his wife's family, the Posts, would have inherited the farm. But James held on and outlived her by a day or less. I don't know. Honestly, I haven't thought about that."

He did think about it later, when after his marriage to Anne Lupton they moved into the room where the murders had taken place. They did not stay for long. "One night, I heard footsteps in the hall, then the door opening," he recalled. "I did not look up, of course, but I felt someone was looking down at me. I think he wanted to see who was sleeping in his bedroom."

What William's moving to this farm in the summer of 1854 said to me was that there was life after death, that the business of farming this land went on. John would later tell me this himself, although in a totally different context: "It goes on; it has to go on."

It was said by others, too, most notably his brother, Henry. Henry once told John, "John, if something happens to you, I'll come home." This struck me as so extraordinary that almost every time John and I sat down to talk, I brought it up.

"I don't know why that surprises you so much," he said once, laughing. "That's just my family."

A portrait of William, painted in the 1870s, shows a refined-looking dark-haired man. He bore a closer resemblance to his grandson Bill than to John. William's wife, Sarah Elizabeth Havens, is pretty in her portrait. William moved onto the farm in the late summer of 1854, after a court proceeding in which his father, also named William, was appointed to handle his son James's estate. According to Bill Wickham, an arrangement was struck that allowed William to take over his brother's eighty-acre farm. In return, he gave up all interest in the Wickham land a half mile to the west, where Bill lives today.

Three years later, William married Sarah, who was from the South Shore. In 1859, two years after their marriage, William's father died. By then, William and Sarah had begun a family. Three children were born, James, William, who was called Will, and Julia. James was John's father; Will was Bill Wickham's father. Julia never married, but because of the many deaths in the family, she was like a mother to John and his two brothers, Henry and Parker.

Having not sought reelection as the county's district attorney, William Wickham continued to practice law and lived on his new Cutchogue farm. John's only knowledge of his grandfather's life is what Aunt Julia told him. John, in the notes he collected over the years, wrote down some of these stories:

> Lawyer Wickham, as he was commonly called, besides being attorney for the Long Island Rail Road, was also representing the Shinnecock Indian Reservation and upon an occasion a delegation of braves came to see him. Julia said that each of them in coming through the south dining room door of the house completely filled it. If she was so impressed by these Indians when her own brother James was six feet one inch and broad to boot they must have been big. It's a pity that virtually all of the men on this reservation perished salvaging a ship off the South Shore. . . . A final story of Julia's was that she had never heard her father call her mother Sarah but once. It was always Mrs. Wickham. However, on this occasion he had unexpectedly come home late at night after the household had been locked up and all asleep. Apparently he wandered around the house and finally in desperation shouted "Sarah" under her window—it worked.

John knew William had died from a cut on his hand. He fell while walking to the house from the train station on Depot Lane, John told me. The cut became infected, and he died of blood poisoning. I found a newspaper clip, and late one fall afternoon, when he was closing up the farm stand, I read it to John. The clipping was from the *Long Island Traveler*, March 4, 1881.

It was a cool evening, the sky clear. He stopped what he was doing and listened.

"'We have to record today the sudden and sad death of William Wickham, Esquire, of Cutchogue,'" I read softly, "'the senior partner of the law firm of Wickham and Case.'"

He laughed. "The Cases have been friends with the Wickhams for years and years."

I continued: "'There is an almost tragic character in the circumstances of his sickness. On Saturday, the nineteenth, he returned from Riverhead on the evening train and in walking down from the station to his residence slipped on a bit of ice. In falling his hand struck on what seemed to be a twig or the standing root of a small bush which had been cut off. It penetrated the palm of his hand, but the wound did not seem a serious one.'"

John fidgeted; he could see where this was going.

"'During last week it pained him quite severely and was swollen and inflamed, but he continued to use it assiduously in his writing, and continued to consult professionally with those who called on him till late Friday afternoon. That night, pronounced symptoms of lock jaw ensued when Dr. Terry, the neighboring physician, was called and doctors Carpenter, of Jersey City, and Preston, of Patchogue, were telegraphed for. But all efforts to save his life proved unavailing.'"

I looked up briefly. John was whisking something out of his eyes with the back of his hand.

"'He went into a spasm from which he never came out, and on Sunday he died. His death must needs be a matter of public interest to Long Island. His long experience at the bar of this county and through the state, his pre-eminent legal ability and his extended practice, as well as the prominent official positions he has held, have made him the best known man in Suffolk County.'"

John looked up, smiling now. "Aunt Julia certainly conveyed to me that last piece of information. I think my cousin Bill would agree with that assessment of our grandfather."

I continued to read. "'His character was a strong and marked one. His will was inflexible'"—he let out a big belly laugh—"'his honorableness distinguished, his unobtrusiveness almost a peculiarity. His self reliance never wavered and nearly always unfailingly won for him success. He was a great friend of the poor man and he espoused his cause as gladly as he did that of his wealthy clients.'"

I slowed down to concentrate on the last few sentences.

"'No man was ever more thoughtless of the rewards which his services entitled him to. Fatigue and labor and loss never deterred him in his cases. He was more just and generous to others than himself.'"

I stopped for a moment, and we watched the cars passing by in front of the farm stand. It was late, and dark now, and a warm home beckoned at the end of the lane.

"'Truly,'" I read, "'he was a good man, and we have met with a great public loss.'"

A big man, John stood and leaned against a wall by a shelf of pies. An aerial photograph of his farm was anchored to the wall near his head. He folded his arms across his chest, thinking deeply.

"Does any of this surprise you?" I asked.

"Not at all," he said. "He's the man I always imagined him to be." He did not know what else to say. He drew the doors down on the farm stand and walked quietly to his car.

Looking down the long lane toward the house, he stopped and leaned against the car door.

"I can see William in all of my children," he said, then got in the car and drove toward the house.

# PART THREE

# Heaven and Earth

*This is the immense threat—that when we lose one set of connections we end up severed from all connectedness.*

—TONY HISS, *Encountering the Countryside*

*Harvesting by hand on the North Fork, July 20, 1936. Photograph by Charles Meredith. Courtesy of the Southold Historical Society.*

TEN

# Ernest Tuthill

"POP WAS A good farmer, I would say that. He grew up doing farmwork, because what else was there to do? For him, there was the Tuthill farm. Oh, I suppose he could have done other things, but I'm not so sure he would have seen it that way. It's not like today, with people having so many other options."

"Pop" was Ernest Tuthill, a jug-eared man with a big round head and an engaging smile. He lived near the top of Elijah's Lane, in the big house on the hill that sits north of the tracks. This was the heart of Tuthill Town. His history lay all around him. He was ninety-nine when he died in May of 1980. He is buried in the Cutchogue Cemetery behind the Methodist church, next to Leila Hallock Tuthill, his wife.

John Tuthill smiles when he talks about his father. On an evening when the western sky turned pink as the sun descended, he sat at the round table in his living room. Soon the house was dark and the night air chilled the room. John is a quiet man, and when I first met him, he seemed to embody the characteristics associated with another age. He lived an older kind of life, not much different from the life his father lived on this same land. He had better equipment, but for the most part the farming was the same, the goals the same, the life quiet and out of the way. John could talk about his family or his work and every so often smile widely and laugh out loud. But it seemed a part of him was hidden away.

"If Pop thought of doing work other than farming, I don't believe he shared them with me. But, you know, he also had other interests. And I think he was a little more social than perhaps I am or some other folks in our area. You can see that in his diaries he kept. Cold mornings, he'd go skating at Wolf Pit Pond. Spring and summer, he'd play baseball with a group of farmers and townspeople. I would say my father was a contented man in most respects . . . most respects."

John's brother Hallock, who lives east of John's farmhouse across open farmland, seemed to me to be the spitting image of their father. Photographs of Ernest and Hallock show strikingly similar-looking men. No one could look at John and Hallock and not know they were brothers, but it's Hallock who looks the most like Ernest.

It was John, though, who after World War II came home and, with the military pay he had saved up, bought the farm of Ralph Tuthill, his father's brother, in Tuthill Town. The farm, stretched along the east side of Elijah's Lane, had belonged to John's grandfather, G. B. Tuthill. After buying the land and the ancient house that came with it, John got married and started raising potatoes and vegetables.

"I enlisted in 1941, before Pearl Harbor," John said. "They had already put out draft numbers. Everyone in Cutchogue and Mattituck got one. So I had a very low number. And I didn't want to get mixed up in farming for the following year if I was going to be called up. So I went and volunteered in the draft. To see if I would be accepted, you know. You went to a doctor first, then if you passed, you went to Camp Upton. All they had there was winterized tents, with a little stove in the middle. Burned coal or wood or something. We froze our tails off. That was some night, that was. And I called up my folks and said, 'I'm in now, I'm in.' I remember before we left in the troop train, my folks did come to bring a few things. They didn't stay long. My dad thought the army was a good thing for me. My mother, she wouldn't cry or anything like that. But she felt it."

The train took him to Alabama, where it was cold, too. The stoves in the tents burned soft coal, and a haze covered the camp like a blanket. In the morning, the soldiers woke up coughing. In June 1941, six months after he left home, he stepped off the train in Mattituck for a visit. He was in uniform and looked sharp as a tack. He went back to the house on the hill where his father and Hallock were farming. Home only a week, John did farm chores, too, the way he had always done. Then he left again for Alabama.

After Pearl Harbor, that December, John was shipped to California. He spent Christmas Day on the base, and he remembers now thinking about his home on the North Fork, missing his family. While he ate a special meal on the base, the family in Mattituck went across the road to his cousin's house, where his aunt Florence cooked a holiday meal. Every year, the routine was pretty much the same: Thanksgiving at Aunt Ruth's in Peconic; Christmas at Aunt Florence's; and New Year's Day at Ernest and Leila's house.

Training in California, John wrote home often, asking about the family and the farm and especially about his share of the income. Four years later, in the fall of 1945, John was stationed in Hawaii. He took a ship to San Francisco, then flew in a troop plane back east. Discharged from a base in New Jersey, he took the train to Mattituck.

"I hadn't called home, so they were not expecting me. But at the station in Mattituck, I called and said, 'Well, I'm here.' My mother answered the phone and she said, 'Oh, I'm glad.' Because Hallock had an appendicitis and my father was taking care of his chickens, that long building in the hollow there. It was all full of chickens. That was Hallock's business, along with running the farm with my father.

"So my father came up and got me. And he said, 'Hello, come on home.' So I got home and we carried water down to the chickens. That same day. And I went to work. And Hallock had potatoes to harvest, and at that time we picked them up by hand. So I dug potatoes out there, and we had to load them on the truck, bag after bag. There's one hundred and forty-five bags on a truck. Two or three truckloads every day. And everyone I saw looked so much older than when I'd left. There was a fellow in the city, and I used to play tennis with him when I was in the army in Hawaii. Goldberg was his name. And golly, he called me up one day and he says, 'Tut, we didn't know how good we had it in the army.' Well, I said, 'You don't want to come out here, because I'm on a farm and I'm working every day.' And that's the way it was."

While John was away, Hallock purchased a thirty-two-acre tract east of the home farm for $6,500. A neighboring farmer, Forrest Horton, held the mortgage, a practice that was not uncommon in those days. Hallock's farm had belonged to an Irish family named Burns, but they went broke, and by the mid-1960s, Hallock was having a hard time, too, so he gave it up and found work down on the bay.

Hallock remained interested in the farming history of Mattituck and Cutchogue, and he made me a map showing the locations of the farms around his family's in 1945. On the map are dozens of Polish last names, some Irish names, and English names that are no longer on the North Fork. It seemed as though one world had been erased, the history stripped away and hidden, and another world built on top of it.

The map shows Ralph Tuthill's old farm, and north of it, across the railroad tracks, the big house Ernest Tuthill built. "Pop bought that in 1911, I think, and the year after he got married to Leila Hallock," Hallock Tuthill says.

"The house where John is, that was G.B.'s, and ol' G.B. got hooked on morphine, not because he wanted to but because at that time morphine was a miracle drug, kill your pain. But finally you realize you can get hooked on it. And they had to send him off to Connecticut somewhere and get him out of that. And Ralph was running the farm for a while, with his brothers, and then Ralph went off to the First World War. When Pop got married, he came up towards the Middle Road and moved part of a barn up there and started farming. And built that house where David Steele's family is.

"Well, when you grow up on a farm, you farm, I guess. Quint, my other brother, couldn't get off the farm fast enough. He was more inclined to get off the farm than John or I. When John left for the war, I bought this little farm from ol' Burns. And I farmed with Pop while John was away. When John came back, it was just in time for him to stand up for me at my wedding. So he and Pop farmed together. In those years, Ralph was still on the home farm, and John and Pop farmed north of the tracks. And then John got married, and Ralph bought over Nat Tuthill's and moved his dairy business over there. It was a bigger farm and bigger barns and everything. And so John bought from Ralph and moved back onto the home farm.

"For me, I couldn't see life as a farmer. Those years, the business was changing rapidly. There was a big change in equipment, and that took money, and I couldn't see it. And running help was always a problem. You got to be pretty damn tough to run help. But there were dozens and dozens of farms round me in those years, and those folks seemed to make a go of it. Go straight up my road and you'd hit Oregon Road, and there was Mahoney, Hannabury, McBride, the Shalvey brothers, Domaleski, Bonkoski, Keleski, Zaneski, Kaunekas, Berkoski, Zimnoski. Skinny and Scrubby Robinson.

"And the Dutch farmers, Duryee and Wycoff, they'd moved out by the time I was along. Hamiltons, Robinsons, Lauders, Wiggins . . . Some said the Dutch came out from Brooklyn after the Civil War. That was the area called Tustin, on the north side of Oregon. They say it was wild— good gosh, brambles and briars, and rough country. And there were Hallocks up in there, and Uncle Billy Tuthill was up there and ol' Bus Tuthill. And down toward Wolf Pit was where Nat Tuthill was, and that's where Ralph ended up.

"Down Elijah's, of course, there was our home farm, and up across the way was the home farm of Charles Tuthill, Sparky and Les's pop. Elijah Tuthill, my great-grandfather, had land in and around here. He had quite a piece of ground at one time. He kept adding on pieces. His land got eventually divided up between Herbert Tuthill and G.B.—they was the two boys."

Across the Middle Road from Ernest's is Stanley and Leslie's home, which was built by Herbert Tuthill, their grandfather. Their land was always great potato ground. ("The glacier left terrific

*A photograph of the members of the Pequash Club taken sometime in the 1940s. Several Tuthills are in this picture, plus, in the second row standing, fourth from the left, is Russell Fanning, Jeanne Tuthill's mother's brother. Photographer unknown. Courtesy of the Southold Historical Society.*

soil behind that Tuthill house," one farmer said. "Those boys would get potatoes the size of grapefruits.")

Today, their farm is a vineyard. The two brothers still live in the farmhouse, which sits in a low spot next to a cluster of old chicken coops. John Tuthill has coffee with them on weekday mornings at nine. Most Thursdays, John Wickham would make an appearance, usually a few minutes late, and the four men, all roughly the same age, all old-time farmers with long histories behind them, would sit and talk and drink coffee. John Wickham was the only one among them who no longer raised potatoes, but no one held that against him.

By the mid-1940s, most of the farms along Oregon Road from Mattituck to Cutchogue were owned by Polish families. The Irish families who had farmed along Oregon Road (some old-timers say, in referring to the farm families on Oregon Road, that they lived "in Oregon") were disappearing slowly, sometimes selling their farms to the Poles who worked on them. But even in 1945, with all the changes of the war years, there were enough Tuthills to hold down Tuthill Town.

"Some said Tuthill Town went from the Main Road in Mattituck, up Elijah's, across the Middle Road to Oregon," Hallock says. "Others said it didn't include Oregon. It was a place without boundaries, but we knew where it was and who lived there."

Hallock and John's mother was Leila Hallock, and she was born in Nebraska. Her parents were from Cutchogue (her mother was a descendant of William Wells; her father was Jacob "Jakie" Hallock), but they moved to Nebraska, near the town of Edgar, after the Civil War, hoping to homestead a large piece of prairie land. "My mother's mother was Mary Wells Hallock, and things happened out there that frightened her to death," Hallock says. "She said one time she had seen an Indian peeking in a window."

The couple and their children returned to Cutchogue, where they bought a farm near where their families had always lived. Years later, Leila married Ernest Tuthill, and her sister, Florence, married Charles Tuthill. The two families lived across the road from each other.

"Pop used to say the only people that was worth anything was farmers. I guess it was because what you needed, you had. You didn't need a store. You raised different kinds of crops all the time. Potatoes didn't come in big until the twenties and thirties. My grandfather raised two acres a long time ago, but potato growing wasn't much around here. Asparagus was a big crop around here at one time. Cauliflower was quite the thing around here, has been for a long time. We used to ship it in barrels, you know. My father says he used to catch a rabbit once in a while on the spring pole and he'd put it in the top of the barrel of cauliflower and send it over to the city and they'd pay him for it. Can you imagine?

"My father was kind of a raw-boned, rangy fellow, surprisingly strong. He didn't look like he was, but he was. His hand would make two of mine. But he wasn't very efficient. If there's any harder way to do a job, that's the way he did it. Everybody said that. And he was never very venturesome, far as that goes. He'd let the darn weeds get ahead of him; then he'd send us kids out there to hoe and practically ruin the crops to get the weeds out. And my grandfather, who worked for my father a lot of years, my grandfather had two or three kinds of hoeing. Just plain hoeing, you can just brush along. And stub hoeing, where you'd have to kind of bend and really stub; you had to get down there and pull the weeds and work at it. The weeds would get so darn bad, and good gosh.

"But there seemed to be time for other things. There was Terry Tuthill and Luther Tuthill, who farmed on the Main Road on the way to Cutchogue. Terry was Luther's son, and Luther used to play on the ball team with my father. My father was quite an athlete, really. He says Luther was the catcher. Pop used to play on the town team. Left field. I guess he could handle it pretty good. But Luther was a catcher. He couldn't run worth a darn, but he could hit like a son of a gun. He could hit a home run all right, but otherwise forget it, he'd never make first base. My dad, one time they put their bicycles on in Mattituck and rode over to Medford, and rode their bicycles down to Patchogue, and played a game of ball and went back to Medford and come back home again. Cutchogue and Mattituck was a different sort of place then. It really was."

Before and just after the war, it seemed there were more Tuthills farming on the North Fork than any other family. Tuthill Town included Jesse Warren Tuthill, Terry and Luther Tuthill,

George Tuthill, Uncle Clarence Tuthill, Uncle Billy Tuthill, Phillip ("Phip") Tuthill, Ralph Tuthill, and Ernest Tuthill.

East of Tuthill Town were the Hortons and the Wickhams; members of both families lived on either side of Alvah's Lane where it met the Main Road. "There was a Miss Wickham there, and opposite was Miss Jenny Horton. They used to have signals when they got old to see that each one was all right. Miss Jenny missed the signal one morning, and, by gum, they found Miss Wickham dead in the house, and Miss Jenny always felt so bad." (Miss Wickham's name was Frances Post Wickham, and she was the daughter of Henry, the brother of the murdered James. He named his daughter, born the year after the murders, after his former sister-in-law.)

"Pop had milk, too, but he couldn't compete against Nat Tuthill, because Nat was too efficient. Pop sold milk around the area. He had a little route, and he'd go down Bay Avenue with his horse and wagon and sell milk. Sometimes he'd get his brother Ralph, who was just a young fellow then, to run the route. And Ralph says he'd grab two or three bottles for two or three houses in a row, and throw a rock at the horse to keep him going. And he'd get home in half the time it took Pop to run the route.

"But Pop, I give him credit. We never suffered for anything . . . no we didn't. We didn't have a heck of a lot. We killed pigs in the wintertime. But we didn't have much meat around the place. Smoked ham, of course, and the ham would get pretty strong in the summertime, I'll tell you. But it's something to eat. I used to say, If I ever get off on my own, I'm never gonna eat cream potatoes again. We used to have them morning and night. Now, I love them, of course. Mother was a very efficient little woman. She'd be sitting there and I'd say, 'What are you doing, Ma?' 'Trying to make something out of nothing,' she'd say. She could make a potato salad that was out of this world, I'll tell you.

"There was church on Sundays at the Presbyterian church in Cutchogue. There were Tuthills from New Suffolk, Tuthills from Tuthill Town, and Tuthills from all over. And on nice days, Pop liked to go picnicking. Go up to the Sound, build a fire, cook your hot dogs and stuff. And once a year, Pop wanted to take a long ride. Sometimes I don't know how we ever got home again. As a kid, I didn't know where the thunder we were. He contemplated going homesteading in Canada, but he gave that up."

Ernest Tuthill kept records of every penny he spent, and every penny he took in. He also noted weather and temperatures, as well as such household tasks as when he turned on the furnace or cleaned out his barn. He wrote in pencil, in nice notebooks, and John retrieved them from a cardboard box in a dank corner of the brick milk house by the kitchen door. A lot of the old farmhouses on the North Fork had milk houses and summer kitchens ("The summer kitchen was to keep the flies out of the house, where you ate," John told me).

Ernest seems to have begun his record keeping soon after the turn of the century, keeping notebooks for income from his "Sprouts" and other books for "Milk" income. A ledger for January 1907 is broken down in two columns:

| JAN. | 1 | Cash on Hand | $29.28 |
|---|---|---|---|
| | 4 | Brussell Sprouts | 13.12 |
| | 8 | Brussell sprouts | 3.11 |
| | 11 | Apples | .90 |
| | 14 | C.E.D. Box | .20 |
| | 21 | Apples | .25 |
| | 26 | Apples | .50 |

For expenditures he noted:

| JAN. | 6 | Sunday pipe organ | $5.20 |
|---|---|---|---|
| | 8 | town taxes | 6.67 |
| | 14 | Initiation fee IOOF | 2.50 |
| | 14 | Wedding Present | .98 |
| | 15 | Doctor Peterson | .15 |
| | 18 | Hair Cut—Clarence | .05 |
| | 22 | Medicine | .75 |
| | 26 | Laundry | .06 |
| | 28 | Horse shod | 1.00 |
| | 31 | Lecture Ralph and I | .50 |

In brown Harvard notebooks, Ernest compiled personal entries. For the first few days of January 1914, he wrote:

1. Had our usual "blow out." Twenty one people here to celebrate. A nice cold day. Skating on small ponds. Have not had a bit of snow so far this winter. Have only seen a few flakes.
3. Terrible hard rain and wind.
4. Cloudy and rainy.
5. First snow about 4 inches.

On the thirteenth, he noted a "terrible cold wave" had arrived "and the worst wind and dust storm I ever knew." On the twelfth, his son saw "Dr. Pete. for first time, has a bad cold. Is 8 months old." The fourteenth was the "coldest day in years." On the fifteenth, his mother "operated on for cancer at Hempstead Hospital." In June of that year—one month after James Wickham, his neighbor, died of blood poisoning from a cut hand—Ernest made this entry on the twelfth: "Began picking strawberries. Had Dr. P lance my hand as it was all swelled up and awful sore, have had Ralph come up and milk for me."

In spring months, he noted when he cut rhubarb, when he turned his cows out to grass, when corn was planted, and when strawberries were picked. He reveled in the details of his farm life. In summer months, he said of some days: "Fine hay weather today, cut first hay"; "Usual picnic down on our bay beach, good time and fine cool day." He enjoyed his life, in a way that was perhaps characteristic of a simpler time.

Over the years, the Tuthills in Tuthill Town died off or sold their farms. Some moved away to try farming in other states. Soon the only Tuthills farming in Tuthill Town were John and Stan and Les, his cousins. Then Stan and Les sold their farm, and John became the last one, the end of the line.

Both Hallock and John lost sons. William Ernest Tuthill, Hallock's son, died in 1972. Edward James Tuthill, John's son, died in early 1973. People who knew the brothers in those years recall two deaths, two funerals of only children, almost back-to-back. Hallock said he never thought he would see the day when there would be no Tuthills farming, and no Tuthill boys growing up on this land.

*Noble Funn, who came to Cutchogue when he was a teenager to work on farms.*

ELEVEN

# Workers

IN THE EARLY part of this century, southern black men began arriving on the North Fork to work

on farms. Potato harvesting was labor-intensive—the potatoes were bagged by hand in the fields,

the heavy bags then stacked on the backs of trucks. In the beginning, it seemed most of the men

who arrived in Mattituck and Cutchogue came from the same part of Virginia; one came, then an-

other, then more from the same small farm towns. Soon, they, too, had their own community. Oth-

ers, though, came from all over the South—the Carolinas, Georgia, and as far west as Arkansas.

They came alone in buses or trains, but most came in small groups any way they could get here. They arrived in time for the spring planting and stayed to dig and bag potatoes. Many lived in bungalows on the farms on which they worked, others in overcrowded camps that soon acquired reputations. The luckier workers lived away from the camps. The camps were a trap.

Most of the workers left the North Fork in the winter to return to their home towns, making their way back in late March or early April to begin seed planting all over again. For many of the workers, the farm families they started off with kept them on for as long as they wanted to stay. Many workers raised their children on these farms, living in the same small houses and bungalows for years.

In the late teens and early 1920s, there was a Ku Klux Klan chapter on the North Fork, as there were chapters all over Long Island. Here, a few of the farmers and local businessmen were active members. But today, looking back at this period and wondering what it was like, it seems the KKK members were more interested in keeping Catholics away than the black men who bagged their potatoes.

"My father told me there were Klukers out here, and they didn't like the Irish all that much," said one old-time farmer. "Some of the biggest farmers went to the meetings, but you never heard them doing anything other than holding meetings. It was like a social club where people talked about 'foreign elements' coming into the country. But what my father said was they was against the Irish."

A thin, elderly black man with long, strong arms, a handsome face, and intense dark eyes, Noble Funn arrived in the late 1920s. He was from Virginia, and he learned of the North Fork from his older brother, who had come up earlier to hand-bag potatoes. He went straight to Cutchogue, the farming community his brother had told him about, and he went to work for a family named Glover, who farmed on the eastern edge of Cutchogue. The day he arrived, he went to work, and he stayed working for the same family for the next sixty years.

In those years, black workers were spread out at dozens of farms. When they were not working, they walked back and forth to meet one another, go fishing in the bay, or attend services at the new Cutchogue Baptist Church on the Middle Road, bought and paid for by the workers themselves. The white clapboard church, with a handsome bell tower, sat on a tiny plot of land that had been owned by Frank McBride, Sr. The McBride home farm is due north of the church. The white building was a model of the simple rural church many of the blacks had known in their hometowns.

North and east of the church by a half mile was the big labor camp on Cox's Lane. It sat in a hollow of trees and was made up of small bungalows, one after the other. There, in 1960, Edward R. Murrow shot some scenes for his exposé on farmworkers, *Harvest of Shame*. The documentary was greeted with derision among the farmers of the region, who thought it made the camp out to be far worse than it was and made them look bad for being a party to it. Others say the camp was a horror—overcrowded and filthy.

In Cutchogue, Funn avoided the camp. It was not for him, and it was not for his friends or his brother, either. He stayed away from it the way a man might stay away from trouble anywhere.

Funn worked hard for the Glover family, and after he retired, he was allowed to stay in the bungalow. He and his wife, who was herself raised in a small bungalow behind a farmhouse in Mattituck, live there today.

"I never went a day without workin, no sir," he says. "And I can remember some days when I like to not go to work!"

He laughs hard as he recalls the days of bagging potatoes in the field and working behind horse teams. "All I remember is the work. You'd get up early and you knew what was happening that day. You went straight to the fields, and there was work all day with the potatoes. The machine pulled the potatoes out of the ground, but you had to pick 'em up and put them in bags. Then someone come along and pick up the bag and put it on the truck or the wagon.

"All around you in the fields was people you knew. I had friends who worked on other farms and some of 'em were from Virginia, and others were from the Carolinas or Georgia, places down south. We'd see each other workin, or sometimes walkin through town. Sometimes on Sundays. I had a friend who worked for Mr. Wickham—Nathan Harris. Nathan was from where I was from in Virginia. He was good people.

"And Nathan, he liked to fish and I liked to fish. I'd walk over to the Wickham farm and meet him and we'd cut through the fields down to the bay there. On the way back, Mr. Wickham would see me and he'd say, 'You got anything for me, Noble?'"

He laughs at the memory. "Oh, I do like to eat fish, any fish."

Eddie Clark arrived thirty years ago. He was born in Arkansas, and he arrived in Cutchogue when the labor camp on Cox's Lane was still open. He refused to live there, he says today.

"It was a hellhole. A bunch of shabby cabins up next to each other," he said. "I didn't much care for the folks who lived there, either. Too much booze, too much fightin.

"In '64, I was first in Florida. I was twenty, twenty-one. It was a camp called Mexico City. Near Homestead. Man, what a place. There was so many kinds of people, from all points. Every part of the South. Any race you wanted. Mostly men. But there was a share of women, too.

"I didn't know how to take it. It was a strange place. Like nothing I'd seen or been used to in Arkansas, I'll say that for the place. It was wild. At night, it got crazy. Mornings, you shopped in the company store. That's where you lost all your money, that and on liquor.

"There had to be a thousand people in this place. There were bungalows and each bungalow had six people. You went there and they'd tell you where you were staying, which bungalow. It was all piecework. The whole thing was piecework—depending on how many tomatoes you could pick, that sort of thing. You'd be out in the fields picking, and you'd load baskets onto a mule train and they took it to the packing house. Whoever was grading gave you a ticket for each bucket you filled. You'd get there early in the morning, just as they was spraying. You could see this spray on the plants when you went out to pick. You had to work like hell to make twenty bucks.

"I paid the guy who got me there, that's how it worked for me. The contractor brought people

*A page from the family album of the Funn family.*
*Noble Funn migrated to Cutchogue from Virginia*
*and spent sixty years on the Glover farm.*

to the camp. Guy who brought me was Walter. He got fifty bucks a head. Walter's job was to get people. I knew him growing up in West Memphis. He was good people. He was maybe twenty-five when I met him. He brought a group with him, eighteen or nineteen of us. We were all friends.

"We got to the camp, and I was surprised that everyone was pushed in together. There was one shower, women on one side, men on the other. There were whole families there. Kids, too. Some too young to go to school. I was with my group off and on for three years. I heard about potato work in the north, north of Norfolk. So the group I was with, we went there on a bus. I remember the weather and the mosquitoes. It was too cold in the morning, too hot in the afternoon. The mosquitoes were as big as birds. They'd eat you alive. So we went back to Florida, to another camp.

"People got killed that first year in the camp. I'd say two, maybe three. One I seen myself. This group of guys was messing around before work. The argument lasted all day. At the end of the day, this guy stabbed him. When he walked in the house, he stabbed him. He walked out of the house and dropped dead. Once I seen a guy's head in a garbage can. A Mexican head. I seen a guy get shot. Mexican guys were shooting dice. A guy comes in with a shotgun. One guy run off and the

*Eddie Clark, the Arkansas-born farm worker now working for David Steele. He first worked for Byron Horton, a descendant of one of the first Englishmen on the North Fork, for fifteen years, living in what amounted to a shack beside a row of storage barns. "I don't expect to live long," Clark said. "Everything that can go wrong with me is pretty much going wrong."*

guy with the gun couldn't catch him, so he killed a guy just sittin in a truck. I saw a guy laying on the ground, a dog eating his intestines. The cops would sometimes come and take away the guns and knives. Down there, they don't care. No way anybody cares.

"You were on your toes all the time. You were always looking. You went together to the bathroom and the shower for protection. You always did this. None of my group got into trouble. Some turned into drunks. Cause that's all you did—work and drink. And everybody ripped you off. There wasn't a bar there. Just a liquor store on the side of the road. I had to get out.

"Some of the guys, when it was too hot down there, when it was hurricane season and nothing to do, they'd take a bus up here. Somebody told me about Cutchogue, so I came. They say you could make decent money. You could make one hundred dollars a week. People were nice and there was plenty to do. There were houses you could live in. That appealed to me very much.

"One of my group, Robert, who grew up in Forrest City, Arkansas, he and I came here by Greyhound bus from Virginia. We went to that camp on Cox's. There were contractors in there who brought people in. One was from Virginia, and one was from Arkansas. There was a church near that camp and some of the people would walk over on Sundays.

"The local farmers would not allow the contractors to give you the paychecks. There was not that 'I give you what I want' from the contractors. We got the farmers to pay us directly. I only stayed there part of one season; then I went to work for Byron Horton."

Photographs of the camp show bungalows set close to one another, old wheelless cars sitting in mud, and clothes hanging out on lines strung between trees. One photograph shows a woman with two young children, a boy and a girl, the boy wearing a sports coat as if it was Sunday morning and they were heading for the Baptist church. A small black dog runs behind them. Other photographs show a fire that destroyed a bungalow on a fall morning in 1961, killing three persons.

Working for Byron Horton—the grandson of Forrest Horton, the man who farmed and held mortgages for farmers around him—mostly entailed grading potatoes. Horton raised potatoes on his land on the west side of Bill Wickham's farm. The farm is on a flat plain. This western half of Cutchogue was, at one time, the home of a number of Hortons, but by the late 1960s there was only one remaining, Byron, and he was later to sell off his farm and move off the property.

Eddie moved into a shack alongside a hedgerow behind the Horton farmhouse. He and Byron got along well, except when they didn't. Once he hit Horton so hard in the face, he knocked him flat on his back. But they remained on good terms for the fifteen years Eddie lived in that shack, which was testimonial to the fact that Eddie knew the business.

"In those first years, '66 to '69, I went back to Florida to work in the winter. Then I decided no more of this. I stayed in Cutchogue. I didn't go no place. Everybody was farming then—there was nothing but farms, all the way out to Orient Point. John Tuthill was farming up and down Elijah's Lane. John had all that—where all those houses are now. So many farms are gone. One bad year, when potatoes were like two bucks a hundred, knocked them all out. Did in a lot of farmers.

"So I knew if I stayed, I'd be all right workwise. My friend Robert was a gambler. He stayed one season and left and went to Vietnam. He came back. I seen him back home, '69, '70. He seemed okay. But another friend of mine from back home, Frank, stepped on a land mine. I seen him on that trip, too. He was deformed in the head. You could see the stitches all across the top of his head, like they had to sew it back on. The draft was going on then, and the whole time I was in Cutchogue, people were looking for me. I wanted to go into the marines. But they wouldn't take me. They said I had a curved spine and high blood pressure.

"I was back here, and when Byron went and sold his farm, I went to work for John Tuthill. Then David Steele took over the farming, and I'm working for him now. There so many less farms now, that's what's so surprising to me. I never would have thought that."

The barracks-style building that sits behind the potato grader by the railroad tracks is the last camp of its kind in Mattituck and Cutchogue. During the hot summer of 1993, it housed a dozen or more people, some of whom seemed to come and go, but mostly it was the same group—nearly all of them southern men with long histories of doing farmwork from Florida to eastern Long Island. Over the summer and into fall, I stopped by early on weekday mornings or on weekends to talk to these men.

Their boss was a muscular man with a limp named Carl Beamon, who in turn worked for the business concern that owned the grader. I thought the barnlike grader a time capsule of another life, another place—it was this grader that David Steele, with his long vision of the fading farm life on the North Fork, told me should one day be a museum.

"Soon it's going to be all over. There'll be no one planting potatoes. There'll be no need for the grader. Just leave it the way it is; don't change a thing. Don't even bother cleaning it up. Just put a lock on the door and let it be."

*Anne Wickham on the couch in her Cutchogue home.*

# TWELVE

# Spring of 1987: Transition

IN THE MID-1980s, after a half century of managing the farm, John Wickham began to slow

down. He had developed heart problems, clogged arteries, mostly, which made him tired. But

looking at him, you did not see a man with problems. On any given workday, in the barns, in the

field, sitting on a tractor, talking to customers at the stand, John Wickham at nearly eighty was the

same man his family and friends had always known. He worked all day, his face brown by mid-

summer, his hands calloused, hands as big as pie plates, and at night he read history books and farm magazines and wrote letters to friends in which he talked about peach-tree grafting and family genealogy; then he slept and woke up early and the day began again.

"As a Calvinist," he told me once, "you learn to take what life gives you and you go on."

He was not afraid of failing health. God in heaven awaited him were he to die, and as a Christian he believed there could be nothing more magnificent than that, nothing at all. Besides, he was too hardy to be frail, too strong, both mentally and physically. At almost eighty years of age, he could do any work on the farm he could do at twenty, but now, in this time of transition, he began to think more and more of Tom.

John and Anne had three children, all gifted in different ways. Parnel had lived upstate with her husband, Stan, and they had moved back after the death of their daughter, Diana. Both college professors, they sought other work near home. They buried their daughter by the family plot in the Cutchogue Cemetery; there was no leaving Cutchogue now for Parnel. Jack—his real name is John—lived in Baltimore with his family and ran his own business. Another engineer in the family, Jack had a very precise view of how things should work, and this conflicted with the nothing-is-working-today nature of work on a farm, so Tom, also an engineer, was given the responsibility to take over from their father.

For twenty years, Tom, tall and lanky, with a streak of humor deep inside him, had tramped around Asia. Like his father, Tom's nature kept him away from suit-and-tie office work. He liked the outdoors, and he liked mechanical equipment, and he had forged a successful life showing Asian farmers how to irrigate and cultivate their crops. Along the way, he met a Singapore-born woman named Gekee, and they were married. They had a son, Jonathan, a spirited and bright boy who early on revealed his own gifts, which lay, of course, along engineering lines but also along more artistic lines. While living in Asia, they read letters from home about John's health and the work on the Cutchogue farm, and it seemed to Tom that the time had come for his return.

The spring of 1987, John's brother Henry, the youngest of the three Wickham boys, died of cancer. One cold and damp evening, sorting asparagus at the farm stand a few days after his brother's death, John told me that Henry had been his best friend all of his life. His death had taken the wind out of him. The loss registered on his face. I knew John had also had recent heart surgery—a balloon on the end of a catheter had been snaked up through an artery near his heart, then expanded. Physically, he felt better than he had all winter; then Henry died.

The brothers had been roommates at Cornell. They seemed to me to be very different men—Henry worldly, urbane, and sophisticated; John very much inclined to love his family's history and the farm. After Parker, the oldest brother, died while still in his twenties, the two brothers had become even closer. It had always been known between them that John would farm; it was never a question, and certainly not after Parker's death. But Henry had not left it at that, and on a return trip to the farm he said loudly and clearly that if something happened to his brother he would come home. This had cemented the bond between them, and it meant the farming would go on.

In the context of the history of the remaining farm families on the North Fork—the Wellses in Aquebogue, Marty Sidor, John Tuthill, Bill Lindsay, Bobby Rutkoski and David Steele in Mattituck and Cutchogue, the Lathams in Orient—this was one of those statements that resonated deeply. Within this family, it had profound historical roots—back through their grandfather William, all the way to Parker and Joseph.

The generations in this family were connected so closely, I had to wonder if there had been a time when it looked as if one of the links might break. No, John didn't think so. Once I mentioned the story of John Tuthill's son's death, and John said he remembered that day as one of the saddest he could remember.

A few days after I saw John sorting asparagus at the farm stand, a memorial service was held for Henry at the Cutchogue Presbyterian Church. This had been a family church from when it was founded in 1732 until 1861—the line of buggies on the day of James and Frances Wickham's funeral in June of 1854 ran from this church two miles west to the Presbyterian cemetery in Mattituck—when a fissure opened up within the congregation over the minister's abolitionist views.

"My grandfather was clerk of the session of the church at the time of the split in 1861," John had told me a few weeks after his brother's death. "This minister was an abolitionist, and evidently some members felt he was ranting too much about it. A secret meeting was called by some members to get rid of the minister, and my grandfather was locked out of that meeting. I think I can imagine how William would have felt about that, being locked out of your own church. So he took the minister, a Reverend Sinclair, and half the congregation and they built a Congregational church across the street."

South of the church, almost in its shadow, was the house Joseph Wickham bought in 1698.

"I'm told this incident rankled my father quite a bit, because as far as I know, he did not go back to the Presbyterian church. When I was a child, the Congregational church was still open, but hardly anyone was there on Sunday, and it was forced to close. When we were children, Parker, Henry, and me, my mother thought we were too wild and needed religious training. She said, 'Get cleaned up, brush your hair, put on a fresh shirt,' and she took us to meet the minister, Mr. Beebe, who baptized us. So we went back to the Presbyterian church—this was more than sixty years after my grandfather walked out—and I do believe that took some strength on my mother's part."

Inside the church the morning of Henry Wickham's memorial service, a flutist played softly as the pews filled up. John and Anne sat with Anne's sister, Virginia, who was Henry's wife. The Reverend James Barr read from Ecclesiastes, Martin Luther's "A Mighty Fortress Is Our God" was sung, and everyone filed quietly out into the spring sunlight.

As he awaited his son's return, John went about farm business. In Baltimore, Jack waited, too, wanting to discuss the business of the farm with his brother after he had settled in. His father had managed the farm since 1930. Now, more than a half century later, another generation was to step in. Parnel saw her father going downhill ("He can hardly put one foot in front of the other," she told me one afternoon that spring) and she worried that her brother, busy in Sri Lanka, might put off his return.

"In their letters, my parents would tell Tom that everything was all right at home, don't worry," she said later. "But I didn't think it was all right. There was doubt in my mind about Tom coming home. We all in this family have a serious commitment to whatever we undertake. So I was unsure if Tom would stop what he was doing. The idea he would stop what he was doing and come home and farm is still remarkable to me."

While he waited, John wrote down his thoughts about his family and put them in his folder. It seemed clear to me that spring that John had spent a great deal of his life thinking about his father, James. He was a child barely five years of age when his father passed away. By comparison, he often pointed out that his father was twenty-three when William died in a second-floor bedroom of the house. It fell to James to run the farm. But within two years, between 1912 and 1914, everything changed in the family—first Will died, then Sarah, his mother, then James, the second son.

"I was a young child, and it may seem odd to you today, but I can remember some things from when I was very young. I have flashes in my mind of things that happened when I was four. I guess you could say I wanted them to stay with me because they have meant so much to me," John wrote.

Will and James were married and had families, while Julia lived on the home farm. Although his father had been educated at Yale and had been a well-known lawyer in public life, James wanted only to be a farmer.

After their father's death, James and Will worked the Cutchogue farm and another farm bought by their father at Hashamomock, in the eastern part of the town. On a wide neck of land overlooking Peconic Bay and Shelter Island, William Wickham had bought a heavily wooded tract of land, and it fell upon Will and James to clear it. They found large quantities of Indian artifacts— spear points, rock weights, arrowheads, and buckets of stone chips—which were shipped off to the Museum of Natural History in New York.

A Polish farmworker plowing up a field near the beach also found some gold coins, pirate treasure, evidently, similar to the treasure buried by Captain Kidd on nearby Gardiners Island—which the pirate later reclaimed from the son of Lion Gardiner. Several coins were given to James, the rest claimed by the worker who had found them.

By the turn of the century, two of William's sisters, Parnel and Elizabeth, were living on the Wickham farm in the western part of Cutchogue, the farm where William had been born, and the second brother, Henry, was living in a home just to the east. When James took over the management of the home farm, as the land between the salt creeks was called, Will arranged to take over the other farm from his aunts.

John said, "In 1912, I was three and a half, I guess. In the house was Julia, my father's sister, and my grandmother Sarah. And my two brothers and my mother and father, Cora and James. Late in the year of 1912, my uncle Will came down to visit his mother because he was leaving for Florida the next day. And this was in, I guess, December. Like my father, Will had no gray hair and he would have been in his early fifties, straight dark hair, looked very much like the portrait we have of my grandfather.

"Well, the rest of the story is, he didn't live to get to Florida. He was taken off the train in Georgia. He had consumption, and he had a real bad spell, and they took him to the hospital. But he didn't live. Then, in mid-May 1913, a few months later, my grandmother Sarah died. Well, she hadn't been sick. I don't know if she had been sick at all. She had a stroke, and she died in the house. I was then about four years old.

"And a little less than a year later, my father got a cut in his hand and he had thought that maybe he had got some spray materials in it and it was giving him trouble. But it turned out to be blood poisoning, the very same disease that killed his father, and he died quite quickly. I don't recall how he cut his hand—it was just an accident—and I suspect that like myself he had thick skin and healed very rapidly, and then things changed. I do remember the crying in the house. We were taken to my cousin's house on the north side of the road, and someone came and told us. It seems odd to me today, but I also remember a few days before my father died, before he cut his hand, he came in and said to his boys that he had lost his eyeglasses somewhere back of the barn. I went out looking, and I saw them in some grass and I bent down to pick them up and it was a butterfly.

"But I look back at that time, and in less than two years, 1912 to 1914, Will had died, then Sarah, then my father. They say things come three in a row. By my sixth birthday, there were no men in the house. I've always maintained I was brought up by women, and remarkable women. I recognize both my mother and my aunt Julia were excellent managers. I always felt, and Henry felt this way, too, that we had two mothers—our mother, Cora, and our aunt."

At the time of his death, James Wickham was well off as a farmer and landowner, but also because of other investments. Prior to his death, James had sold an oyster business he owned, including profitable leases to bay bottom, a boat called the *James A. Marshall,* and oystering equipment. He also owned scallop-opening shops along the waterfront in New Suffolk, south of the farm, and had a financial interest in most of the scallop boats that plied the waters around Robins Island. A forty-foot scalloping boat called *Eva* had been sailed into the creek behind the farmhouse just before James's death. There it remained for years, until it rotted away. When he was a much older man, John went clamming at the top of the creek and raked up metal fittings from the *Eva,* and like so much on this farm, it reminded him of this man he had never really known.

John, in his own writings, said of his father: "He was a dealer for the J. I. Case Company and had a Case touring car. It had to be cranked by hand and it fell to his sister Julia to do the cranking after his death, but Cora drove it. That car was subsequently sold, but in all it traveled 240,000 miles. He was also agent for the Aspenwall Potato Planter Company, the first mechanical potato planter. He also secured the first carload of Hoover potato diggers sent to Long Island.

"In those years at the time of James's death, crops on the farm were far different. About ten acres was in asparagus, which was sent to the New York market by the Adams Express, and to the Hudson Canning Co. in Mattituck. Probably about twenty acres was in cabbage for seed and this was sold to the Thorburn Seed Co. in New York—and finally there was a substantial acreage in timothy hay. This was stored in the big barn and on rainy days in the fall and through the winter it was pressed into two-hundred-pound bales in a 'jump press.' Men would fork hay into a boxlike structure open at the top. When it was loaded, a cover was clamped on and there was a big wooden wheel with a long rope wound around. A team of horses would pull out this rope, forcing a pair of knees to raise the bottom of the press to make the bales. Men would then insert the two wire ties, hook them and then back off the wheel a little, let down a side and roll out the bale. They were sent to New York to feed the horses that pulled the horsecarts. These were the main crops—wheat and corn were also grown for the livestock and at times there would be six or eight hogs butchered and hung up to cool."

After James's death, a court invested title to the home farm in Parker and Henry, seven and four years of age. John was given interest in the farm at Hashomomack and land near Patchogue that had been in his grandmother Sarah's family. But three small boys could not run the farm, so within days of her husband's funeral at the Presbyterian church and his burial at the Cutchogue Cemetery in the same plot with his parents, Cora arranged for a neighbor to lease the farm.

"We had a neighbor, a friend of our family's, named Harry Fleet. He had been a widower for a relatively short time, three or four years. And had really quite a small farm, just across the hedges. And my mother engaged him for one thousand dollars a year—which in 1914 was an appreciable amount—to manage this farm, to keep everything here going. And he was an expert cauliflower grower, and an expert cabbage-seed grower. And it worked very well.

"He did this for years—ten, fifteen years. Then another farmer took over, and he grew strawberries and potatoes, but he didn't raise any cabbage seed. He also grew cucumbers for pickling and had a field of dill right alongside our lane, and he did the whole operation right on the place. He had it for two or three years. Then he wasn't making any money. You see, farmers did very well during and immediately after the First World War, but by the early 1920s, agriculture on Long Island was in trouble."

Another man, Carlton Dickerson, took over the running of the farm until 1926 or 1927. But prices remained low, and soon Dickerson was in trouble. So Parker quit college after the summer session of 1928 and returned to Cutchogue. He just wanted to be outdoors and on his own, he told his brother. Back home, he worked in a garage the winter of 1926–1927; then as spring approached, he started farming on his own.

"Parker was enthusiastic about livestock. He was very much interested in registered Jersey cattle. I was going off to Cornell, and he had had a room reserved that he, of course, no longer needed. So my brother Henry and I took that room and were roommates. You know, three boys growing up together on a farm, they can get close. We were very close. Henry was smaller and a different sort of man from the one I am, but we could not have been better friends. I'll say this, Parker was better looking than I am . . . than I was. But if people didn't see us together, they usually mistook us. We were both tall, slim, with blond hair. Parker, who was the oldest brother, he was very much a person in his own right. I mean, he had a tremendous amount of energy and was the hardest-working man I ever knew, and he was the best man to work with I ever knew. Nothing was too much. He was always taking more than his share of the load—always.

"Because of his love of livestock, Parker raised Jersey milk cows and sold milk at the roadside. There was a large dairy in New Suffolk, and Ralph Tuthill had a large herd in Mattituck. The fall of '27, he was married and he built a new home alongside Wickham Creek, next to the Fleet property. Her name was Margaret Lane. Parker called her 'Miki.' Her mother was Marion Horton Lane, and the Hortons married the Tuthills, so she was a Horton and a Tuthill.

"By '29, Parker was operating the entire farm. I remember that year very well because I worked for him. Henry didn't. Henry was never interested in farming at all. But it was just because he didn't have a chance, as the youngest brother. I mean, had it worked out, he would have been farming. That year, '29, was a critically dry year. We had a real drought. It didn't rain from the fifteenth of April until August. And at that time, we decided that the barn ought to be reshingled, and I basically reshingled the whole north roof myself."

In his notes, John wrote of this drought: "It was not only dry this year it was hot, and in ridging potatoes on a hot afternoon one of the horses dropped dead just where Henry Fleet's house stands. Water was poured over the horse but he was gone. The potato crop was so poor that in a four acre field east of Dam Meadow Pond Parker put the entire crop of about 120 bushels on a new Dodge truck he had just bought."

In the spring of 1930, John was a senior at Cornell, rooming with Henry. On the North Fork, there was an early spring, and Parker planted seventy acres of potatoes, starting on St. Patrick's Day. He and Margaret now had two sons; their second, Stephen, was born on Christmas Day, a few months before planting started. In April, John returned to Cutchogue from college and, for the few days he was home, worked for Parker.

It was a warm spring, dry again. The brothers got along well—one a happy college boy studying engineering, the other a contented farmer with a four-month-old baby boy named Stephen and a three-year-old son who was named after Parker's father but from childhood was called Jimmy. From his new home on the creek, Parker could see the green expanse of the farm's eastern edge, a ridge of land like a series of knobs where the horses had been buried, and south of that the low land called Shell Bank. Farther south was a line of trees and the blue opening of the creek into the bay between two sandy fingers. From his second floor, Parker could see the dark mass of Robins Island in the middle of the bay.

On the morning of April 5, John and Parker were working in the big barn. The Cutchogue Fire Department, which occupied a building just west of the farm, had only recently installed a siren, and a few minutes after twelve noon, it went off. Neither of the boys had ever heard it before, and the sound was electrifying. They raced to their car.

"I said, 'You drive,' and Parker said, 'No, you drive.' It happened to be my car. And I drove. He said, 'You drive,' so I did. And we got to the head of the lane just as the fire truck went whizzing by, and we pulled out right behind it. I was about a half mile east and, of course, couldn't see ahead of the fire truck. And one of our men, one of Parker's workers, Florentine DeJesus—we called him 'Flip'—had gone out before the fire truck and turned east, and just at this moment he ran out of gas. He slowed down to about ten miles an hour.

"Anyway, the fire engine pulled out and went to the left and passed him. But when I got up there, there was another car coming from the east and there was simply no place to go. And not only that; I learned many years later that there were two kids on bicycles off to the north side of the road. So there was absolutely no place to go. And I hit the brakes, and you've got to remember that in those days there were only two-wheel brakes. The car slid around, and I corrected and got around this car somehow, and I still don't know how I got around it.

"And then it went into a worse swing the other way and just flipped right over on the highway. And my brother was thrown out when it flipped over. I was in the car. It slid along for about fifty or one hundred feet, upside down on the highway. It ground off the top of the radiator, and the windshield and all the rest. It was a LaSalle roadster, no protection on the top at all. When it stopped rolling, stopped sliding, I was upside down on the highway, head and shoulders on the highway, and my feet still up on the pedals, the steering wheel still in my hand, although the steering wheel was all broken up.

"And everybody thought I was finished. But I was perfectly conscious and so forth and I asked how Parker was, and they heard me, so they rolled the car off of me. I got up, and I had a little cut on my head where the steering wheel broke up and my jacket was torn a bit, but that's all. They were trying to resuscitate Parker. He had a little bump on his forehead but nothing else. But he had broken his neck and died immediately. Yet he looked fine. I walked back to the house, or someone drove me . . . I don't know. My mother heard the commotion, I guess. She was there. You can't imagine what that was like for me. It sounds odd, perhaps, but I had to be doing something. That afternoon, I went back planting potatoes with a three-horse team alongside the lane."

The *Riverhead News* ran the following article on April 11, 1930.

Cutchogue and other villages in this section were plunged into sorrow last Saturday afternoon when James Parker Wickham was almost instantly killed as his car rolled over while he was responding to an alarm of fire, he being one of the firemen.

The tragedy was the worst that has happened in this vicinity in several months, and grief was all the more pronounced because of the popularity of the young man who met such a swift death at a time, too, when he was endeavoring to be useful and save others from possible trouble and expense.

John, a brother of James, was driving the car, and it is believed that brakes applied too suddenly caused the car to turn over.

The victim was thrown clear, and it is understood his neck was broken. John was pinned beneath the car, but he escaped with a few cuts and bruises. Later it was learned that the car ahead was stopping because it was out of gas. And the fire, it was ascertained, was only a brush fire at that and didn't amount to much.

Mr. Wickham was well liked by all who knew him and the sympathy of the entire community goes out to his entire family. He was only 23 years old, a son of Mrs. Cora Wickham, and leaves a widow and two small children, James Parker and Stephen Lane. Another brother, Henry, also survives.

The funeral was conducted Monday afternoon by the Rev. F. G. Beebe of the Presbyterian Church. It was one of the largest ever seen in Cutchogue, the firemen turning out in a body. The pallbearers were Preston Tuthill, Charles Lane, Carleton Wickham, Roy Glover, Stanley Case, Donald Robinson, William Wickham and Eliot Barteau.

Often during that spring of 1987 as John awaited Tom's return, he spoke about Parker's death. Over the next three years, he would talk about it more. Once he said, "My father's death made Parker a farmer; Parker's death made me a farmer. Although I had a chance, yes, but on most farms only one of the boys has a chance. Parker was the oldest and he had the chance. It didn't make any difference how I felt. It had suddenly changed. You know, I have always felt my life was spared, so I have had to think about what I would do with it and how I would live it."

In late spring, Tom returned. A drought had settled in, and Tom immediately went to work moving irrigation pipes and maintaining pumps. The pumps ran eighteen hours a day to keep the orchards wet. We drove around the farm early on a Saturday morning a few months after he returned, and we stopped to check the pump that pulled freshwater out of Dam Meadow Pond.

"I knew the time had come for me to come home," Tom said. "I really enjoyed the work abroad. It was enormously challenging for me. But I walked away from it. I am home because I wanted not to get out of touch with the farm. I began to see more and more that there was a clear role for myself. I came back to farm. There was no doubting I would."

*Tom Wickham and his son, Jonathan.*

THIRTEEN

# The Wheel of History
# and Indian Summer

IN THE LATE summer of 1993, heat that held on like an enemy began to dissipate, pulling back

from the dry earth and fleeing out to sea on a northwest wind. Nights grew cool, and welcome rains

began to fall. August had been bone-dry. During a normal August, nearly four inches of rain fall

(3.8 inches according to the climate center at Cornell); this August of 1993, just over an inch hit

the earth. On the twenty-fifth of the month, the sky covered over with black clouds, but nothing

came of it but .15 inches of water, not enough to quell the dust. Farmers who gathered at the grader alongside the Cutchogue railroad tracks talked about almost nothing but the dryness.

September, though, brought rain and lower temperatures. On the tenth of the month, the sky thickened with clouds; by the middle of the day, it was raining hard. More than an inch fell by nightfall, and it was raining on the morning of the eleventh when David Steele got up to start his pumps. Water shivering in puddles on the farm roads was a surprising sight. Tom Wickham was up early, too, priming his pumps to get them going, wondering if the dry spell was over. It rained again on the seventeenth and the eighteenth, and then, suddenly on the twenty-second, thunderclouds rolled across the North Fork and a hard rain began to fall. By the following morning, more than two and a half inches had fallen, the ground was saturated, and some folks were complaining it was too much too soon on too dry a ground.

The heat was an unwelcome distraction for Tom. Angry at the state of politics in the town, Tom, a lifelong Republican and the son of a lifelong and active Republican, had announced he would run for town supervisor. After his return from Asia, he had been elected to a seat on the town board, and he had watched the bickering and general nastiness between the two parties cripple any efforts to accomplish something. So he decided to run for the supervisor's post, but not as a Republican. He had come to loathe partisan politics—what had the two major parties accomplished in a town of not much more than twenty thousand residents? The parties were employment agencies, not idea factories, so he decided to form his own party, United Southold, and campaign for the top job.

"My feeling is I can accomplish more as an independent than I can as a Republican or, for that matter, a Democrat," Tom said one afternoon at the farm stand. Bumper stickers had appeared around town with the party's logo, and the two parties, hoping to block Tom's election, joined together and sponsored a joint slate of candidates.

Tom's father was no stranger to town politics. He had been a longtime member of the Southold Planning Board and had been active in Suffolk County planning affairs. Along with a small number of public figures, John had helped create the county's innovative farmland preservation program. The goal had been to save thousands of acres of fertile ground on eastern Long Island.

"From where I sat," John Wickham told me, "I could see what was coming. Once in the fifties, I went to a potato growers meeting up west. I heard some of the growers talking about selling to developers and looking for farms farther east. All kinds of farmland in western Long Island was going out of production as suburbanization spread. After that meeting, I came home, and over breakfast the next morning, I said to Anne, 'We've got to get out of potatoes and look for other ways to stay in farming.' That's when we went into fruit in a big way. The risk, though, was that it took so long to get a crop we could sell. With what's happened to the potato industry, I can see we made the right decision."

He was also the father of the North Fork's wine industry, having shown a young couple looking for land to grow wine-producing grapes, Alex and Louisa Hargrave, that his experiments with table grapes applied to them. (John was a lifelong teetotaler. He grew only eating grapes.) The couple bought an old potato farm in Cutchogue, planted the first grapevines, and soon other growers followed.

Even as John contemplated his son's entry into town politics, he was looking back at his family's past. For quite some time, it had rankled him and other members of the family that New York State, in willful violation of the Treaty of Paris, had confiscated his ancestor's large Cutchogue farm, Robins Island—which, other than some run-down buildings on it constructed by twentieth-century owners, was untrampled and wild—and land near the head of the river in Riverhead and auctioned it all off. The fact that people Parker had feuded with as a public official had ended up with the property seemed to prove that politics and jealousy were at the bottom of everything.

At a time when the German owner of Robins Island was talking about bulldozing its woods and ringing the island with expensive homesites, the heirs of Parker Wickham brought a lawsuit in federal court seeking remedy for the 1784 seizure. Because Parker's Riverhead holdings were now, two centuries later, covered by a downtown business center, asking for that land back was impossible. The situation was much the same on his former farm in Cutchogue. Most of what had been called Wickham Neck was now an eighteen-hole golf course; the rest was expensive housing. If traced through the records, the title to all these holdings went back to an improper seizure. No one in the family wanted to bring actions against owners living on developed property, but Robins Island was another story. It was unoccupied, its only resident a caretaker who lived on the mainland.

Jack Wickham flew up from Baltimore for a press conference held at a barn on the bay southeast of the farm. "It may be more than two hundred years ago," he said, summing up the family's feelings on the suit, "but it was wrong and we want the courts to recognize that it was wrong." He said the goal was to win back the island and turn it over to The Nature Conservancy for preservation.

As a boy, Jack had worked on Robins Island when his father was responsible for planting cover crops for pheasant hunters brought over by the island's owner. "We kept a tractor over there because we used to cut the trails on the island when it was maintained as a game preserve," Jack told me. "Once, the track came off the tractor. To get it back on, you'd take out a pin. You would put a bar against it and drive it out with a sledge. My father was hitting it. He hit it with a glancing blow and the hammer hit me just above the eye. A lot of blood came gushing out. It knocked me right down. My father was upset, sure. But he was in control. We had to wait for the boat because the caretaker had gone off somewhere. So we waited on the dock. But it turned out all right. No bones were broken."

"That scared me to death," John told me later when I brought up this incident. I pictured John sitting anxiously on the dock with his injured son, waiting for a boat to materialize, wishing he could ghost himself across the narrow race to New Suffolk.

The lawsuit would not have been possible without the work of Dwight Holbrook. *The Wick-*

*ham Claim,* his book published by the Suffolk County Historical Society, had proven that the confiscation of Parker Wickham's land had been illegal, even in the context of the confusing days after the British had been evacuated on ships from New York Harbor just ahead of armed mobs.

But did it matter two centuries later?

Holbrook, as part of the legal action initiated by the heirs of Parker Wickham, drew up detailed charts showing dozens of descendants, all of whom would be affected by the outcome of a suit that returned Robins Island to the heirs. The core of the suit did not seek profit, only that the land would be left alone. It was for this reason that the plaintiffs in the suit formed a group called Robins Island Preservation Fund, Inc., to push the Wickham claim.

While John Wickham felt strongly about the unique merits of the suit, he felt just as strongly about keeping Robins Island, held by his family for three generations, in its natural state. He was certainly not antibusiness; it just seemed to him that some things should stay as they were, and he saw the value of saving an undeveloped island, of which there were few others anywhere in the Northeast.

To press the suit, the plaintiffs hired Bertram E. Hirsch, a Long Island attorney who represented the upstate New York Oneida people in their fight to reclaim ancient tribal land. Hirsch argued that, because of what had happened to Parker, the title to Robins Island was clouded by the 1784 confiscation. In the spring of 1989, he asked a federal court judge for a judgment declaring the preservation fund the owners of the island. Two years later, the federal court ruled against the preservation fund, saying, in effect, that the heirs of Parker Wickham were two hundred years too late in filing their lawsuit. The decision was upheld by the United States Court of Appeals. Hirsch's move to take the suit to the United State Supreme Court was blocked when the justices voted not to hear the case.

The decision of the United States Court of Appeals, filed in the fall of 1991, was a well-written document that could have been authored by a group of history professors. In the decision, the three justices wrote of "deeply rooted historical events" that were "not widely celebrated today— the systematic confiscation of property belonging to those Americans who refused to join the Revolution." The justices noted that while it could be argued that the Americans did not live up to the terms of the Treaty of Paris, neither did the British. They stayed in territories they were required to evacuate, and they kidnapped slaves to take back to England.

"When, in 1791," the justices wrote, "Thomas Jefferson requested a statement from the newly arrived British minister . . . regarding whether Great Britain intended to honor its treaty obligations requiring the evacuation of American territory and forbidding the taking of slaves, he was told that the king 'was induced to suspend the execution of that article, on his part, in consequence of the non-compliance, on the part of the United States, with the engagements contained in the fourth, fifth, and sixth articles of the same treaty.'" These were the articles that dealt with confiscations of land held by Loyalists such as Parker Wickham.

By 1794, John Jay had negotiated an agreement with England in which Jay agreed that the Americans would "cease punitive measures" against former Loyalists in this country. "As revolutionary fervor cooled," the justices wrote, "the enforcement of the Treaty of 1783 became more consistent. Loyalists who had fled the United States felt secure in returning. In 1789, Joseph Parker Wickham received 2,800 pounds sterling from Great Britain as consideration for the loss of his father's estate. Two years later, he returned to Long Island where he resided for the remainder of his life."

From the point of view of the three justices of the United States Court of Appeals, the island could not be returned to Parker Wickham's heirs. The justices wrote: ". . . we are unaware of any statute of limitations which would provide for a two-century-old action for title and possession of real property. . . . Reason tells us that a claim to property long unprosecuted is lost."

In late October, the Republican-Democrat coalition trying to keep Tom Wickham out of town hall brought up the subject of Parker Wickham's loyalty to the British, suggesting this somehow meant something about Tom Wickham. It was the low point in the coalition's inept political campaign.

Few people in Southold were listening to the blatherings of the major parties, however. On election day, Tom and his United Southold party were swept to victory.

*Summer of 1994: the workers at the Cutchogue potato grader. In the center of the picture, in the darker T-shirt, is Carl Beamon, the longtime boss of the workers, most of whom live in a barrackslike building behind the grader.*

# FOURTEEN

# A Cold Winter

IN THE FALL the weather turned cooler, and by December a deep cold had settled in. Farm

ponds froze quickly, and the edges of salt marshes turned white with ice. Skies were clear. Week-

day afternoons, kids in hockey skates slapped pucks around on Wolf Pit Pond, the spring-fed hole

that sits below Ralph Tuthill's old dairy. Storage barns on the North Fork were stuffed with pota-

toes as prices per hundredweight held steady, if a little low. The potato men sold truckloads out of

storage.

One afternoon a week before Christmas, I stopped by the grader in Cutchogue and watched the men work. Inside the old building, temperatures were a little warmer than outside. The men were wrapped in worn-out sweatshirts and thin secondhand coats, with wool hats pulled down low. One man's bare toes stuck out through the ends of his sneakers. As the clanky grading equipment pulled potatoes out of a truck and sent them along a system of conveyors, passing under a water spray that hosed off dirt from the field, the cold air filled up with tiny clouds of dust.

Carl Beamon shouted loudly and someone pulled the plug. The noisy conveyors stopped running. "You got to listen to me when I'm tellin ya what to do!" His stroke-damaged arm dangled at his side. He was shouting at a man hiding beneath a worn hat. "You can't be droppin bags there and leavin 'em for somebody else! Pick 'em up, man! Pick 'em up!"

Walt Zilnicki came out of what passed for an office in a corner of the grader to assess the shouting, rolled his eyes at me, and said softly, "So what else is new?"

Some of the workers were broken down. Carl's job was to shout his way through this group and get them to bag the potatoes. Walt answered to the owners of the grader. Their job was to market the farmers' potatoes; Walt's job was to keep the machinery working, which on some hard days took a magician's skills.

On this afternoon it seemed that most of these men were either hung over, their heads heavy as cinder blocks, or numbed from staying up all night in their camp building watching an old black-and-white television with a coat hanger for an antenna.

Some North Fork farmers have grading operations in their own barns. For farmers like David Steele or Bobby Rutkoski, this grader is the last one in the area where they can get their potatoes bagged. In years past, when potato acreage was high, there were other graders along the railroad tracks in Cutchogue, but they have long since been closed up. The potato world on the North Fork has shrunk, down to this last building and these few men.

"We're the last of the Mohicans," Walt said, shaking his head at the old equipment. He chatted briefly with Carl and shouted for the machinery to be turned on again. The dust in the air was thick and settled on your tongue. He had a disgusted look on his face, as if he was trying to figure out which part of the rackety grader would break down next. Earlier, in the fall, he'd had to shut down for several days to search for parts.

Walt has a dim view of the future for the potato men. How many more years could they continue to raise a crop and then line their trucks up outside this grader?

"You get a bad year like '85, some crap like that, and half the boys now in potatoes'll quit. The acreage'll be cut in half. I telling you right now. There's no reason to be doing this if you can't make no money. We're getting killed on taxes, killed on regulations, killed by bureaucrats who want to look at our pesticides, how much we're paying people. How they gonna feel when there's no food to eat? Ask them big shots that!"

This pocket of potato growers are edgy. Their hope every year is that some other group of

# The Steele/Tuthill Family

*David Steele seeding a hay field on the old Horton farm.*

*David and his son, Kyle, in the pickup.*

*David and Kyle in David's shop.*

*David working on his tractor.*

*David and Eddie Clark preparing chemicals.*

*David and his three children, Kyle, Kristin, and David.*

*Kyle driving the flatbed.*

*A break in the work: David, his worker, Angel Lopez, and young David.*

*John Tuthill driving the truck without a door.*

*John Tuthill helping Kyle blow out the birthday candles.*

*John Tuthill working on a plow at the edge of a potato field.*

*David Steele harvesting potatoes, his son behind him.*

*Young David helping with the harvest, his father driving the tractor.*

*Kyle Steele working in the barn; next to him is one of his father's workers, David Valle.*

*Cutchogue farmer Tony Chituk chatting with Kyle and David Steele.*

*David Steele going through the kitchen door.*

farmers in places like North Carolina or Delaware will be hurt by weather or bugs or some other calamity and that as a result yields will be way down, driving prices up for farmers on the North Fork. It's all a crapshoot, year after year. A good year and you get hopeful for another good year; a bad year and you hope there won't be two in a row.

Walt helped load ten-pound bags onto a truck that had backed up to the south side of the building. Once again, someone hit the button and the clanking stopped. Jimmy Wilson, a soft-spoken, sweet-faced black man from rural Georgia who lived in a home a half mile away on the Middle Road, came out from behind a stack of potato bags to see what had gone wrong. What I knew about Wilson was what David Steele had told me: He'd run this grader himself for a long time and knew a lot of the history.

But he had been reluctant to talk to me ("There's nothin I know I wanna tell you today," he said once as he shoved bags onto a rig that weighed the potatoes) and I hadn't pressed it.

"Think you can fix it?" I asked him.

"Oh, heck no." He laughed. "What you doin here again today?"

"Looking for you."

He laughed again. "Oh, is that right? I got my own life to live, and I can't see what good tellin you is goin to do for me."

"Have you gone home in awhile?"

"Georgia? What are you talking about?" he said. "I have a family in New Jersey, if you must know."

Carl came around from the half-empty potato truck on the north side of the building and began barking orders again. In a moment or two, the machinery went on and potatoes began moving along the conveyor. The north wind blew through the building, shivering papers nailed to the wall.

I knew one of the men was named Frank Bryant, and I had seen him often walking around Cutchogue. He is tall and very thin, with a broad smile. The next morning, I arrived at the grader before the machinery was turned on, hoping to find him. He was inside, waiting to start work and trying to keep warm. We chatted for a few minutes, and I asked him where he was born.

"I'm from Alabama," he said softly, looking around for Carl to show up and moving his feet up and down to keep warm. His shoes looked too tattered to be worn. He explained that he'd met Carl years ago in Florida and rode a bus with him to Cutchogue to grade potatoes.

Another worker, Irvin Whidbe, sat on a stack of potato bags next to Bryant. When he heard what we were talking about, he said, "I worked in Virginia. That's where I learned 'bout potatoes."

"That's all I know," Bryant said. "All I know is potatuhs. But I can't complain."

"I can," Whidbe said, pulling on the torn collar of a holey sweatshirt. "I'm from Elizabeth City, North Carolina. I was sawmillin. Not bad work. Me and my old lady split. We had problems. I just left. Took off. I went to Florida and met Carl there. Carl, one day he just drive up to me and ask me what I'm doin. I heard so many people talkin about Florida. They said there was work. Climate was good. I got into trouble when I got there. Fightin. I wound up cuttin a guy. I don't remember much about it now. But I did meet a lot of good people in Florida. People just tryin to make it work. Know what I'm sayin? A guard I met at the prison called me by my first name. His mother came round when I got out and gave me a job. Pickin cucumbers near St. Augustine. There's a lot of heat there. That's the problem.

"People say, 'Where you from?' when you first show up in the field. Most of the people I met were from the South. Mostly black men there. Some black women. They lived in huts. We was makin three seventy-five an hour. I lived in a camp like this one here. There was four, five guys in a room. I can't remember their names. People come and go. I didn't keep track. I worked there three months or so. Then I met Carl. At a little place where people went. Carl was lookin for workers. He asked me what I'm doin. I said, 'Man, I'm doin nothin' new.' He say, 'You wanna work?' I said I didn't work no grader before.

"I left with him. We drove to Molasses Junction. There was a potato grader there. I went right to work. It was noisy and so dusty. I remember the dust. We lived in a camp. We tried to keep it clean, you know, 'cause them inspectors would come around. We'd load the potatoes right on the truck. There weren't no bags like we do here. You call that bulk. I had a certain amount of weight I had to do. We'd do ten trucks, man, by twelve o'clock.

"They'd go to the potato-chip factory. We'd stay till April, then we'd go to Virginia on the eastern shore. Another camp. Man, you seen one, you seen them all. People'd come and go. They tell you all these lies 'bout where they been. Some were on the lam. They'd tell you what they want to tell you—that's the point. We leave there in August and come here. Carl brought us here. We first worked for one potato guy in Southold, but he's out of business now. I've been here ever since.

"I still in touch with my wife. Her name's Georgia. She still in Elizabeth City. We got four kids. Two boys, two girls. My oldest boy, he's twenty-six. He's in Germany in the army. I call Georgia now and then." He grimaced. "It's tough."

"Man"—Bryant sighed—"that is tough. You never go back and see them kids a yours?"

"I see them in New York City. They look good. My other son got a scholarship. My oldest daughter, she got a scholarship."

"Oh, that's good," Bryant said, smiling. "That's very good."

"Georgia, she married again. He's a cop. So I can't really just drive down there and go knockin on their door."

Bryant piped in. "I would not do that, Irvin. How come you left that woman?"

"She gave me an ultimatum. That was it. She was a good woman. She was. But, you know, I'm workin. I got money in my pocket. Twenty bucks. That's it, man. That's . . . all . . . I . . . got."

Two days before Christmas, I saw Tom and John and they mentioned that a Wall Street investor was in the process of buying Robins Island from the German developer who had owned it for more than a decade. Years of effort by environmentalists to get Suffolk County to buy it as a nature pre-serve had come to nothing. The Wickham lawsuit was a footnote in a long battle, and now a new owner no one had heard of had stepped in.

"I think this could be all right," Tom said. "He's talking about keeping it as it is and using it as a family retreat."

I knew John had not been well. His heart was giving him trouble again. At dusk, a few days after Christmas, the temperature in single digits, I drove past the farm stand. The front doors were up, the light flooding the darkness by the road. The family station wagon was parked alongside the stand, and I stopped and found John inside. He looked pale, exhausted.

"Right after the first of the year," he said, leaning against a bench, "I'm going to North Shore Hospital for heart surgery. The doctors tell me it's a fairly straightforward procedure." The north wind whistled through the stand. He listened for a while, then said, "Winter came on strong, did-n't it?"

A month before, just after Thanksgiving, John had first mentioned he was not feeling well. The angioplasty he had undergone soon after his brother Henry died, which had worked well all these years, seemed to have given out. He felt run-down and winded.

There's a tightness there, he said.

On that day, he invited me into the house to talk, and we sat by the fireplace in the sitting room, looking out the windows toward the barn and the flooded valley of Wickham Creek below. Over the previous few months, he had mentioned several times that he wanted to know more about his father's death.

"I don't have an image in my mind of my father," he said. "It's funny how I can see my uncle Will—he came to the house to say good-bye to his mother before that trip to Florida when he died. And I have an image of Sarah, my grandmother. This is odd, of course, because they both died before my father. Yet I can't see him. I can see the farm, but I can't see him.

"The year my father died, our farm went over to the hedge on the east side, and from the high-way—including some twelve acres north of the highway—to the bay. This was all our property. My father also added a great deal of salt marsh over in what they call the Great Meadows, which is where we have our cranberries and so forth. And in addition, over on that side of the farm, I in-herited some land from Fred Tuthill, who lived in the house Jack now owns. Fred was quite the character. He played the violin. In that house, Jack found a black mantelpiece. It seems that the year that George Washington died, many people in this area painted their mantelpieces black."

I asked him about his earliest memories of the farm itself. He said he could see twelve hogs hanging from a big willow tree down by the creek, stacks of wheat on either side of the front barn doors, and a row of hundred-year-old pear trees near the house.

"My mother always said that had my father lived through the First World War, he would have been a millionaire. Because he was that smart. He was a terribly hardworking man, and astute. He owned a row of scallop shacks along the bay in New Suffolk. There were fourteen shacks. Scalloping was a big business, and this was the center. I have heard, but I have no way to justify it, that my father put up the money for practically every one of the boats in the scallop fleet. The shacks were all rented out. And each one had a little duckwalk and the sloops would come in to this duckwalk and load the scallops onto wheelbarrows. Then they'd wheel them into the opening shop, where there were counters on both sides with holes cut out for the discarded shells and so forth."

I asked if he remembered the last summer he worked for Parker, the summer of 1929.

"We didn't get back as a crop the seed potatoes we planted in the spring. They burned right up. And not even the weeds or grass grew, it was so dry. West of the lane was potatoes. I remember so clear the potatoes we had east of the pond, maybe three and a half acres. We put the entire crop on one truck. On three and a half acres, we got one hundred and twenty bushels. Mostly marbles. They were Green Mountains or Irish Cobblers.

"You know," he said, pausing for a good long while and thinking again about his brother's death, "you don't kill your brother without thinking about it a million times."

The summer after Parker's death, he went to church one Sunday morning and met Anne Lupton, who was playing for the regular organist, who had had a baby. Meeting her helped him to forget his brother's death.

"When we got married, I spent a lot of time thinking about how to run this farm. This farm has got a lot of land good for lima beans. This is one of the few areas of the country where lima beans can be grown. And before the Second World War, there was a very substantial market for lima beans in the Baltimore area. It was an excellent market, and we drove trailerload after trailerload to Baltimore. Then all of a sudden, we just quit, in probably the mid-1950s. We went from fifty acres to zero in one year. That was in part the motivation to go to peaches. They take the same kind of land as lima beans, what we call 'down-neck land,' a sandy soil. Good bean land is good peach land. It's also excellent land to grow early tomatoes on, and early melons, early sweet corn."

He looked out the window and talked about his father.

"He must not have been feeling well, because my mother wanted chicken for dinner. So she took the shotgun out and killed the chicken. But my recollection of my father is all blanked out. I hadn't realized it was blanked out until many, many years later. I went to a funeral for another officer of our church. And I was an officer. I would have been in my thirties, probably, or maybe forty. And this chap died of a heart attack, and he was a big man, ruddy face, and it's never my custom to go up to an open casket. But because I was a fellow officer, I felt I ought to. And I took one look at that guy in the casket and I barely got out of the door of the church, and I broke down and sobbed like a child.

"It must have made me think of things I'd blanked out. But to this day, I have no memory of seeing my father after he was dead. But I know my mother well enough to know she would have taken her children to the front of the church to say good-bye to their father. I know that. That's clear in my mind. So anyway, one of my friends took pity on me after that funeral. She lived next door, and she invited me to the house for a while. But I was . . . I was dumbfounded. I had no way to understand it. It was completely unexpected. I mean, I didn't just weep, I broke down.

"Oh, I knew my father was sick—very, very sick. Because he had blood poisoning, and the doctor asked us boys to take the bloody mess down and bury it, which we did. I remember that."

I had found the newspaper story of his father's death, and several times I brought it to the house to show John, but always I held back. It seemed too strong on the details of the death, and on these late afternoons, so cold now, it struck me as inappropriate to dig the story out and show it to John. Besides, I was not sure he really wanted to know more—he had his memories, what few there were, and he held on to them like priceless treasures.

The account in the *Riverhead News* of May 21, 1914, read:

### POISON IN HAND FATAL

The many eastern Long Island friends of James Wickham of Cutchogue were shocked to hear of his death last Friday. He died of blood poisoning of less than a week's duration.

A week or so before he stuck a thorn in one of his hands. The tiny wound festered and he opened it with his pocket knife. It is said that his physician was in the house at the time and warned Mr. Wickham against using an unsterilized implement for such a purpose, but Mr. Wickham, which is quite natural, laughed at the doctor's admonition. Shortly afterward, however, it was learned he had blood poisoning of the most virulent form. It spread up the arm with alarming rapidity. A day or so before his death a New York specialist operated on the arm, but it was too late to save Mr. Wickham's life.

Mr. Wickham was one of Cutchogue's wealthiest and best known men, and he was generally regarded as a good citizen. He was 56 years old, and is survived by his widow and three children.

Largely attended funeral services were conducted Sunday by the Rev. Mr. Beebe.

I wondered if there was someone still alive on the North Fork who remembered Cora taking her three boys up to the coffin. But there was no one.

John's health had continued to worsen, and I began looking for him at every chance so we could chat—a few minutes at the stand, a few minutes at the house, once outside the post office. He was weakening, yet it seemed this strong man could hold on and dig himself out of the hole and be fine once again. There would always be another long afternoon of listening to him by the fireplace, I was sure of that.

At a party at Parnel's house on New Year's Day, I asked about John. Parnel said her father was too tired to come. Perhaps it's the bitter cold, I thought. Wickham Creek was locked in ice, and

*Parnel Wickham-Searl.*

there were sheets of shifting ice across the water, from the back of the farm to Robins Island. Maybe he just couldn't bear to walk outside to the car for the short trip to Parnel's.

"He wants to talk to you," Parnel said as guests gathered in the warm kitchen. "But he's really feeling it. The doctors are telling him the surgery should go well. And he's very strong. He has that going for him."

A few days into the New Year, I saw Anne in the village and she said John was doing fine, that the surgery had gone as well as anyone could have expected.

"The doctor said John is unusually strong," Anne said, looking relieved. On January 4, Anne hoped to go to the hospital to visit her husband, but it was snowing.

Days later, John was brought home, but it was not to last. By the third week of January, new concerns had arisen and he was back in the hospital. Meanwhile, the weather worsened. By the end of the month, temperatures were below zero some nights. When he was home again a few days later, I called to chat.

"Parnel was driving me to the doctor for my checkup," he said, "and quite suddenly I got dizzy. This is the first time I've ever been sick like this." I told him I wanted to come over and chat, perhaps over the weekend, but he said no. "I'm still a little tired, but I'm feeling stronger. I'm feeling stronger every day."

Wednesday morning, the twenty-sixth of January, I saw Tom at the post office. John was sitting forlornly in the station wagon, dressed up for a trip to the doctor's. He rolled down the window and smiled. "I'm tired," he said, his voice hoarse. "I'm not getting my wind back.

"Come over on Saturday," he said. "And don't delay."

That night, I spoke with Tom, who had just been sworn in as the town supervisor, and he sounded concerned, the jagged edge of worry creeping into his voice. "He has fluid around his heart. He can't catch his breath. It really wears him out. The doctor gave him some medication."

It seemed he was not getting better. Yet each time I spoke with him, he said, Don't delay. Come over as soon as I feel better.

On Wednesday, February 2, I called Anne. "He's in bad shape," she said. "Last Sunday morning, he had a stroke. It was very sudden. The prognosis is not good; he's not conscious. On Saturday night he got up from the chair to come in for supper. Jack and Mary Lou were coming over. And he fell down. We took him down to the hospital."

The next morning, I drove down the lane, the ground frozen solid, and parked behind the house. No one was home. The creek was locked in a heavy crust of ice. I stood by the car, looking back up at the house, when a flock of geese suddenly jumped up from the edge of the creek and passed noisily overhead, turning sharply to the west, toward the big open meadow by the edge of the woods where the Indian fort once stood.

At 2:30 the next afternoon, Jim Fogarty, who works at the police department and is a volunteer fireman, called. "Hey, I don't know whether you heard or not, but John Wickham died this afternoon, about an hour ago."

On the following Monday, an overflow crowd poured into the Presbyterian church in Cutchogue. A simple wooden casket sat at the front of the church. Anne Wickham gracefully walked in, followed by Jack, who looked stunned by his father's death. They sat in the front, and Jim Barr, who had met John forty-five years before when he worked as the minister in this church, stood up to speak. For some time, Barr had been working on the farm, doing jobs for John and Tom.

He read from I Corinthians, the eighth chapter of Romans, and the fourteenth chapter of John, which read, in part: "Let not your heart be troubled; ye believe in God, believe also in me. In my father's house are many mansions; if it were not so, I would have told you. I go to prepare a place for you."

I thought of John and his two brothers attending their father's funeral here, and John attending his brother's funeral. Someone told me that John on the Sunday morning after Parker's death sat in a front pew, his face in his hands. When services were over and everyone had filed out, he sat there alone, his head bent over. That April morning, his mother waited for him outside to drive back to the farm.

I knew that Stephen Wickham, Parker's younger son, who was four months old at the time of his father's death, had died a few years later when he was hit by a car while walking home from school. His ghost seemed to be in church this morning, along with the ghosts of James Wickham and William Wickham. It did not take much for me to picture the Loyalist Parker Wickham walking across the road from his house in the hollow to sit in these pews.

"John stated," Barr said, "that when it came time for his funeral, and if I had a part, he did not want a eulogy listing all the things he had done. He said to make it as simple a service of worship as I could. And to make it short."

Without listing the accomplishments of the deceased, Barr said simply, "You know them, and I know them. He lived them, and he did them." In his conversations with John, Barr said that John talked about the Pilgrims—"He felt a close kinship to them and their faith, because they had a willingness to come to a wilderness in a strange land"—and about his death, and that he "believed God created a life beyond this life. But he was not in a hurry. He hoped God would let him remain here as long as possible.

"He believed history had a purpose. He loved the beauty of this North Fork. He wanted future generations to love that beauty. He was a pioneer. We thank God for John's life. God was extravagant in creating such a man."

After the congregation sang one of John's favorite hymns, "A Mighty Fortress Is Our God," a large crowd followed the Wickhams to the Cutchogue Cemetery. It was cold and sunny. I thought about the obituary of John's paternal grandfather, William, which ended, "Truly, he was a good man." The crowd stood around the granite obelisk with the names of deceased family members engraved on its four sides, a prayer was said, and Anne led her family back to the cars and home.

A month or so before, Davis Steele had sat in a car with John and driven the dirt roads of the Wickham farm. On this cold morning, he stood with the crowd around the graveside. "John was always saying he'd drive me around the farm. Ziggy and I went over. He loved that farm. He knew every inch of it. With most farmers, it's about getting by, getting to the spring planting again. With the Wickhams, it was never about money. There's all that history tied up in their land."

*John Tuthill in his barn.*

# FIFTEEN

# A Wet Spring

TOWARD THE END of March, I took my son, Andrew, to a Little League game and ran into David

Steele. He looked restless, as if the winter, the coldest in years, had gotten to him. The bay had

only recently lost its ice, but the ground was damp and in wooded areas the earth was still hard. Of-

ficially, it was spring, but potato planting was two to three weeks away, and the expectation of it

showed on David's face.

"We can't start now," he said. "Ground's too wet. You plant now and you get dirt clods.

You'll be married to them for the rest of the year. We need some wind and some warm nights to dry up the ground."

On cold mornings, he had driven the roads that linked together his potato ground, mapping out the next few weeks. Most farmers are pessimists; the future always looks rather grim. If there's a season for optimism, it's the spring, when planting is about to begin and the hope is that this year prices will stay high and some decent money will be made.

He had driven around Ziggy's beautiful pond, which along the fringes still held a thin coating of ice. Sometimes he took the dirt road south to the Main Road, past the second freshwater pond in the chain and up to the knob of Manor Hill, and from there east to Bill Wickham's barn, where David cut his seed potatoes.

Cutchogue starts at the point south of Ziggy's pond, where the land dips into the shallow ravine that crosses the Main Road on the east side of Manor Hill, then continues south to the bay. This north-south line is not the actual dividing line between the hamlets of Mattituck and Cutchogue, but the changes in the land right there are a signal to me that I am coming into Cutchogue.

This line, ending at a small creek on the bay, is the western edge of what had been called the Broadfields. The creek on the west side and the creek on the east side form a neck of land, and it was on the east side, in the woods overlooking a wide part of the creek, that the Corchaugs built their log fort. This was Indian land, occupied for thousands of years, and cleared over the centuries to make room for crops.

Manor Hill levels out quickly on its southwest side, where the Elak family now farms. Near the center of the hill is the childhood home of Ralph Solecki, an archaeologist who did extensive diggings on the Fort Corchaug site. On the hill near his home, he found ancient chipped stone pieces worked by the Indians who lived here before the Corchaugs came. This hill is a promontory on which native people could survey the world around them and watch for attackers.

Driving east along the Main Road, you pass between the knuckles of Manor Hill. The pond, the second of the two small kettle-hole ponds in a north-south line, is on the north side of the road. The road then rises out of the ravine carved by the glacier's meltwater to the flat, fertile top of Fort Neck. This is all open land on the south side, although in the summer of 1994, its future was up in the air.

On the north side of the road is the Pellegrini Winery, which was erected on old potato land owned first by a succession of English farmers, then, by the turn of this century, by Polish farmers. East of the winery building is the old Horton farmhouse, and east of that is the farm of Bill Wickham. Proceeding east, the land drops slightly, through another shallow ravine, as the road climbs and bends to the east toward the center of Cutchogue.

Hallock Tuthill's map shows the families who lived there east and west of Manor Hill. Along with a number of Tuthills, there were families named Grabowski, Kruk, Baginski, Downs, Dickey, and many others. The Downs family owned Fort Neck for generations. They lived in a home old-timers say was grand, but today there is no sign of the house.

"You'd look around in the years after the war, you'd see families you'd known all your life . . . you'd see them giving it up," Hallock told me. "Prices being what they were, you know. You'd look around, see everything changing, and you'd have to wonder."

As he farmed, David has thought about the changes that occurred in years past. He learned a lot talking to John Tuthill, and it has made him wonder about his own future. But this spring, as every spring, there was planting to consider, and there were so many variables to factor in, including the weather.

Thirteen years before, on April 6, 1981, half a foot of snow pushed along by forty-mile-per-hour winds had raked the North Fork. It is a date every potato farmer left seems to remember with great clarity. For most, their seed was already in the ground, and the wind and the sudden drop in temperatures had wreaked havoc. Many lost their entire planting and had to begin again with fresh seed. Today, many farmers are superstitious about the date and won't start planting until after April 6.

"That was a terrible storm," David said. "Everybody got killed. I'd just finished up the day before. That year, we began planting on March twenty-second. The seeds froze with all that wind." He grimaced. "If there had just been a little meat"—he curled his index finger to make a tiny hole—"around the eye of the potato, we'd have been all right. Instead, we replanted without fertilizer."

The cold winter this year raised hopes that potato beetles might be fewer. "You'd think the cold winter would do a job on them," David said. "Like in Maine, where they don't have 'em. Still, you know, we gotta wait. Conditions have to be just right. The ground's still got ice in it along hedgerows and places out of the sun. Next week, we'll start."

The morning of April 8 was cold and windy. During the night, the wind had howled, and by sunup temperatures hovered in the low thirties. The rainwater that sat in puddles along the long dirt road that leads down to the Kurkoski farmhouse had caps of thin ice over it. I knew David would be planting north of the farmhouse.

I parked behind the house, near a big storage barn Ziggy built when he was still farming. I noticed Ziggy's car was gone. Most mornings, Ziggy and his wife go to Mass at Our Lady of Ostrabrama, the Polish church built by immigrants, including Ziggy's father, east of his house on Depot Lane. It is an ornate old-world church, in sharp contrast to Sacred Heart, which is smaller and sits near the center of Cutchogue.

Older Poles say their fathers were inspired to build their own Catholic church, using what little money they had made farming, because the Irish at Sacred Heart made them stand in the back like second-class citizens. Many old residents say the complaint is probably true, but then some members of old Irish families will quickly add that they were given the cold shoulder by the old English families. ("When my grandfather Owen came here from Ireland," Frank McBride told me, "he could hardly get anyone to do business with him. Now that's a fact. Even my father said, when he went to their little schoolhouse on Oregon Road, that the English kids would have parties and the Irish kids weren't invited. It really hurt his feelings.")

I found David loading potato seeds into his planter. He was bundled against the north wind, in brown overalls and several shirts, his hat pulled down tight.

"You dressed warm enough?" he said, laughing. "'Cause I gotta say, it's still damn cold out here. That wind howled all night. I knew it would be tough going this morning."

Eddie Clark, the front of his overalls ripped open at the zipper, his wool hat yanked down hard over his ears, helped with the loading.

"It's been so wet, we can hardly get anything planted," David said. "We've worked maybe two partial days. It's frustrating. But what can you do? You can't fight it. We don't decide when we want to go planting, no way. But if you want your early varieties dug up in August, you gotta plant now."

"You know," Eddie said, "it was twenty-nine when I got up to David's house this morning. Man, and it's April! It's damp, too. It's like you can't stay warm when it's cold and wet like this."

The sky to the north was lead gray, and the trees north of the Middle Road were shrouded in early-morning mist. It was quiet by Ziggy's house, set well back from the road. It sits halfway between the Main Road and the Middle Road, farmland almost all the way around it, and it feels remote here. It is all open land in a straight line to the east, broken only by Alvah's Lane. Walk east and you cross Horton land and Wickham land, rich farmland all of it, down the glorious spine of the North Fork.

Here, and along the northern fringe of Cutchogue, you see what the North Fork still is. It is farmland, but it is farmland with an uncertain future. On this very land, some boneheaded planners had proposed running an extension of the Long Island Expressway all the way to Orient Point. Others talked of building a bridge from the North Shore of Long Island to somewhere in New England. Proponents of the bridge labeled the North Fork the "dead end" of Long Island. They wanted this farmland entombed in concrete and asphalt.

Several times, I had asked David about the future of potatoes here, and he generally said the same thing: "Give us another two-dollar year and the few who are left will get out. People talk like we should just do this even if we aren't making money. That's just stupid! If I wasn't leasing this land, who would? How many people you know are lining up to be potato farmers?"

David has equipment at his house, at John Tuthill's, and in the belowground barn behind Bill Wickham's house. He was also renting a section of a big barn behind the former Horton house. Next to that barn, buried in the vines, sits the wreckage of the chicken coop–like house where Eddie lived during his years working for Byron Horton. There are four other growers using the Horton barns, too—Marty Sidor, Paul Kaloski, Bill Lindsay, and Bobby Rutkoski. Their farmland is a patchwork, here and there, whatever can be leased or is still in families.

North of where David and Eddie were working this morning, a tractor turned the soil. "That's

John Tuthill," David said. "I was his right-hand man for twenty-four years. Now he's my right-hand man. He's eighty years old and still out there. He's been working since five-thirty."

When David worked for John Tuthill, he learned what he needed to know to run a potato farm. Their relationship worked on another level, too. David did not have a father around, and John had lost his son. Over the years, John never talked about Edward.

I watched John work up and down this tract, turning the damp soil, his head down and a warm coat pulled up around his neck. I wondered what he thought about on mornings like this, sitting alone in his tractor.

Fertilizer was added to the planter from another truck. The fertilizer was dropped in the ground first, then the potato seeds. There was a bumper sticker on the back of the fertilizer truck:

WHEN YOU GRIPE ABOUT THE FARMER
DON'T TALK WITH YOUR MOUTH FULL

David climbed up on the tractor, and Eddie huddled on a narrow platform behind the planter. In his gloved hands, Eddie held a broomstick to be used to feed the seed potatoes down to the teeth that drop them into the wet soil.

Looking into the wind, David said, "Every time you start out in the spring, you wonder where you'll be in the fall. In '85, we lost a lot of guys. There was a huge crop up and down the East Coast, which pushed prices way down. Zeneski went out. They were up on Oregon Road, where that sod is now. Romanowski . . . Domeleski . . . You had guys in their sixties who lost their retirement money."

Before he pushed the tractor forward through the soft, wet earth, a pickup pulled up behind the barn and three men jumped out to talk to David. Sensing that a few minutes would be eaten up in conversation, Eddie piled into David's truck to drive to the deli for coffee and buttered rolls.

"We can't do nothin in Riverhead," one of the men said dejectedly. "Ground is saturated. All mud. I'm hearin Delaware's behind, too."

"They've had a lot of rain, too," David said. "With their clay soil, the ground stays wetter than here."

"And North Carolina," another man said, "it's only sixty percent planted."

"Everybody's behind," David said with satisfaction.

"At least you're workin," the first man added. "We had a thunderstorm just Tuesday mornin."

"Missed Cutchogue completely," David said.

"We can't do nothin. Shit. Damn ground's like mud."

By midmorning, David stopped planting and we got in the fertilizer truck to drive to the grader alongside the tracks to refill it. He moved slowly up Ziggy's farm road.

"Got to be careful," he said as he turned east on the Middle Road. "I wouldn't want to trail any chemicals out on the road. Some do-gooder'll come along and get on my case. Truth is, they put more chemicals on their lawns per square inch than I do on this whole farm."

Still, he said, it was prices that each year determined who was alive and who was dead.

"It all comes down to prices. Talk to Ziggy about that. He'll tell you he had good years and just horrible years, one right after the other, almost never two good years in a row. If we could just tack on thirty percent every year like everybody else does, there wouldn't be any houses out here, just farms."

At the grader, Jimmy Wilson weighed the truck on the way in, then again after ten tons of fertilizer had been loaded. He wrote the numbers down on a pad, which showed Marty Sidor had loaded up earlier in the day, along with Frank McBride and Rutkoski.

"Old Rut got started?" David said.

"Yeah," Wilson said in a southern voice, "he just left, as a matter of fact."

Heading back down Ziggy's farm road, David pointed out the ryegrass he planted as a cover crop on the west side of the road. Last year, it had been potatoes; this year it would stay in grass as a hedge against beetles.

"They'll have nothing to eat on their side, so they'll have to come over the road to eat my potatoes," he said.

On the tractor again, David pushed north into the wind. He was planting an acre every time he went up and down a row. Nearing the railroad tracks, he turned the tractor around, guiding the planter behind him until he was lined up the way he wanted to be.

"When I first got started, I heard there was twenty-five, thirty thousand acres of potatoes, numbers like that. Now there's maybe seven thousand. People don't know we're still out here."

*The picture of dignity: Frank McBride, the last Irish farmer in Cutchogue, behind his house.*

# SIXTEEN

# Tustin, Oregon, and Canada

FRANK MCBRIDE'S FARM is at the east end of Oregon Road, where a community of Irish used

to live. His farm is a tract of heavy ground that runs north from the road to an upturn of sand and

woods that overlooks Long Island Sound. On clear days, the thin line of Connecticut can be seen

in the distance. It was across this water that the English traveled in their first voyage to the North

Fork.

Frank's grandfather Owen arrived in the United States from Ireland after the Civil War had gotten under way, found work where he could find it, and bought this farm in July of 1863. Throughout the town that summer, young men were being mourned who had died fighting in the war. There were occasional parades in support of the war effort, but mostly life went on as it always had, one season after another. Soon after buying his land, he began to clear it of trees.

In those days, the area of Cutchogue near the Sound was an out-of-the-way place. The colonists were said to avoid this part of the North Fork; their lives were centered on the flat lands alongside the salt marshes and creeks of the bay. This part of Cutchogue was far from the center of life along the main east-west road farther south.

Once the land was cleared, Owen found huge boulders buried under the surface near where the wall of ice had stopped and the meltwater accumulated in a large and shallow lake. A house was built alongside what is now called Oregon Road—what was then a narrow cart path. Here men and women lived Irish lives, and many spoke Gaelic back and forth. A man like Owen could live and work his land along this stretch of good ground and think he was in a part of Ireland that had mirac-ulously been blessed with fertile soil.

Reading the histories, talking to old-time residents, it seemed to me that Oregon, like Tuthill Town, was a place by itself. Old maps show it had its own schools and a meeting hall where farm-ers gathered to hear talks on current events or farming practices. In his diary entries written after 1914, Ernest Tuthill jotted down brief passages about his evenings spent listening to lectures. The first members of the black Baptist church in Cutchogue say that before their church was erected in 1924, worshipers met in the meeting hall on Oregon Road.

I asked John Tuthill about the farms along Oregon Road being a community separate from Cutchogue. "Travel in those days was slow, and communication was slow, so they did make certain neighborhoods, you know. I guess you could say that it was like Tuthill Town, in that people who lived there knew where it was. There was what was called Oregon, certainly, but farther east in that same area, they used to call it Canada. That was simply because it was considered so far away, which is why Oregon got its name. It was just far away. There was Tustin, too. Well, that's part of Oregon, right up where the old schoolhouse was. I don't know why it was called Tustin, but it was famous for being rough country—catbriers and trees and brush. So the farmers that took over there cleared it up."

Frank McBride does not know what his grandfather found when he came here. "What I know is what I been told, which is that my grandfather bought this property in 1863. I never got down to really doing anything to nail that down, you know. There were Irish here, that's a safe guess. None of the Poles yet. They stepped off the boat later, and I remember one old friend of mine telling me about a farmer named Hallock in Orient, and he had a worker who could speak Polish. And he'd send him in a horse and buggy to Greenport. The boat from Poland would be arriving at a certain time in New York, and he'd take the train in and sit on the dock. When all these Polish people come off the boat, he'd stand there and tell them, 'You come on, get the train with me. I'll take you down to Ori-ent, you're going to have a nice job on the farm.' And these guys would all jump on the goddamn train with him. Maybe six, seven at a clip. And then they'd get to Greenport, and they'd jump on the goddamn buggy and bump, bump, bump nine miles to Orient.

"In years past, lots of years ago, there were Mahoneys up here and lots of other Irish names," McBride recalls. "And a Drum family, and Kelly, Garvey and Haggarty, Hazard, Lindsay. Further south, towards Cutchogue, there was a Burns family. They was Irish. That's the land Hallock Tuthill's living on now. The east end of Oregon was Irish; go further west a half mile, a mile, and that was Tustin and then the top part of Tuthill Town, and those were old Yankee farms along there. Tustin was all wooded. They said there was every kind of damn animal there ever was up there. And my father says when he was a boy, which would have been back before the turn of the century, they used to come up there, cutting wood. He says they used to stay up there; they used to bring their lunch with them. And sometimes they'd sleep up there.

"My guess is, Owen bought the home farm from a Tuthill. There was grants back in those days, big tracts of land. I think this side of Depot Lane was a Tuthill grant. I figure Owen was born in 1838, so he was twenty-five or something when he bought the home farm."

He died December 11, 1913, and is buried in the Sacred Heart cemetery, which is directly south of the farm. Owen's wife was named Margaret McBride, and she died February 29, 1932. She was ninety-two years old. Frank believes they came to Cutchogue together. Owen had four sisters, and they left Ireland, too.

"My grandmother's maiden name was Sammon. Not S-A-L-M-O-N, but S-A-M-M-O-N. Salmon is an English name. We don't have any English blood, God no. My mother would be spinning in her grave at the very thought. The Sammon family came over during the blight in the early 1840s. There was terrible suffering then. They came to Riverhead, in the northwestern part of the town, so called Dublin because of the Irish there."

Margaret, the oldest daughter of the Sammon family, married Owen McBride in St. Patrick's Church in Southold on June 15, 1865, and moved into his farmhouse on Oregon Road.

Margaret's sister, Catherine, married a man named John Reilly, and they farmed near Calverton, the part of Riverhead that was once referred to as Dublin. The couple had fourteen children. Frank never knew Owen, and Margaret died when he was a boy. "I know they was very hardworking people," Frank says. "Grandma had a little garden up by the Sound. She used to walk up there every day. I remember on Mondays she used to make cookies and she would give them to us. She had a briar patch up the Sound where she'd pick berries, maybe back of where my irrigation pump is, up in the good heavy ground up there.

"She had gooseberry bushes up there. And she had raspberry bushes. And I know when we went to plow the whole thing up. My father says, 'Oh, God, we're going to plow up Grandma's bushes.' And we went and tried to dig them all up and bring them back and plant them here, and I guess we did; we moved them around two or three times. I don't remember my grandmother talking about Owen. I know he had a stroke. And I remember my father telling the story about him having a stroke and being incapacitated for about twelve or thirteen years, to the point where they had to bathe him and do everything for him. He couldn't farm. He couldn't do nothing. He was an invalid. And there were nine kids, my father and eight others.

"They'd leave one boy home to run the farm. And they'd take three boys, my father, my uncle Dan, and my uncle Jim; they'd go to Southampton, and they would work on the estates over there for the millionaires. And they'd spend the whole summer over there working. I remember my father telling that story. And then they'd be stable boys over there. And they'd take care of the horses and the carriages and keep them up. And they'd be there all summer. My uncle Owen would stay home. I guess he was the one left.

"And one summer, my father was out riding around, as I understand it, and lo and behold, he sees these two Irish girls out walking, too. And he got to know one of them, and that was my mother. She was born in Galway, and she came to America when she was seventeen. She never got a chance to go back and see her parents, and it hurt her very badly. She worked for a family in Brooklyn as a housemaid or a governess or something. And one summer, she came out to Cutchogue to a family who had an estate on the bay. And that's when she ran into my father. She was a real pretty lady. She loved to dance the Irish jig.

"Uncle Owen died young. Uncle Jim died in 1930. Uncle Dan married Elizabeth Holland and farmed for a while up on Twomey Avenue in Calverton. That left my father home with the farm. And my father, of course, bought this farm and bought another piece of land down here and dug out all the stumps. Think of that, now. He bought this farm, where I'm farmin, in 1937. It was put into the estate of my aunt Mamie McCarthy, the whole farm. After my grandmother McBride died, it was such a conflict of the brothers and sisters getting into an argumental problem that they made her the executor. And they then put it into her name—Mary McBride McCarthy, my dad's sister.

"And then in 1937, I was in high school, and, uh, one day the principal of Mattituck High School came to class and waved me out of class. I said, 'Oh my God, somethin happened.' And I went down to the office room, and he takes me into his little room, on the side. And my mother and Henry Fleet, who was the president of the Mattituck Bank, was in there. And my mother says, 'Mr. Fleet wants to ask you some questions, Frank.' And I said, 'What is going on?' She said, 'You know we want to buy the home farm.' I said, 'Yeah, I know that.' We were talking about a mortgage. So Henry Fleet says, 'Well, what's your intentions? When you get out of high school?' Well, I told him, 'I'm only a junior.' No, I was a sophomore at the time. Maybe fifteen. And I said, 'Well, I intend to farm.' And at the time, we had just bought a tractor, or two tractors. And we had some machinery, and I had been going home from school and cultivatin and doing different things. And I told him my intentions. And he did, he gave us the mortgage. And they bought the farm from my aunt and paid the estate off.

"There was, of course, problems with my dad's other siblings. It's always that way. Oh, they had a terrible time. But my aunt Mamie stuck with my father on it, and says, 'No, he was the one.' And Uncle Dan, he made a lot of noise, but he couldn't put up any money. They never spoke. They never spoke. Well, to make a long story short, when the papers were made up for the mortgage, my mother and I and my father went up to the bank to sign the papers, and they made me sign as a cosigner. I'll never forget when we were leaving the bank and Henry Fleet sarcastically said, 'Well, I suppose I'll never see the damn money again.' And my mother, who had a problem with them Yankee families, she turned around and she said, 'You'll see it.' This was the fall of 1937. I'll never forget—I graduated in 1940, and my mother took the last payment up and gave it personally to Henry Fleet and threw the damn thing on his desk. She paid the whole damn thing off in two years. Seven thousand five hundred dollars."

In mid-April, the cold and dampness held on as if the coldest winter in years refused to yield to spring. The plowed ground along Oregon Road was wet and clumpy as Frank McBride planted early potato varieties on a piece of land that ran north to the bluffs. Early one morning, looking cold and glum, he steered past a huge boulder protruding like a broken piece of earth and whipped his rig around and headed south again, back toward the road. South of him, the land sloped gently downhill all the way to the bay.

With his own land, plus the leased land that stretched along the road, McBride had four hundred acres of ground to plant before the third week of the month. He is one of the largest potato growers on eastern Long Island. His former neighbors, the families his father and grandfather might have known, are gone, as he pointed out to me when he drove along Oregon Road. The once-grand home of the Mahoney family, sitting diagonally across from McBride's, is today a fallen-down mess with brush growing up through the floors.

The other families Frank's father and grandfather attended Mass with and with whom they shared a buggy or a truck ride to the meeting hall to hear a talk on world affairs—they are gone, too. Some of their land was sold to Polish farmers, many of whom worked for English farmers like Hallock in Orient, or on some of the large farms along Sound Avenue west of Mattituck, before saving up enough of their paychecks to buy their own farms. Most of them are gone now, too. The land is either out of production, in sod, in a small acreage of wine-producing grapes, or leased out to growers like McBride. This is one of the few remaining places on eastern Long Island where open farmland runs unbroken to salt water.

On another cold April morning, McBride sat in his truck and pointed out the fading history around him. Up to now, he had planted 180 acres of potatoes; the remaining work had to be done, and soon, and this weighed on his mind heavily. As always, equipment was breaking down just when he needed it the most. Ain't it always this way, he said.

"We're jumping around because you've got to work with the weather," he says. "It's wet, you know, and sometimes you have to move because there's certain fields that's got puddles in them, and you can't plow that field, so you go further on with a pickup and find a field that works better. It means we got three or four trucks that are equipped and with seed. So you might have to have an empty truck and switch to another variety of potato. You got to keep changing. You change with the weather. This is a pain in the nuts, but I mean, this is something you've got to do and you've got to be equipped to do it.

"We got an inch of rain the other day, which was unfortunate. And now I talked to one of my friends over in Bridgehampton, and he was quite surprised that we planted last Friday at all. 'Cause they got two inches of rain in Bridgehampton. That was Wednesday. And they couldn't plant; they never turned a wheel Friday. And we did, but boy, I'll tell ya, we slipped on. I couldn't use my big tractor with the four-bottom plow, so I had to use one of the smaller tractors with the three-bottom plow. I couldn't pull, couldn't get the grip. I got four tractors with plows. I got four-bottoms and I got three-bottoms. When it's wet like this, you can't get the traction, and you can't plow the right depth. And you can't make no time, so you cut down one bottom by using another tractor and it can maintain the right speed and the right depth. You want to maintain eight inches in depth. Then we pull a buster to smooth it out. So we're trying, we're trying. If it would only dry up.

"We did plant all the Superiors; we've got about ninety acres of Superiors, the early varieties. Then the next early variety would be the Sunrise. So we got that out of the way. Now we're planting six fifty-sevens, which is a Norwich. It's a very heavy yielder. Then one or two of the growers that we buy from in Maine called us and told us there's a new variety called St. John's, which was just introduced about three years ago. And it's still in the stages of being developed. The seed farm up there, they just give out like fifteen bags to the growers, who'll then plant 'em; then they'll build up seeds from that.

"Anyhow, I managed to get one hundred and fifty sacks from one guy. Now, one hundred and fifty sacks, there's about twenty sacks to the acre. So we got some others from other people and we ended up with like one hundred and twenty-five hundredweights. We planted around fifteen, sixteen acres of this new St. John's. It was just beautiful. And some yields. We tried to get it last year, but we couldn't locate any. It will produce. And it's a pretty potato. It's got a shallow eye. You know, like if you're peeling it, you don't have to go digging out the eye. You know the housewife is going to think about that, 'cause there's nothing worse than peeling a potato and have to keep digging out the eye."

McBride watched the land around him change, as his father had watched the families around him change. He does not like much of what he sees, and he worries for his sons, who farm with him, and for their children. From his perspective, change seems always for the worse.

West of Depot Lane in Cutchogue, he had fifty-eight acres that ran together into a beautiful potato operation, complete with its own irrigation pump. Then the land was bought by speculators hoping to sell off lots for $250,000 a piece, and McBride lost the land.

"The land became industrial, and the pump goes with the property that's being developed. And they made me take my engine off; they made me take my five-hundred-gallon tank off. They didn't want any agriculture on it. They didn't want any oil on the property. I gotta go there and skim off some of the topsoil and haul it away and all this bullshit.

"So I'm renting in the area to try to make up for the lost acreage. I got twenty-three acres down by the railroad tracks, and I got thirty-six acres closer to Oregon Road. Another farm nearby, it belongs to the Krupski brothers. They rented it out as a sod farm, and the sod business is in the cellar, too. They're not making any money, so they gave it up. It just laid there idle. So I approached them and asked them if they wouldn't rent it to me. We went to school together in Oregon; we all know each other real well. And in fact, they raised potatoes up until the bad year of 1985. And they sold all their equipment."

At the eastern end of Oregon Road, McBride pointed out where the Shalvey brothers, "Irish boys like myself," once raised potatoes. "And they went farming and they lost their shirts in the two-dollar year, and rather than go completely broke, they both quit and went out and got jobs. Eight of my best friends went broke the two-dollar year. It just wiped them all out. I mean, they lost all their money, all their pin money. Rather than mortgage everything, they just said the heck with it and quit. I lost a great deal of money that year, and to make that up, I had to sell a piece of property to a Greek.

"Past the Shalvey brothers, west along Oregon Road, was the old Russell Drum farm; that was another Irish family. Then the Comisky farm, Mike and Mary Comisky. They're all dead and gone. Another Polish family was neighbors to them, and they all quit farming back in the seventies. One boy went to work for the county, another's a priest, the other works in Riverhead, and one of them works on televisions. Past them was the Hannabury operation. It was all farms then, believe it or not. I farmed it till last year, and then a million-dollar house went up. I farmed another piece near here, too, until the owner got a bit snotty with me and I told him to shove it."

He pointed out where a grand home used to sit, now just a weed patch surrounded by potato fields. "When I was young, ten or twelve, this was the old Haggerty farm. Several other families lived on this land at one time or another. The last one was the Urban family. And old Leo Urban, he's living in Florida right now and he's a little bit older than me, but a good old friend of mine; comes up to see me every year. When my dad was a boy, the Garveys farmed this land. There was an old house up there and the old Irish used to go up there at Thanksgiving, and they'd play a game called forty-five. It was like poker, I guess. A dozen guys would all take off, and they'd go up there for a week. And Mike Hand, he was a great Democrat. He had a store in Cutchogue and he'd supply the turkeys—twenty or thirty turkeys.

"And they'd all stay up there and sleep there and not come home for days. And I remember my mother, she'd make a great big pot of chicken soup. And then she'd put the cover on the pot and she'd put me in the back of the 'mobile, and she'd say, 'Hold that cover on,' while she'd go up the bloody road. And she'd drive up that road, bumpity, bumpity, bumpity, and I'm trying to hold the damn cover on without spilling the soup. My father was up there the whole time. They never stopped the game from the time they started until they stopped. They had wine, they had cider, they had whiskey, they had beer. And then at Christmas, they had another one. And my mother used to hate it, because nothing would happen on the farm. She said, 'The whole farm is going to hell, Frank.' John Lindsay owned that house. They used to call him 'Purdy.' Purdy Lindsay. Awful nice man."

Across the road from Owen McBride's home, his son, Frank Senior, bought property that ran all the way down to where the town dump is today. There, Frank McBride, Sr., sold a small tract of land to the group that erected the Baptist Church of Cutchogue. McBride knows his father brought a man up from Virginia named Thomas Carter, and just after planting had started, that man's granddaughter, Frances Wilson, died. The funeral was held at the Baptist church. Mick said he remembered Frances "as a very pretty little girl" and her father as "the nicest man you could ever meet."

West of Owen McBride's house were the farms of people named Garvey, Bileski, Lupton— "we used to walk by the Lupton house because Elizabeth Lupton used to play the cello, and we liked to listen"; the Deneski and Bonkoski farms—which, when McBride was a boy, was owned by a man named Moore. "He used to have violets, and walking by his house after school, we'd go in and steal them violets and he'd run out and chase us." The Peter Kurkoski farm was the first piece of land bought by Ziggy's father, and that's where Ziggy spent his childhood. And west of that was the old Oregon Road school.

West of the old elementary school was where an even older school was erected. And past that school was the upper end of Tuthill Town, where, when McBride was a child, an oddball of a man they called "Bluejay" Tuthill used to chase schoolboys down the road. And past that was the home farm of the Sidor family, where this spring Marty Sidor and his son, Chris, were finishing their planting.

"My father went and sometime in the 1930s, he bought that old one-room schoolhouse and dragged it down the road with a tractor to our farm. Finally, it got so dilapidated, we smashed it up. And on the boards, you could see these names carved on them. And I'd say to my father, 'Who is that?' And he'd say, 'That's Oscar Robinson. And that other one, that's one of the Tuthill boys.' My father used to laugh and say there was guys who were thirty years old coming to school. Whiskers down to here. My father was born in 1884, so we're talking 1900, 1905.

"And my dad also talked about getting along with the Yankee families in the school and how it upset him so. When the Yankee kids had their parties, they never invited the Irish. It was always their own kind they invited to the party. The Yankees, when they heard the Polish church bells ring, they'd say, 'The pigs are going to church.' They treated us the same way they treated the Polish. They thought we were a bunch of pigs.

"But all that's gone now. That's the part that sticks in me: that it's all changed so much. Goddamn, I'm thinking about that and I'm saying, How come it did? People have no understanding what so friggin ever where their food comes from, and I guess they don't much care, either. They just never think about it. But I think about the names who was up here and how they're all gone. And you know I'm not feeling sorry for myself one iota, 'cause I can work and I've always worked, and my sons, they can work.

"Our farm, it coming to my father and all, there was repercussions, you know, within the family. And I think about that, too. My father died in 1959. Uncle Dan was still living, and then one of his daughters, Alice, we bumped into each other someplace, and she says, 'You know, my father would love to come down and see the old place.' And I says, 'What the hell, bring him down.' 'Well,' she says, 'he hasn't been back because of all the problems.' And I says, 'I don't care, bring him down. I got no quarrel with him.'

"And she brought him down. He'd been working for the highway department in Riverhead. He was in his eighties when he come down that day. So he came and I took him and I drove him around, all over the farm. Took him in the old house, of course, the place Owen bought and his children were all born in. And he cried. He looked over everything and he told me stories. And he cried."

# SEVENTEEN

# Corchaug Pond

As April ended, the weather began to improve, and by the first days of May, warm, dry air arrived like a welcome guest. David Steele, Marty Sidor, and Frank McBride all had their fields planted, and David, his eye on the next few months, began wondering whether the cold winter was a harbinger of a hot, rainless summer.

I saw him one afternoon near John Tuthill's house, and he asked if I had seen Tom Wickham. "I was wondering how he's doing now without his father," David said. "That's gotta be tough, what with his town job and all. How's he going to run that big farm?"

Jonathan, Tom's son, was soon to return home from MIT, where he was completing his sophomore year. Jonathan's cousin Stephen Searl would be on the farm, too, along with Stuart Wood, a Westhampton Beach High School English teacher who had worked for the Wickhams since he was a teenager. These days, he repaired machinery, but he could do anything.

When I saw Tom at the farm stand on a Saturday afternoon in early May, he said he did not foresee a problem being both a busy farmer and a town supervisor. He missed his father, but, like other family members, he did not display his emotions. The family had had hundreds of people back to the big house by the creek after the graveside service, and then it was over.

I thought of the story John had told me about plowing the potato field near the house the afternoon of his brother Parker's death, and how his mother's comment—"Let the horses run"—had over the years come to mean life went on: Let your feelings go; get on with it.

With planting over on the potato grounds, I knew I had a few weeks to talk to the farmers about other subjects. One of the subjects I wanted to discuss concerned the Indians who had lived here for thousands of years and then—to use a verb often employed by nineteenth-century historians—"disappeared" from the landscape. I wondered how these men could have written this, but they did, over and over. The simple truth is that the "history" these historians pursued was, at best, incomplete.

Many farmers were interested in the native people. Some old-timers told me about a Cutchogue man named David Hannibal; he'd lived in a shack south of the Main Road, near a freshwater spring. One spring morning, I found his gravestone in the Cutchogue Cemetery, in a section Hallock Tuthill had told me was kind of a paupers' ground.

In talking about his father's and grandfather's lives on Oregon Road, Frank McBride had mentioned his father's arrowhead collection—"Oh, it was a beautiful thing, just a beautiful thing"—and how heartsick he was that it had been lost. Many other farmers had collected boxloads of artifacts; some were framed and displayed in their living rooms, others left in their barns. Lyle Wells of Aquebogue framed his collection, and looking at it today reminds him that someone was here long before William Wells arrived from Connecticut.

The Englishmen who arrived on the North Fork in 1640 were, in the agricultural sense, the inheritors of the land from the Indians. Tom Wickham, Lyle Wells, and John Tuthill all still farm, all within a relatively short distance from where their ancestors arrived as the first white men. As much as I wanted to know the stories of these old farmers, I wanted to learn more about the Corchaugs. How could a people live on the North Fork for thousands of years and then just fade away? As June approached, I began going out on weekend afternoons looking for arrowheads along the edges of freshly plowed fields.

Ken Homan, who runs the busiest seafood market on eastern Long Island, on the Main Road in Cutchogue, is an avid collector, and every time I spoke with him about Indian matters, we talked about the Corchaug people. He wondered if it was possible to find out with any certainty what had happened to them. They could not have all died from the diseases brought by the English. Some must have survived—but what happened to them?

Did the English move them onto swampy tracts alongside salt creeks, where over the generations they died off? Did they flee west into the pine forests, or north across Long Island Sound, the Englishmen's North Sea, into New England? Or, perhaps across the bay to the wide, open meadows at Montauk, on the tip of the South Fork?

Ken knows well the thick woods along the creek at the edge of Fort Neck where the Corchaugs built their primitive log fort. On a cloudy day in late spring, Ken took my son, Andrew, and me to the woods, and after walking through thick undergrowth, he showed me a ridge of pushed-up earth perhaps a foot high that ran perpendicular to the creek. This was the south wall of the fort, and near one corner a hole had been dug.

"People come in here and dig for stuff," Ken said. We walked along the edge of the salt creek. "Over there," he said, pointing south toward the bay, "if you walk by in the summer looking for clams, you can feel the cold water bubbling up. That's what would have brought the Indians here, plus easy access to the bay in their big dugouts. And in the winter, they could have gotten out of the wind by going well up into the woods, where a spring comes up, near where the road is now."

It began to rain when we walked back into the woods where the fort had been. We stood in the middle of an open area, the ridge to our south. This had been the middle of the fort. To our west would have been a planting field; to the east, the creek. The ground was thick with rotten leaves, but kicking them away revealed pieces of shells ground into the soil. Thousands of artifacts had been retrieved from the site, some of which found their way into the Indian Museum in Southold. Older town residents tell of farmers selling arrowheads found on this property.

Ralph Solecki, who grew up on the promontory of Manor Hill, dug on this site as a young man and found countless artifacts, some of which suggested that the remainder of the Pequots had come to Cutchogue after the massacre in 1637, seeking refuge.

Solecki, who teaches archaeology in Texas and has not lived in Cutchogue for years, said the creek sites near his childhood home continue to fascinate him. "I was finding stuff in Cutchogue in the early 1930s," he says. "So I read up and found the early reports on the fort on Downs's farm. The fort was all but gone by the 1660s, and a cartway was put through it. When I started visiting the fort, I saw the embankments. The woods were cleared then and it was mostly pastureland. It's very lucky, too. Had that creekside been heavily farmed, the fort would have been erased.

"I talked to Mr. Downs, and he confirmed everything. He said the embankments had been higher when he was younger. The tradition in his family was that a fort of some kind had been in there. My sense is that it was a base camp built after the Pequots were beaten. I think I'm correct, because right in the middle of the site, I found Pequot-type ceramics. It seemed to me that after the massacre some of these Pequots fled to Long Island. Or perhaps they were brought to Fort Corchaug and incorporated into the tribe."

But by 1710, just seventy years after the arrival of the English, the Corchaugs were all but gone, Solecki told me. "Gone," he said, could mean a lot of things, from emigration to death from diseases, their remains buried in fields where, in some cases, they would later be plowed up by farmers. (Many farmers have found skulls and bones on their farms.) But he believed that as a group on the North Fork, the Corchaugs had ceased to exist. The town census of 1698 lists forty Indians living in Southold.

John Strong, who teaches at Long Island University's Southampton campus, said it was conceivable that a number of Corchaugs might have moved to an area on the South Shore in the town of Brookhaven, called Poospatuck. "It had a reputation as a remnant place, with natives of different backgrounds living together," he said.

At the University of Connecticut, Karen Kupperman and Kevin McBride both felt that the Indians might have been here all along, even if they did not show up on censuses. "It would not be uncommon in New England not to mention them," McBride said. "Diseases would account for, in some cases, a ninety percent mortality rate. And competition for land would have pushed any remnant groups to other places occupied by native peoples. So, from the English point of view, the natives were no longer a part of the land they now occupied."

Later that day, in an open field alongside another Cutchogue creek, Ken and I found a number of chipped quartz pieces. "I think this must have been a really productive field for the Corchaugs," Ken said.

The rain had stopped; the ground was wet, and small rivers of rainwater flowed downhill toward the creek.

"You come here after a rain and you see quartz chips and shell pieces all over. Seeing all the stuff that's been found, you get the feeling there was a thriving group of people on the North Fork who had pretty good lives. With the woods, fields, and the creeks filled with shellfish, there must have been a lot of food to eat."

By the early 1760s, Southold's natives must have been few, because there is evidence that Ezra L'Hommedieu, a man who had a keen interest in Indian matters (and the man who, twenty years later, would buy Robins Island at a state auction after it had been seized from Parker Wickham), tried to broker a deal to bring the remnants of the Montauk Indians in East Hampton to a tract of woodland on the North Fork called Corchaug Pond. This land had been given to the Corchaugs by the town fathers in 1685; six years later, the Corchaugs were removed from this tract and settled on a nearby hook of land now called Indian Neck.

For reasons lost to history, the effort to bring Montauks—and perhaps a remnant group of Corchaugs living with them—to Corchaug Pond failed. But Samson Occom, a Monhegan Indian preaching among the Long Island Indians, was leading an effort to raise funds to build an Indian school somewhere in New England, and he kept the land in mind for the site of his school. Occom evidently liked the site and thought the people of the North Fork would have been good neighbors. (Dartmouth College, the school envisioned by Occom, was later erected on a site in New Hampshire.)

A letter written in 1767 by Nathaniel Walker, a minister friendly with Occom, reads: "Mr. Occom tells me that there is a large tract of land on Long Island on ye North Side not far west of Southold, which was formerly offered to the Montauk Indians for Montauk, and which he thinks may be procured for a small sum which is handy for fish oysters clams, so that much of the youth's living might be obtained therefrom. Salt hay enough for large stock, and all the barons of the island for their range in summer. Will it not be worth while to look after that land and send the advantages of it, if they are great, or worth considering. You know the good temper of Long Island folks."

Even as L'Hommedieu was trying to relocate the Montauks to the North Fork, and as Occom was considering the same site as the future home of an Indian school, a small group of "Southold natives" drafted a letter to New York officials in Albany, begging for help to get back land they believed had been reserved for them. The letter shows the Corchaugs were still around on the eve of the Revolution, although they had been reduced to indentured servants.

SOUTHOLD AUGUST YE 27 DAY 1764

Honored—we thy poor subjects and natives of the township of Southold do earnestly request and beseach your favor and protection in our extremity who are destitute of friends and money and are deprived of our land and all other necessary priviledges so that our wives and our children due cry for bred and we can't help them by reason of being—indet [indentured] and our masters won't let us go to their relief—all—de prive us of the fishing and clamming only in the town where we belong we have never had any bricks and blankets or seeds that was free as our neiboring governments have. We with our sanity do humbly entreat thee to help us who lie at the feet of thy mercy.

Seventeen names were signed, with *X*'s next to them.

| | |
|---|---|
| Samuel Gohe | Josiah Beeman |
| Sary Hay | William Hannibel |
| Elizabeth Hannibel | Mary Hannibel |
| Sary Toby | Daniel |
| Geny gebry | Harry |
| Prince Cuffey | Stephen Hannibel |
| Elizabeth Cuffey | |
| Sary Shee | |
| Mary Garden | |
| Esther Samson | |
| Sara Beeman | |

The letter found its way to Cadwallader Colden, the colony's lieutenant governor. Colden's papers show that one month after receiving the petition, he asked the Southold town clerk to inform him of which properties in the town had been reserved for the Indians. The answer came back that Indian Neck, and not Corchaug Pond, was considered Indian land.

But in late September of 1764, a letter signed by the owners of the neck arrived on Colden's desk. In it, they suggested that another parcel had been reserved by the town for the benefit of the Indians. In this letter, they copied an entry in the town records, dated August 3, 1685, in which the town fathers voted "that the Indians should have a planting Field laid out for the use of those Indians of Right belonging to this township at the East side of the Meadow now belonging to Mr. Thomas Mapes Senior, near a Place called and known by the Name of Corchoague Pond which field is to run South from the Highway to the value of one hundred and twenty acres. . . ."

The town record went on to note that the Indians living on this tract could cut wood only within the reserved area and could not fire a gun anywhere else without permission from the town. These rules applied to no one but the Indians. The size of the reserved tract indicates the number of Indians living as a community in 1685 was very low, most likely fewer than fifty.

The owners of Indian Neck pointed out that they had deeds to the property that were grounded in the original patent creating the town in 1640. Thus, they argued, the Indians had the right to live only at Corchaug Pond and nowhere else in the town. Out of kindness, the owners informed Colden, they would allow those Indians who were "truly descendants of the old Southold tribe" to live on the neck and plant crops, provided no other Indians lived there and the land was not leased out to whites.

To investigate further, Colden commissioned an attorney to travel to Southold to conduct interviews. While the limited paperwork that survives from this time shows that the town could not—or would not—help the attorney in his efforts, the attorney solicited statements from older residents that showed the Indians had lived at Corchaug Pond until 1691, when they were removed to Indian Neck. The statements were notarized by the town justice, Parker Wickham. (One of the owners of Indian Neck listed in the petition to Colden was Samuel Landon, a relative of Jared Landon, who bought the large Wickham Neck farm from the state after it was confiscated from Parker Wickham.)

The lawyer sent to the North Fork was John Tabor Kempe, the colony's attorney general. In his writings, Kempe showed concern that the Southold Indians had been unfairly treated. He even hinted in his correspondence that he believed the original patent for the town might not hold up to a court challenge, a point that, had he pushed it, would have spawned panic over the hundreds of deeds held by town residents. In a letter to Colden, he did make clear that he did not believe he could help the Indians, with whom he could not communicate, but who, he argued, had the same rights—"as the King's natural born subjects"—as anyone else in the town. And while he had been informed of the existence of documents related to lands reserved for the Corchaugs, "I cannot find out the purport of it, nor where it is to be found." Without that paperwork, he wrote, he could not file a lawsuit on behalf of the Corchaugs.

On top of the difficulty of finding documents, he wrote, the statute of limitations prevented the Indians from claiming Corchaug Pond. As for Indian Neck, he said, the statements of old-timers indicated the Indians had vacated that neck by the early 1700s, and because there were no town records giving the Indians the legal right to live there, they could not claim this tract, either. (These statements, like one written by Richard Terry, showed the presence of wigwams on Indian Neck as late as the 1720s. Terry said the Indians had planted a nursery on the neck "and an orchard and buried their dead.")

In his report, Kempe made clear his feelings that the Indians were not treated the same as white residents of the town—he pointed out, for example, that they were not allowed to cut wood on common lands, as everyone else was. In spite of the legal difficulties facing the Indians in winning a lawsuit to regain their land, Kempe suggested nonetheless that they should sue "in forma pauperis," or as poor people.

If the Corchaugs brought such an action, there is no record of it. It would seem, since Kempe said in his report that he could not communicate with the Indians, that someone wrote the petition on their behalf, then scratched in their names after the X's. Perhaps it was a minister working among the Indians who felt a desire to help them. Occom had been in Montauk at roughly this time, and he might have written it for them; another possibility is a Southold minister named Azariah Horton, who traveled among native communities and kept a diary, although there are no entries in it for Southold.

On March 26, 1765, six months after the petition reached Albany, a lawyer named David Colden wrote to Kempe asking him to again try to help the Corchaugs. His letter reads:

> One of the Southold Indians brought me the enclosed letter from Wm. Nicoll, speaker of the Assembly, which by the governor's directions I communicate to you. The opinion of the Attorney General which Mr. Nicoll mentions was that the Indians could only have relief by sueing in forma Pauperis. There is reason to think the Indians are really ill used, and their poverty and ignorance excites compassion in such a case. You may remember that the Council last year made an order concerning this matter, which was served upon the Southold people, but I think they have not paid the least regard to it. The governor asks sir that you would again consider this complaint, and advise him what steps he can order to be taken for the relief of the Indians as he really thinks they deserve compassion.

What Kempe might have done after receiving this letter is lost to time. There is no record in Southold of the Corchaugs reclaiming land or challenging titles to other tracts. They probably remained as indentured servants, separated from their land. There is very little to tell us what happened to the seventeen who signed the petition.

David Hannibal—there are two men and two women named Hannibel on the petition—died in 1936. He was active in the Cutchogue Presbyterian Church, and when he was buried, he was mourned as "the last Indian."

John Wickham told me Hannibal was born in Southold. "He had all the features of an Indian and he said he was an Indian," John told me. "He was very active in our church, and a very fine man, I must say that of him."

Noble Funn knew Hannibal in the early 1930s. "I would have to say that man was in fact an Indian, 'cause he looked just like an Indian. He lived down from the Main Road in a shack in some woods. I always heard he worked for the Fleet family, but I don't know that for sure. I'd be out walkin in Cutchogue and see him sittin under a tree just by himself, and I'd say, 'Hey, there's that Indian again.'"

Ed Brush, another lifelong resident, showed me the woods where Hannibal's shack was, and I walked through it one afternoon. There were no clues the shack had been there. Near where it had stood, there is a freshwater spring that flows under the road and into a salt creek. I wondered if it was possible that he was the last Corchaug, the very last one.

I told Ken Homan about Corchaug Pond, and that my son and I had found it hidden in an overgrowth north of the Main Road east of Cutchogue. Maps from before the Civil War showed it on the farm of a family named Hutchinson, but modern-day maps don't show it at all. It's little more than a swampy area today at the north end of a finger of Richmond Creek.

Ken said we should put a monument up, a stone marker by the road, telling people this land had once been reserved for the remaining Southold Indians. He said we should engrave on it the names of the Indians who had signed the old deeds, as a way of remembering them.

Maybe people driving by will stop and look at it, he said.

---

*Fall of 1994: Henry Rutkoski holding a head of cauliflower. "I would never sell my farm," he says. "It means everything to me."*

# The Wickham Family

*Tom Wickham driving an old tractor through an orchard.*

*Lunchtime: Tom Wickham cutting pizza with a pair of scissors, his mother, Anne, looking on.*

*Tom Wickham giving instructions to a group of workers by the barn.*

*Tom Wickham drawing directions on the road. With him is his cousin, Rob White.*

*Farm bounty: Tom Wickham pulling a load of apples to the farm stand.*

*On a cool morning, Tom Wickham gives instructions to pickers.*

*Tom Wickham fixing a flat.*

*Stuart Wood, a schoolteacher who has worked summers on the Wickham farm since his childhood, at the wheel of the tractor pulling a combine.*

*Stuart Wood loading chemicals into a tank.*

*Jonathan Wickham, Tom's son, adjusting an irrigation sprayer.*

*On a hot summer day, Steven Searl, Parnel Wickham-Searl's son, dragging irrigation pipe.*

*On another hot day, Jonathan Wickham works on an old irrigation pump.*

*Fruit of the land: Jonathan Wickham in the wagon on a farm road through the orchard.*

*Jonathan talking to a group of apple pickers.*

*Aren't they sweet? Tom Wickham talking to an apple picker.*

*Tom carrying a bag of apples out of the field.*

# EIGHTEEN

# A Dry June

BY THE LATE spring of 1994, the beginnings of a drought had settled in hard. June was hot and

dry, and lack of rain meant irrigation pumps had to be cranked up early and shut off late. This was

true in the potato fields and in the Wickhams' orchards.

Standing out of the bright sun at his raspberry stand one morning, John Tuthill said droughts

were hard work for the farmer, and more expensive, considering oil tanks next to pumps had to be

refilled every few days. "They're always harder on the farmer," he said in his soft New England

accent.

*Henry Rutkoski holding a photograph of, from right to left, his father, John, himself, his brother Edward, and a friend, Edward Blasko.*

"But you know we can irrigate here, and that's not altogether true for potato farmers in other places. So in that sense, we can often come out ahead when it comes time to sell our potatoes. At least that's what we hope, anyhow." He smiled under the brim of his cap. "We'll just have to see this fall if prices are good, that's all."

I saw Frank McBride sitting in his pickup by the wreckage of the old Oregon Road school, his pump on one side of it squirting oil, and he looked weary, the lack of rain beating him down. He had pumps scattered up and down Oregon Road, and keeping them going was hard work. In hot spells, he told me, everything that can go wrong, will go wrong. It was a rule.

"It's hard keeping machinery going," he said, hardly smiling. "What with all this work, I got two sons who farm. I got a grandson who's crazy about it, and another grandkid coming up."

He pushed his cap back, a line of sweat appearing across the middle of his forehead. "Oh, boy. I'm very worried about our future. I don't see it continuing. No one's makin any money. Yet every damn spring we keep on doing this and every few years we get into a real nasty drought and I think, How can we keep going?"

Earlier in the spring, someone had vandalized David Steele's irrigation pump by the railroad tracks, and he was livid about it. Just when he needed it the most, it was out of commission and sure to cost him a couple of grand to get it repaired, a couple of grand more than he had right now. They poured sand into the engine, he told me, and I could see in his face a keen desire to booby-trap the pump so that if someone tried again, they'd hurt themselves.

*Orient farmer Ed Latham and his son, Dan. "I've been here a long time, and there were a lot of farms between my place and Riverhead," Ed said. "Now you can count them on one hand. When I got started in forty-four there were thirty-five farmers in Orient and now there are two."*

"This sort of thing never used to happen around here," he said one morning as he moved irrigation pipes in his nursery in the field west of his house. The sky was blue and clear, the air hot. It was not yet eight in the morning.

"Boy, do that when I was a kid and if you got caught you'd be taken care of, no questions asked. Now the way they coddle criminals, it's no wonder this stuff keeps happening." He explained that he'd called the town police, but he wondered out loud what good it would do. You can't keep a cop posted on my pumps around the clock, he said.

David and John Tuthill, working together most mornings, kept track of rainfall amounts, and they knew by the third week of June that it had not rained hard since the middle of May. Moving long sections of aluminum pipe on David's potato land was tiring and time-consuming. The only farm on which it was fairly easy to irrigate was Ziggy's. The system, in which water was pulled out of the pond and pushed through underground pipes to wellheads in the potato fields, was testament to Ziggy's farming and engineering skills.

Not many North Fork farms had ponds to pump water out of. John Wickham had done much the same thing as Ziggy had done, taking maximum advantage of Dam Meadow Pond to water his orchards. Throughout June, I could hear the Wickhams' pumps going late into the night, and I knew Tom or Jonathan was leaving the house at ten or eleven o'clock at night to shut them off. Hot, dry work brought out the frustrations in farmers, and some days the best policy was to stay out of their way.

Late on a hot afternoon in June, I saw Tom and Anne closing up the farm stand. I could hear their pump running south of the house. For a few moments, Tom talked about the frustrations of

*Lyle and Susan Wells and their children, Jessica and Matthew, on their Aquebogue farm.*

government ("It's not like a farm or any other business where if you want to get something done, you do it," he told me) but said that overall he was glad he had been elected town supervisor. He seemed the rarest of public officials—one who wanted to accomplish something.

"How's Jonathan doing?" I asked Anne, and she said he was glad to be home from school and was talking about perhaps skipping a year and working on the farm instead. In a family where almost every member had an advanced degree in something, Jonathan's desire seemed revolutionary. "But Tom needs him now, too, so he's very glad he's here."

A local farm service had drawn up a list for me of who was farming on the North Fork this spring. It did not include farmers to the west, in the town of Riverhead. The Kujawski family raises potatoes on Sound Avenue in Riverhead, and I'd driven past their farm for years, admiring their well-kept fields. Not long ago, the Long Island Lighting Company had proposed building two nuclear power plants on the Sound a short distance from the Kujawski farm on Sound Avenue. The construction, which never got off the ground, would have wrecked Sound Avenue, which runs east and west along Riverhead's northern edge.

Like Oregon Road in Cutchogue, there were schoolhouses on Sound Avenue, but they are long gone, along with dozens of old farmhouses that collapsed or were bulldozed. One of the oldest, owned for generations by the Hallock family, was turned into a farming museum. Among the many farms along Sound Avenue, there are a number that have abandoned potatoes and branched off into serious vegetable growing, like the Wells farm and the Schmidt family's operation. Lyle and Susie Wells raise more than two dozen vegetable varieties. The Schmidts raise specialty crops—

*In their Mattituck storage barn: Fran and Bill Lindsay and their children, Wayne, Lisa, Michael, Billy, and Matthew.*

cabbage, spinach, different types of lettuce, beets, parsley, celery root—and plant and cut until frost kills the crops.

The list of potato growers in Southold was short: Paul Kaloski, William Lindsay, Jr., Frank McBride and sons, Henry Rutkoski, Robert Rutkoski, John Sidor, Jr., Martin Sidor, Robert Sidor, David Steele, and Tom Wowak. The list of vegetable growers was longer: George Conway, Doug Cooper, A. and H. Domaleski, Edward Harbes, Peter Harbes, Mike Konarski, Jr., Joseph Krukowski, Al Krupski, Jr., Fred Lappe, Dan Latham, Fred Lee, Fred Terry, John Tuthill, and Gene Wesnofske, Jr.

"The list seems to get smaller every few years," said Dale Moyer, who drew it up and who has worked with the farmers for years. "There were so many more potato growers just a few years ago. But I think the ones you have now, they're the ones who want to hold on as long as they can."

On another hot morning, McBride, known for outspokenness and blunt assessments of the future, shut off the pump next to the old schoolhouse building. The pump had been squirting so much oil, he feared it might catch fire. "All I need now is something major to go wrong; that's all I damn well need," he said. "It's June, and there might be three months of hot and dry ahead, and I can't afford anything to up and quit on me."

Before climbing back into his truck and heading home, he spoke of the summer of 1993, hot and dry, and said this was now two in a row. "Only this one's startin out worse," he said, pulling away in a cloud of dust, the red taillights of his pickup fading into the darkness of a hot evening.

The next morning, David Steele was working in his nursery field west of the house. Since sunup, he had been laying out irrigation pipe to wet down the soil; later a crew would come and dig up a number of trees. "You have to wet the ground before they can dig," he said. "It makes things a lot easier."

I asked about Eddie, whom I had seen the previous night riding through Cutchogue on his bicycle. I had stopped him and asked how he was, and he'd said he was feeling lousy.

"He's sick again," David said, feeling the shortage of help this morning. Angel and David, two Puerto Ricans, were working with him, but there was a lot to do, and not having Eddie around was a loss.

"He went to the hospital a few days ago with swollen ankles, swollen wrists. He's bad off. He's got to take care of himself, but I've said that before, and he's got to do it on his own. You know he's already lost one kidney. Now the other one's giving him fits."

At the southeast corner of the field sits another pump; the one that had been vandalized had been hauled away on a truck for repairs. David tinkered with the pump to crank it up. "I had this one down on the Main Road. It works pretty good. You know, they put sand down the pipe and the dipstick." He shook his head as if he still could not believe it. "Once, someone ran a wire from one railroad track to the other and shut the gate down. That's the sort of prank these assholes do. It happened between nine-fifty and ten at night. The gate was down till the following morning."

The pump fired up and smoke billowed out into the cloudless sky. A minute or two later, sprinkler heads in the field began to spout tiny fountains of water. "One speck of sand in there and you have to tear the motor apart," he shouted. "I didn't have insurance on it. It's opening up a can of worms to tear a motor apart. Things are tough enough. I don't need this bullshit."

Late in the month, the heat held tight. For days, thunderstorms rumbled by on both sides of the North Fork, like express trains that don't stop. It rained hard in Connecticut, just to the north, but nothing here. It had become a bad joke watching dark thunderclouds roll by in the distance, too far to do any good.

Just after seven in the morning, a Tuesday, David and his two workers, Angel and David, hauled pipe to the east side of the potato field on the north side of the Middle Road. Bill Wickham's thick woods stood in the distance, dark and gloomy. This field stretches north, and is connected to other fields, potato-to-potato, over Oregon Road and all the way to Long Island Sound. To the south, we could see the dark line of Ziggy's big barns. In the southern sky, wisps of white clouds zipped across the sky. The ocean is that way.

David, riding in his white pickup, the back filled with rubber boots, buckets, a winch, a tire, and some empty cans, talked to Angel and David (pronounced daVEED) about laying out the pipe. Done with instructions, we headed down Ziggy's long dirt road to the pond behind his house. Soon this pump was up and running. Only the end of June, and David had already gone across Ziggy's field three times with the irrigation system. The system stays in one place for three hours, then is moved.

"When I was young and working with John," he explained, "if you watered three times in a season, that was a lot. This year is really bad, and last year was bad, too." When he was certain the pump was running well, we headed back to the field on the north side of the road. Nearby, John Tuthill picked raspberries in a field for sale at his stand.

His health better, Eddie was cutting hay and straw on the flat plain of Fort Neck. It is owned by a man named Baxter, and most of the farmers call this Baxter's farm. After starting up the pump on the old Horton farm, we went to find Eddie, but he was not at Baxter's. "Maybe he's out getting coffee or moving equipment," David muttered.

"He could be up on Elijah's Lane doing something," David said. "There's a lot of stuff he could be doing. Broke the transmission in one of the tractors yesterday cutting hay, which is typical for us. Just something else to do."

The big barn behind David's house was filled with bales of timothy hay, which David sells to the horse people. We stopped by on the way back from the Baxter farm. Passing over the railroad tracks, David stopped to talk with John Tuthill, who announced that Eddie had gone off for a doctor's appointment.

"He can't piss again," David said. One more problem on a problem-filled morning.

Late in the day, I found Eddie turning the tractor into the Baxter farm. He pulled a cutter into a field in which the hay was waist-high. In seconds, the cutter was clogged with hay and he had to climb down from the tractor and shut it down.

"This is the third tractor in two days," he said disgustedly, jiggling the hydraulic lines that connected the tractor to the cutter. "Man, everything's falling apart. Like me, I guess. Kidney's going. Gallbladder's not much better."

A half hour later, the cutter was freed of hay and he tried it again. Now it worked. He began cutting through the tall hay, diagonally to the Indian woods. As he cut the hay, dozens of purple martins suddenly appeared from nowhere and filled the sky around the tractor, dive-bombing the specks of grain dust the cutter kicked up into the air.

*Sigmund "Ziggy" Kurkoski by his barn.*

# NINETEEN

# Potato Ground

ON A BLISTERING afternoon, I drove down Ziggy Kurkoski's long road and parked behind his

potato barn. The pump by the pond was running; so was the pump on the north edge of the old

Horton farm. To the east, water shot out of sprinkler heads on the Wickham farm. The sky was free

of clouds, all blue, and back by Ziggy's house it was quiet except for the humming of the pump.

This summer, David Steele's potato operation was stretched over three farms—Tuthill's,

Kurkoski's, and the old Byron Horton farm. His hay and straw were planted in the field south of

John Tuthill's house, on Bill Wickham's farm, on the Baxter farm, and on various jib pieces—odd-shaped sections of plowed land missed by the potato planter.

Most mornings when Ziggy and his wife returned from early Mass, Ziggy looked around for David. David, it seemed to me, reminded Ziggy a little bit of himself when he was a young man farming. Ziggy watched carefully, even if he was not involved himself. He knew how many times the irrigation system had been walked across the property by the beginning of June; he listened when David started up the pond pump. In early fall, he would watch and help if he could when David loaded the big storage barn floor to ceiling, front to back, with potatoes.

Like a number of old-time Polish farmers on the North Fork, Ziggy grew up in a household in which his parents spoke Polish. He could speak it pretty well himself, but English was more useful than Polish. Marty Sidor's father, Martin senior, grew up speaking Polish on his Oregon Road farm, but, like Ziggy, he found at an early age that Polish was something spoken by older people, or by the priest at the Polish church on Sundays.

"Peter Kurkoski was my father," Ziggy told me. We sat on a small porch on the west side of his house. A welcome breeze blew through the house, and every few minutes we could smell the pond in the back, which was now low because of all the pumping. "He came from Poland in, I would guess, 1912. I think he was around twenty-one years old, eighteen, something like that. He came by himself. When he got off the boat in New York, he went to Jamaica, where there was other Polish people living. And he got a job working on trolleys. He was getting fifty cents an hour. He lived in Jamaica, by himself.

"The only thing I remember him saying about the trip over was that it took a month. When he left there, he wanted to get on a farm. That's what he wanted to get. So he worked in Jamaica for a while, made a few bucks, and he came out to Peconic. There was a big farmer there by the name of Smith. He had a Polish name, but I guess no one could pronounce it, so it became Smith. He got a job working there on his farm. Fifty dollars a month. And living on the farm, in like a house. If you could call it a house. He worked there and then in the winter months he never got paid. It was just for board. He had to feed the animals and things like that, just to stay.

"He worked there probably around eight years, ten years. Saved himself a buck. Then he came to Mattituck and he worked for C. H. Wickham. He sold, you know, plows and things like that. And he had a small farm, too. So my father went in with him for thirds. Wickham gives him the fertilizer, he's got to supply the horses, and he's got to feed them, and then he'd get a third of the profits. And he lived on that farm, too. And got married when he was living in Peconic, so he came with his wife. Her name was Antoinette Durkoski, and come to think, I think he met her in Jamaica. And she came out with him to Peconic. This is the 1920s.

"So my father and mother, they made some money, and he came working over here for Bill Wickham. Or Bill's mother, I guess. I think Bill's dad had died by then and his mother was running the operation. So he came to Cutchogue and rented some land from Bill's family, and there was an old house up by the Middle Road, an old Wickham house, very old it was, and we all moved in there. Now that house is on the village green in Cutchogue and it's a museum. But back then, that house was up on the Middle Road. And the farmland ran from that house all the way back to the Main Road. A big, beautiful piece of farmland. But my father only rented half. And another man rented the other half.

"And, because he was saving his dollars, my father bought a farm up in Oregon that was nothing but woodland—thirty acres. It was near where the old schoolhouse in Oregon was. They called that area Tustin. It was the next farm east from the schoolhouse. And it ran up to the Sound. It was my father's first purchase. And he cleared the whole thing. They worked; years ago, people worked hard.

"I was born in 1918, and I can remember living in that Wickham house. Two families lived in that house, too. My mother and her sister lived there. There was three kids on our side, and on my mother's sister's side, there was two kids—all in that house. Which was maybe why my father bought a piece of land covered with woods that would take years to be able to farm.

"My father bought the land in Oregon with his sister's husband. He was a farmer. It was a seventy-acre farm that Georgy Reilly owned. So my father and his brother-in-law bought it from Mr. Reilly and they split it in half. And then in eight years, they cleaned it right out to the Sound. We lived there eight years, and all I can remember is clearing woods. We cleared it with a team of horses. They cut the trees down, and for the briars they had what looked like an ax, but it had a long blade. And they cut it down and they would dry it and burn it. And we would pull the stumps right out of the ground, with the horses. We had stump pulleys to pull out the stumps. You used to work the handle back and forth. It was hooked up to one tree, then hooked up to the stump, and you'd keep pumping and crank it out of the ground.

"And there was a man named Lipman in Greenport, and my mother and father went there to buy work clothes. He owned this farm, my farm today. So they made a deal with him. He was maybe having financial problems, and the deal was he'd take the Oregon farm my father had just finished clearing, and my father would take this one, which was sixty-three acres. I think he may have had to take a mortgage out, too. My father was a worker, that's all. Small man, maybe one hundred fifty pounds. He would never look back. Just keep going, and he made it. And boy, his brother-in-law was the same way. He used to do carpentry work to bring in some income, and then five, six o'clock, he'd come home, while it's still light, and he'd go out and start cutting trees. That's how they worked in them days.

"This house was on the farm when we bought it from Lipman. And the real beauty was, the land was all cleared. But it was very different from Oregon Road. When we was living there, it was nothing but Poles. Oregon Road was Polish Street. All the farms but a few were owned by Poles. There were some Irish farms, but mostly they were being sold and the Poles were buying 'em. People sometimes say the Irish lost their farms, but mostly they sold them.

"Our neighbors in Oregon were Frank Bileski. He was next door. Dan Rutnoski lived across the street. A Joe Heleski, a little east. Steve Fitzer was next; and then there was an English fellow by the name of Moore. He lived around in there. Then Bonkoski. Keep going east and you have the McBride family. Everyone had horses, so in addition to potatoes, you had to raise hay, you had to raise corn. When you just pulled the stumps out and the first time you plow it, you can't plant potatoes in there because the weeds will take over. So there would be buckwheat, because buckwheat grows fast. That's how they lived.

"When we left Oregon, I was fourteen. I just went to grammar school, because we were needed on the farm. That was the same for everyone. Even when I was in school, we did an awful lot of farmwork. Well, you cultivated in the morning; you walked down and cultivated until eight-thirty. You would wash and then run to school. We had a path through the woods. Charlie Tuthill owned it, and it was woodland. There was a lot of walkin in them days. I mean, you plowed. In a day, you'd plow two and a half acres, from morning till noontime. And then in the afternoon, you'd plant. If you plowed all day, you'd probably do five acres. And you walked all that. Back and forth, back and forth. Me and my brother Stanley. That's how we grew up."

There were five children in the family, two boys and three girls, living first in the Wickham house, then the house on Oregon Road, then on the big farm by the pond. From a modern point of view, that house seems small, too, considering seven people lived in it. But Ziggy said no one thought of it as small, and none of the five children thought of their parents as poor. They made a living, some years a good living. There weren't new bicycles or anything like that, but no one ever went to bed hungry, never that. In fact, no one of Ziggy's generation remembers anyone on a farm going hungry, even in the worst of years. Going hungry was a contradiction on land this rich.

Peter Kurkoski was an optimist when it came to the future. He invested in the new Polish church when it was built on Depot Lane, a lot of money for a farmer. But it was money well spent—for the Poles, it was their own church, their own priest, their own Mass. No more standing in the back of the Irish church. As farmers, everyone was pretty much in the same boat; no one was materially better off than anyone else. The first farmers who bought mechanized tractors and cars were the talk of the town.

"When we moved in this house, there was no heat. No lights, and we had lights in Oregon. So when we came here, my God, we were kids, you know, so we didn't like it from the beginning. There was nobody to play with. No kids around. It's so far back from the road. We moved in right in March. There was a stove in the house, like a potbelly. And we always had plenty of wood. We had three horses, two cows, and we used to have around four or five pigs. Chickens. This was the Depression, '31 or so, when we moved. They were hard times. Potatoes were seventy-five cents a hundred. But I think there were good years in there, too, 'cause my father was selling out of storage, maybe four dollars a bushel. I just remember forty-five cents a hundred. That's the lowest I can remember. That was '34. We had a couple hundred dollars. We had chickens; we had eggs. But nobody had luxuries, either, or any extras."

When the family lived on Oregon Road, farmers sold potatoes in barrels, carting them to a dock on Mattituck Inlet, where they were loaded on a boat bound for Connecticut. Later, after the move to the bigger farm, Peter Kurkoski dealt with potato brokers like I. M. Young and a number of others. He would haul the potatoes to the railroad tracks in Cutchogue and load them in bins; later, workers would dump them into hundred-pound bags.

"My father liked Cutchogue. That's where he wanted to be. He was satisfied when he got this farm. This is what he wanted right here. He died in '65, and by then, just me and my brother Stanley was farming. This is good land, and my father knew that, and he hoped Stanley and I could keep everything going. The trouble here is not the land. The trouble now is the taxes are so high. You can't live on a farm if you're not working the farm.

"Dave, I like him farmin it. But how's he gonna keep doin it? I'd like to see the land like it is now. I wouldn't want to see houses on it. But what are you going to do if your taxes keep going up? What are you going to do with the land? You know, there was nothing but potatoes here twenty years ago. Potatoes, cauliflower. Long Island was doing good."

From the back of Ziggy's farm, a dirt road snakes east, down through a patch of low-lying woods too irregular to farm. Then the land rises again slightly to the back of the former Horton farm. Follow this pickup road and you come along the edge of Bill Wickham's farm, moving south toward the house. Most afternoons, Bill Wickham, a courtly gentleman in his eighties and still practicing law in Mattituck, walks his dog, occasionally kicking up a pheasant in the brush that separates his farm from the winery to the east.

The Horton farm runs from the Main Road straight back, a wedge of flat land between Wickham on the east and the Pellegrini Winery on the west. When Byron Horton sold off the land in the 1980s, the family's farming history ended abruptly. ("No one ever said you got to keep doing the same thing all your life," Horton told me when I asked him about the sale of his farm. "That's just the way it worked out, that's all. It's not good, it's not bad. It's just the way it is.")

A man named Horton, who lived in New Suffolk, built Bill Wickham's home. Bill's father was Will; he and John Wickham's father were brothers. Will died when his son was a child, and Bill's memories of his father are fleeting images.

"The early town records tell a rather interesting story about this particular farm," Bill Wickham said when I stopped by his house one summer evening. "It was a gift from Barnabas Horton to his son Caleb. It went from the cartway, now the Main Road, all the way to the North Sea on the north. So it went all the way to the Sound. The land of Samuel King was to the east, Barnabas Horton to the west.

"Caleb was the third son of Barnabas. He was born in 1640, the year the town was formed by the church group, and died in 1702. Interesting that he was born in 1640, but he never had a home lot assigned to him in the old bounds of the town. In 1669, he was twenty-nine, and his father made a gift and grant to him of a tract of land in Corchaug containing three hundred acres, from the cart-way to the North Sea. And also sixty acres in the Broadfields, which was across the cartway and ran east all the way to the John Wickham farm.

"Upon this three-hundred-acre lot, he built his house, cleared his land, which was all forest, and became a wealthy farmer. The greater part of the farm remained in the Horton family for three generations. David Horton, Jr., son of Silas, about the year 1782, sold it to a John Wickham, one of the nine children of Joseph Wickham, Jr. John willed it to his son William, who was my grandfather's father. He died in 1859. So that's what's so interesting about this farm—that it's only been in two families, the Hortons and the Wickhams. It was much later, of course, that the two wings of the Wickham family divided up. My father took this farm, and my father's sister and brother, Julia and James, took the other farm. This farm is the older of the two Wickham farms."

John Wickham always said he had no real memory of his father. Bill Wickham was eight in 1914, the year James Wickham died of blood poisoning, and he remembers James "as a big guy." By that year, his own father had been dead for two years.

"I was quite young, but I can picture my father. He'd always had five horses, a nice team of workhorses. He had a nice team of mules; they were beautiful. And he also had a road horse, as most of the farmers did, with a fine carriage. He had a one-seated carriage with rubber tires. It was a fast carriage, for a fast horse. Oh, it was a beautiful thing.

"When my father died at the end of 1912, we had to split this farm. The old house on this farm was moved up to the Middle Road. And that's where Ziggy Kurkoski spent part of his youth, in that Wickham house. This allowed, after my dad's death, for there to be two farms to be rented out. The last Wickhams to live in that house before it was moved were the sisters, Nancy and Parnel, my grandfather's sisters."

Will was the last Wickham to farm this land. Bill was not interested in farming the land himself. He does not know, looking back through the window of the past, whether his son, William Shepard Wickham, who died in 1966, would have wanted to farm. There is no way to know what the future would have held for this boy, who was the fifth William Wickham in a row to be born on this farm. The boy's death ended the male line for this branch of the family, the way Edward's and William's deaths ended it on the Tuthill farm.

"Shep was a very bright boy, and I think he would have looked for different opportunities," Bill told me. "I believe he would have been interested in the farming, but I don't believe he would have farmed himself. There is just no way of knowing, really.

"My father was the last Wickham to farm this farm. I was too young when he died and not that interested in it to begin with. But I like it. And I wouldn't let it go for anything. I'm proud of it. I own the original tract first bought by a Wickham. I don't believe there are many places in America where you find this sort of thing."

# TWENTY

# Fire from Heaven

THE DIRT THAT had been sticky in the spring rain was bone-dry by the middle of the summer.

The diary kept by John Tuthill on his desk showed the last rains anyone thought much of had fallen

in May. He filled in details at night, the same way Ernest Tuthill had, in that careful pencil scrawl

of his. John collected his father's diaries and notebooks in a cardboard box and put them in a cor-

ner of the old milk house that sits by the back door. For everyone working in the Cutchogue and

Mattituck potato fields—the Rutkoskis, Bill Lindsay, Marty Sidor, Frank McBride, David Steele,

Tom Wowak—the daily effort was to move pipe around, start up pumps, and send water flying over the low-lying greenery. With pumps running all day and into the night, fuel oil costs for each of them were soaring. No one needed these added costs, not in a business in which making money depended on so many variables, so much that was outside of anyone's control.

The hard truth was they could work all summer and come fall find that potato profits they had been calculating were just wishful thinking. And everyone at their worst moments thought about the last two-dollar year, when dozens of farmers went belly-up.

Inside the work-camp bungalow at the railroad tracks, the air was as still as a crypt. It was so uncomfortable one late July evening that one of the workers slept on the ground outside, hoping for a whiff of night air, a whisper of breeze. The windows were open, the screen door had been repaired, but nothing seemed to work. It was just hot. The grader itself, big and cavernous, with wide doors on the south side, was slightly cooler, and Walt worked repairing the old equipment, replacing what he could, goosing it along with the hope of getting another season out of what amounted to antique equipment.

One of the drivers from Maine who had come down with bags last winter had said the equipment was the oldest he had ever seen. "There's nothing like that in Maine, I'm telling you that for certain," he had said, almost smirking about it. In Maine, they had moved to a sophisticated weighing system; here there were needles on gauges and usually, to be on the safe side in case some government bean counter showed up, the workers went a little heavier on each bag, an extra potato or two, which meant the farmer got paid for a ten-pound bag even if it weighed ten and a quarter pounds. One more nail in the farmer's coffin, someone said.

In the white pickup, David rode each day along the dirt road, sunup to sundown, usually with one of his children in the cab or standing in the back. Each child got a day—that's how it was set up. It was not just for the kids, David, Kyle, and Kristin. It was the way David liked it, too.

The boys could drive the truck when hay was baled, even though they had a hard time seeing over the wheel. In the fall, when it got cooler, they could help dig potatoes, too, standing on the side of the digger with Angel or David, or sitting in the cab with Eddie while their father steered the tractor. The digger was so noisy, they'd have to shout to be heard, but that did not bother anyone.

Several nights during July, as thunderclouds marched noisily by on both sides of the North Fork, lightning bolts had split the gray cloud cover, like flashes of light behind a closed curtain. It was all very theatrical, but nothing came of it that anyone watching a rain meter in the backyard could get excited about. They talked about the rainfall on a night in early July that seemed good while it was coming down, but in the morning there was nothing, no proof it had rained at all. The heat had wicked up the moisture before sunup.

That morning, I drove along Oregon Road, where every sprinkler system was going full blast. The irrigation pump next to the dilapidated schoolhouse was slimed with oil, and there was water pooled around it, as if it had just been shut off. Frank McBride was making his rounds, trying to stay ahead of the heat. North toward the Sound, huge sprays of water shot out of a cannon that was spinning slowly as it watered a large arc of potato field. The potato plants were a foot and a half off the ground.

The previous night I had spoken with Claire McBride, Frank's good-natured wife, and she said her husband was going nuts. "Mick's fit to be tied," she said. "Everything's breaking down. Things are real tough around here right now."

I drove east along the narrow roadway and parked by the abandoned Mahoney farmhouse across from McBride's barn. The house was falling down, the big barn in the back a monument to a family in which a generation arrived that did not want to farm and that was that. Across the way, the MCBRIDE AND SONS sign over the top of Frank's barn shimmered in the heat.

In his office, Frank was sitting with another man, looking weary and beaten down. "Two tenths of an inch is all we got," he said with disgust. "And some people never got nothing."

His son Jimmy came in and said, "I hope to God we get a big thunderstorm today or tomorrow. That's what they're talking about, anyhow."

"Don't mean anything," Frank said. "They say that and you look out and it whizzes by and we get spit."

He sipped water from a paper cup. Frank wore a hat advertising a seed-potato outfit from Caribou, Maine. There were ribbons on one wall of the office from the Empire State Potato Club, which surely must be one of those organizations with a drastically shrinking membership.

"We're burning up engines as fast as we can. Jimmy's puttin a water pump in one now. We got automatic shutoffs on the motors, but sometimes it don't work right. I got a tractor out there with three holes in it this big." He made a circle with his hands. "I'm wore out. Richie's wore out. Jimmy's wore out. We're goin all night. I got a mechanic working on equipment out in the field. He couldn't stand it and left and never come back. Hell, he's my age! On top of that, the fuel pump went out on my pickup. It still ain't fixed. Probably pushed me aside for some big shot with a Lincoln. The only way to get comfortable is to get in Richie's new Chevy and turn on the air-conditioning."

A morning or two earlier, I had heard talk at the grader about rain hitting all around the North Fork. Just another point of frustration, someone had said. It had rained in Calverton. It had rained in Bridgehampton. It had *poured* in Montauk.

For Frank, the summer of broken equipment was another slap in the face. He liked to know where he would be and what he would be doing; sitting around hoping for help from the weather was not something he was any good at. Ideally, his early potatoes could be dug up in late July, which would allow him to get some cash in the house. Frank was one of the few local potato people who did not use the crew at the grader to bag his potatoes. He had his own crew, and on this hot morning they were sitting in North Carolina, waiting for a phone call telling them to head north.

"I'd like to start digging next week," Frank said, his patience running thin with visitors dropping by the barn. "I'd start across the street from the dump, but we got seven pumps running practically round the clock, and it's hard to dig up potatoes with that kind of thing going on. My crew's ready to come. They're done diggin down there. They go to a guy in Virginia Beach, and two guys in Cape Clark, Virginia. Then straight up here when we start up."

One of the genuine sore points in Frank's summer life was housing his crew in a camp in Riverhead. Like nearly all farmers, Frank has hard feelings for the bureaucrats who regulated his life, from camp inspectors to pesticide people. "There's a guy with the Board of Health. He's hell on wheels. He sends his henchmen out to find any violation they can. They have to find a violation or they don't get their lunch money. 'That lightbulb is not working. You have two days to fix it or we'll bring you up on charges.' They can fine you without taking you to court, which is absolutely un-American. How can that be legal? Can you answer me that? It's the same old shit, and the farmer is stuck in the middle, getting it shoved up his backside. I'm sick of it."

This week a local planning group came out with a recommendation that the farms down the central spine of the North Fork be upzoned to twenty-five acres. This would, the group hoped, keep the land in farming and take away the incentive to cover the land with houses. Frank saw it as a direct assault on his well-being. He was not alone, either. I heard it all week from other farmers. Planners hoping to preserve the rural atmosphere of the North Fork saw the land they wanted to save; the farmers themselves were an afterthought.

"They want to save these old farms? Is that it? But what's the point of saving the farms if there ain't no farmers? They're doing nothin to save the farmers! A big-shot politician asked me twenty years ago, 'Mick, what can we do to save the farmer?' I said give us a lower rate of taxes. It's that simple. Don't give those doctors and lawyers who bought up these farms and sittin on them while they're making money in New York City, don't give them a damn break. Give us a break, the people who are working these farms. Saving the farm ain't nothing—you gotta save the farmer."

For the first time in years, many of the local farmers, including David Steele, were not planting fields of cauliflower. There's no point in doing it, David told me, because prices were so bad, you lost money in the end.

It had been a great cash crop, with an auction on Route 58 in Riverhead, where the cauliflower was sold. The season flowed naturally from potatoes to cauliflower, which allowed David to keep his Puerto Rican crew up longer and put money in the bank to offset the uncertainties that always came with potato prices.

"We had the most lucrative business in the world raising cauliflower," Frank said as we walked outside to look over the tractor that had blown apart. "Those farmers in California get Mexican labor for twenty cents an hour and we're paying seven dollars or maybe twelve dollars. They can trim it, cut it, wrap it, and put it on Tiger airlines and it's here in these stores the same day. California knocked us off the map, and no one who ever talked about saving these farms ever thought we'd be all right if we could just sell our cauliflower in the stores. How come no one thought of that? The chain stores bought from California instead of Long Island. It killed us. The Calverton growers had such a thing going with cauliflower. They were doing two loads a day. They died, and I don't hear no one complainin about it. We were making good money. Now tell me, how we gonna make that up?"

Also souring Frank's mood was the current issue of *Agricultural News*, published by Cooperative Extension. A cauliflower farmer on Sound Avenue in Riverhead, a man everyone knew, was selling all his equipment. He was going out of business. "If them guys can't make it, no one can," Frank said. "It was beautiful for so long. A hundred years ago, they used to raise cauliflower and put them in barrels. My father told me they put the barrels in wagons and hauled them down to the Cutchogue station. Jim Hand was the station agent. Special trains would come and take the barrels into the Washington Street Market in New York City.

"Used to have a beautiful pickle works down where the cauliflower auction was held in Riverhead. That's gone. The county closed it 'cause they didn't like the brine. I saw Bucky Hallock the other day, and he said, 'How can you stand it?' I said, 'Forty years ago, we had nothing. Now we got the Labor Department, the Board of Health, the EPA, the Department of Conservation, every goddamn thing you can have and it's puttin us out of business.' Bucky said, 'You deserve a medal for doing this.' And it's gettin worse. No one, absolutely no one, gives a shit.

"Now I read breast cancer is caused by pesticides. That is bullshit! Complete bullshit! Every woman out here would have breast cancer if that was true. They used to do test wells on my property and tell me I was drinking contaminated water. I say to them, I drink more water than anyone I know and look at me. I kicked 'em off my property. People get nasty with us, yet they keep saying, 'Oh, we love the farms. Let's keep the farms.'

"I had guys betting me forty years ago I would not be farmin in ten years. My own brother-in-law said real estate people would buy up these farms and there'd be nothing but houses. That was when my father died. Everybody wants cheap food, but no one gives a shit about the farmer."

He walked back toward the barn.

"If it rains tonight and tomorrow, I might dig next week. And if the dog didn't stop to shit, he'd have caught the rabbit."

On a morning in late July, Stuart Wood, the Westhampton schoolteacher, was in the metal shop in one of the Wickham barns, trying to repair a clutch on a tractor. Like all the family's tractors, this one was a relic, kept going by luck and repairs. Jonathan stopped to help before heading out on his own chores.

"I believe this is an early 1950s model," Jonathan said.

"It has the problem of the clutch not letting go," Stuart said. "You get to the end of a row and

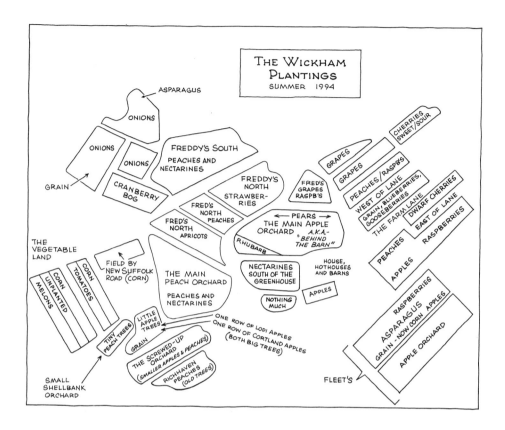

The Wickham Plantings
Summer 1994

you push down on the clutch and it keeps going." He pulled a chain down from the rafters to help wrest the engine away from the rear section of the tractor so he could get at the clutch.

Jonathan had spent the early-morning hours watering in a pocket of peach trees in the southeast corner of the farm, opposite a marina that sits at the mouth of Wickham Creek. As he helped Stuart, Stephen Searl came in looking for instructions.

"I teach twelfth-grade world literature, advanced-placement English, and a class of English One," Stuart said, looking over the tractor. "Working with people to working with machinery—it's very healthy. I came here when I was fourteen. I had a friend who was the son of a minister and his father got him a job here. Then they moved to California, and I tried to get a job here. John said they had enough help, but when I heard my friend was leaving, I came and asked again and John said yes. In those years, we were raising a lot of cauliflower, which took us into the late fall, until heavy frost.

"Then, when I started teaching, I'd come as soon as school was over and work all summer. Graduation was last Sunday night, and I was here Monday morning. Yesterday, I was cultivating on the tractor—melons, tomatoes, young asparagus. Then I fixed the sprayer tractor. And I replaced a starter on one of the trucks. You know, we can do everything here. We've never taken a tractor out for repair."

There is a huge old maple outside the door, on the west side of the barn, probably planted by William Wickham or maybe even one of the Albertsons. Standing here, the view to the south encloses the winding edge of the salt creek. I walked down the main farm road, past a buttonwood tree. At Dam Pond, the pump was running. Farther south, I walked into a cornfield, and here, along the saltwater edge of the farm, near where Lymas, the freed slave, lived, the soil smelled of tidal mud.

Inside the house, Tom was working in his office on town matters. In the kitchen, Anne Wickham and her sister, Margaret White, were having coffee at the kitchen table. The sisters were raised in a large home off the Middle Road just west of Elijah's Lane. Their father was in the seed business. East of them was Tuthill Town.

The sisters grew up with the Tuthill boys—John, Hallock, and Ernest Quintin, who went by his middle name, and Stanley and Leslie, the boys' cousins. All the boys were shy, and it was John, enlisting in the army before Pearl Harbor, who broke out of the mold and left the North Fork. They remembered Stanley had red hair and was always called Sparky; Leslie was called "Pep" from the time he was a young boy.

"Stan and Les used to have birthday parties when they were young, and their mother would invite everyone to come," Margaret White said. "They were just shy brothers, very much in the shadow of their mother. She was a nice woman, too, who very much looked after their well-being. Neither of the boys particularly talked much, not that I can recall."

Tom came into the kitchen and snatched a doughnut from a box. We walked outside and he talked about knocking down peach trees planted by his father in the 1960s and planting young ones. It would take five years to get a crop, but they would produce fruit for twenty or twenty-five years. Stuart continued with his effort to repair the clutch on the tractor.

Outside the barn, a 1940s diesel tractor waited to be used. Last summer, Jonathan had stripped a diesel engine out of a tractor and installed it on blocks by Dam Meadow as an irrigation pump.

Stuart was covered with grease and sweat. He stepped outside the barn to grab a lungful of fresh air. There were five Farmalls dating back to the 1940s to keep working this summer. Two were in operation this morning. Sooner or later, he'd have to look them all over.

"How long do you think you'll be on that clutch?" Tom asked. "There's some spraying we'll have to attend to this afternoon."

"I've almost got it," Stuart said, walking back inside the barn. "I'm hoping by the middle of the afternoon."

"I'll come look for you later," Tom said. He climbed aboard the tractor. It started right up.

*Hallock Tuthill on his homemade stilts. He made the wreaths that hang on the side of his barn.*

# TWENTY-ONE

# John Tuthill and Early Digging

AT DUSK ON a hot July evening, Eddie Clark rode his bicycle east along the Main Road from his

home in the woods. He was wearing his familiar brown cap, with a headset clamped over them.

Near the country club, he stopped and we talked. He said he had missed a lot of work and that

David was having to get by without him.

Pulling off the headset, he smiled and said, "Stevie Wonder. I hate that new stuff."

He held his side and said he had only recently been released from the hospital. "I'm taking different medicines and these patches." He pulled open the front of his shirt to reveal dime-sized patches on his chest. "You know, with only one kidney, this blood pressure thing is really dangerous. I'm trying hard to control it, but damn it, there's salt in everything."

Cars sped by and disappeared into the falling darkness of early evening.

"Honestly, I've been thinking I'm not going to make it. My brother died last October of cancer. My father died young. My mother, she's dead. We got bad lifelines."

The next morning, I found Marty Sidor on his tractor near his home on Oregon Road. I knew Marty had been working with his son, Chris, this summer, and another farmer had told me how proud Marty was of his son. Like a lot of father-son relationships, theirs had had its ups and downs, but Marty felt they had turned a corner. A quiet boy, Chris seemed to have arrived at farmwork after several years of looking for his niche.

"We're getting ready to start digging soon, any day now," Marty said when he jumped off the tractor behind his house. Marty is a soft-spoken man, with brown-black hair and a wide face. Since taking over the farm, he has remained close to his father and his father's brothers.

"My father was Martin, and he came from a farming community near Kraków," Martin Sidor, Sr., Marty's father, told me one night in August as we sat around Marty's kitchen table. "Conditions there were bad and he came here. He started here in 1910. He and his brothers came, Anthony and Jacob. Not only them but all of Poland. Just like Ireland, everyone was coming here. There was a land of opportunity here. And this country wanted them at that time—you know, they wanted farmers and help—so they came over.

"My father was working for fifteen dollars a month, and in the wintertime he got nothing, just food. And a roof over his head. There was the Polish church in Riverhead, and there was lots of Poles around, so I'm sure he felt at home. But he wanted his own farm. I think he met my mother in Riverhead. She was Polish-born, too.

"It wasn't just my dad riding around looking for land. Probably all of them were doing that. He saw this place, and he liked it. It was small, but he kept adding on and adding on. Buster Tuthill, who was right next door, sold twelve acres to my dad. And he was sorry as ever afterwards. And then he had a good-size farm, doing all right. He also bought a piece of woodland, which we helped clean out. All he grew was potatoes, all his life. He didn't care for cauliflower or nothing. Just potatoes."

Maps from the 1880s show the farm was then owned by a man named J. Wyckoff. Across the street from Wyckoff was a farmer named J. W. Duryee. Members of the Lupton family (Anne Lupton married John Wickham in 1933) owned a considerable amount of land at the west end of Oregon, and south toward the Middle Road. Anne Wickham remembers as a little girl that the path home from the Oregon Road school ran by Buster Tuthill's farmhouse, south through some woods and fields to her father's home.

HEAVEN AND EARTH

"We had good neighbors," Martin Sidor, Sr., said. "We had Buster on one side, and a man named Robinson across the way. Austin Tuthill was a little to the east; his son was Blue Jay Tuthill. My father, he was a rough little guy. He wasn't afraid of nobody. How big you were didn't make no difference. He was the boss. He was only five feet five. They had tractors, but still he'd be out there with a horse and a cultivator. When he got his citizen papers, he was forty-four and my mother was thirty-two.

"We were young children when we started to work for Dad. We were all one group. We were stuck together. Dad would do all the deals; he had a smart head on him. We didn't argue with him, either. We worked—we just went to work. If he hollered, what the heck, we just kept working. Times were tough. We didn't have no irrigation. In summers like this, we laid under the tree and just watched things dry up. We went swimming a lot. Everybody else did the same thing.

"Oregon Road, it was all Polish except for the McBrides. Everybody got along. They used to play baseball together behind the barn. Go swimming together and everything. Buster's mother used to come and bring us cookies. We didn't even speak English when we went to the Oregon Road school. The parents always spoke Polish at home. But things were tough; there were tough years. Sixty-two was a good year. I remember '73—that was a biggie. Seventy-four was really bad. So it goes in cycles. Eighty-five was a killer. Sometimes it took everything you had to keep going. But when you're born and brought up on a farm, what are you gonna do?"

In the afternoon, I stopped by John Tuthill's house. He was selling bales of hay out of his big barn. The bales were stacked nearly to the rafters. Inside, the air was sweet-smelling. South of the house, David was baling hay, his sixth-grade son, David, driving the truck. His little head was barely above the wheel. Earlier, the wind had come up from a storm passing by to the north, and the long rows of cut hay rolled across the field like long brown snakes.

When David passed by the house on the tractor, he said, "The wind's really messing us up." It felt like rain; the wind seemed to demand it. But there was no use talking about it. Hay is a quick-growing crop; usually, David can cut alfalfa four times during the season. In a wet year, timothy can be cut twice.

David's face was red from a month of hot sun. Today, he wore a straw hat. "This is a lot of work, but selling to the horse people can be a good business through the winter," he said, "if they pay their bills."

I left David and found John Tuthill at his raspberry patch on the Middle Road. He was in cut-off shorts and wearing a green farm cap perched on his head. As much as he could, he stood under an overhang fixed at the rear of the abandoned truck he used as a farm stand. Every few minutes, someone stopped by to purchase a pint of raspberries. I told him I had walked around the Buster Tuthill farm next to the Sidors' on Oregon Road, and he smiled.

*Jeanne Tuthill, John's wife, behind their home in Tuthill Town. "I don't think people can possibly understand how special the farms are out here," she says. Her grandfather, John Fanning, a member of an old Southold family, was the last Fanning to farm on the North Fork. Some members of the Fanning family were Loyalists and fled the North Fork during the Revolution.*

"Ol' Bus had a sister by the name of Elizabeth," he said. "She taught grades three, four, and five at the Oregon Road school. Quite a nice lady. She married a man, and he used to ride by the school and toot his horn." He smiled at the memory.

I asked him if that morning he'd had coffee with his cousins across the Middle Road. He smiled. Yes, I did, he said. The bachelor Tuthill brothers were quiet, reserved people who lived by themselves and, as far as I could tell, never left their property. After John Wickham's death, John Tuthill seemed to be their only visitor. When they were in the chicken business, they had had a number of customers, but they had given that up, and now they had only each other to talk to, and their cousin every morning at nine.

The three men were related on two sides of their families, the Hallocks and the Tuthills. "I've always found that part of it kind of interesting," John said as he kept busy with his raspberries. "Stan and Les's grandfather and my grandfather were brothers. Their father was Charles Tuthill, and he married Florence Hallock. My father married Leila Hallock. Florence and Leila were sisters. Florence and Leila were both born in Nebraska during the time their parents were homesteading." A large group of raspberry customers drove up.

We arranged to meet at his house, and as I was walking back to my car, John shouted after me. "I heard an interesting statistic today. In 1940, every farmer fed ten people. Now every farmer feeds eighty-five people."

That night, I drove to the Tuthill house. Jeanne was working silently in the kitchen, her apron still on. It was nearly eight. All the windows were up; the house was hot and still. Over the years,

Jeanne had written ages, dates, heights, and other family data on the doorway between the kitchen and the living room. I looked all the way down by the floor and saw the first reference to Edward. He was a child when that mark was made. The pencil marks with his name on them crawled up the doorway, and then they just stopped.

John was at his desk, his diary next to him. We sat at the round table and he mentioned the weather, how hot it was. He picked up last year's diary and read: "'August seventeenth, three-quarter inch rain. A light drizzle on the eighteenth. Fine day, pleasant. Thunderstorm last night, one-tenth inch rain. Hot and humid. Hot and humid. Hot and humid. One-tenth inch rain. Hot and humid. Hot and humid. Thunderstorm September tenth. Thunderstorm last night, three-quarters inch of rain.'"

He looked up. "So there you see. It broke in September." He flipped a light on. "When you have a dry year like this one, there's a shortage of supply, generally, and the prices go up. And if you irrigate enough, you'll have a good crop—at a higher price. And that can cover the difference, all the expenses. Better than on a year when you have a natural rainfall.

"It's particularly true for a crop like potatoes, yes. Yup. Yup. Potatoes is the crop that irrigation got started on around here, because potatoes was the bread-and-butter crop. The major crop here for as long as I can remember was potatoes.

"All around this house was Tuthill potatoes, yes. South was my father's potatoes, west of that was Ralph and Clarence's potatoes. That's right. Not many farmers had their own graders at that time. In other sections of the country, they did, but not on Long Island. There were different grading stations around, operated by different companies. It was the I. M. Young Company that was in Cutchogue. So you went there. In those days, you would start grading about the first of August—right out of the field—then load up and take them to the grader. During the winter, you would take them out of storage when you thought the price was right.

"At times, they would have a certain crop of green stuff. That was brussels sprouts or cauliflower. In those years, there was a cauliflower auction in Riverhead and Southold. At the Southold auction, there were great lines of trucks; farmer after farmer lined up there. There was two lines; one would come down from Youngs Avenue in the north, and another would be lined up along the Middle Road. They'd go in in two lines, and the auctioneer would sell on this side, then he'd sell the other side, see?

"There were buyers in there. Lots of them came from New Jersey, south Jersey. And they supplied different city stores. And of course the buyers had certain favorite farmers that they bought from, because they felt they got what they wanted from them, you know. If the farmer was enterprising enough, you'd have a load at the Southold auction and then go into Riverhead. They used to load freight trains with cauliflower, forty, fifty cars, because Long Island cauliflower was sold all the way up the Mississippi River.

"It just kind of gradually slowed down here, until there was no cauliflower. Dave Steele would send his truck to the cauliflower auction. But then all the other sections of the country got onto raising cauliflower, and other areas took over the market. So pretty soon, there were too few people for the auction in Riverhead and it closed up.

"But at that time, they also raised cabbage seed, so sometimes a field would be designated for cabbage seed instead of for potatoes. Some farmers even raised strawberries. There was an auction for strawberries within my lifetime. And that was wholesale, of course, by the truck load or pickup load. Whatever a farmer had. Another crop was brussels sprouts. When I got out of the army, Ralph was growing brussels sprouts, and we'd pack them, his wife would pack them, and the next day I would take his pickup and go down to the auction with his brussels sprouts.

"But any ground which they call potato ground was all in farming. At that time, many of the fields were cut up quite a bit because there was what you call light spots, gravelly spots—you know, places without irrigation—and they couldn't plant there. So that would cut up the fields to a great extent."

Ralph Tuthill moved into the house John and Jeanne live in today when he got married in 1918. John's grandfather George moved into a house on the Main Road, and as a young boy John remembers his grandfather walking back up Elijah's Lane from the Main Road to do farmwork.

"He worked for Ralph and he worked for my father quite a bit. He'd walk on over here and hoe or cut corn, such things as that. And even if there wasn't anything to do, he'd walk up and visit, or go on over to his brother's place, Herbert S. Tuthill. Herbert Smith Tuthill. The old old-folks way of referring to him was Hubbert. I remember him very well coming up here. This Herbert chewed tobacco, and they would sit there beside the old well, and this Herbert S. would lay his quids on the windowsill. And George Bryden would come along when they was dried out and he'd smoke them."

Every winter in his early years as a farmer, John Tuthill watched other farmers go out of business. There was always a farm auction to go to, where someone was selling off his equipment. "A man had his money in his farm. He didn't have anything else. If he lost it, he lost what money he put into the farm. So he hung on to it, come good times or bad. He stuck it out. The money was in the farm. There used to be quite a number of farm auctions, two or three, maybe five one winter. Some years were worse than others.

"It's economics, but it's also who has he got to take over, you know. If the boy doesn't want to take over, he can get out. At the auction, everything goes. In my own family, there were the sons of George Bryden Tuthill. There were six children. My father was the oldest, and he got a farm of his own. The next one was Frank, and he went to school, and he got a job in New York City. The next was Clarence, and he got into a partnership with Ralph. And they farmed extensively on the old home farm. They became quite big farmers.

"And when they couldn't make a go of it, they split. And there were some harsh words there. The next brother was Raymond, and he got off the farm. He got into the service, World War One, and after that, he worked here and there and he became a cashier at the bank in Cutchogue. So he was out of farming. And the next after Raymond was Ralph, and he farmed after he split up with Clarence, and then I bought his farm. The fifth was Jay, and he hated farming. He said, 'I'm not going to spend my life going up one row and down another.' So he headed for the city. He wanted to go to Detroit to work in the fledgling automobile industry, but Frank got him a job in New York City. He became a salesman for trade magazines. There wasn't land enough here to keep the boys home, so they got off and left.

"And in my generation, there was me farming, and Hallock had his farm, but he gave it up. And Quint went to Hartford to work. Now there's Dave Steele farming here. I think about it sometimes, that I'm the last one of the Tuthills farming. I do think about that once in a while. But time goes on. That's the way it is."

The next morning, David checked the pump on the north side of the Middle Road, directly north of the Kurkoski farm, which was sending water to a field on the south side, through underground pipes. He was in the pickup when the sky went black and it began to rain hard, rainwater washing over dry fields. But it was not enough that the pumps could be turned off.

"We're going to be digging up our early varieties here soon," he said. "I'm just waiting to hear from Walt at the grader when they want to get started, that's all. They get orders and we'll start digging."

He was eager to get going. But once he was through with potatoes, there would be no cauliflower to go on to. "This is the first time in twenty-two years I haven't planted any. Used to be good money in the fall, just when you needed it."

In the early evening, the western sky was a soft pink, the air clear and less humid. The air smelled richly of brown soil. Low clouds hung over the woods on the west side of the Baptist church.

The next morning, McBride's barn was filled with black men filling ten-pound bags and loading them onto a truck. As the grading operation was under way, Frank was digging on high, sloped ground south of the dump. He had already filled the big green GMC truck several times with small potatoes when he stopped to catch a breeze.

"We've got a lot of ground to work," he said. I asked about prices, and he said, "They're okay right now, but tomorrow, who knows? But we gotta dig, and that's all there is to it."

After a few minutes, he pushed forward again, the digger skimming the earth. Weeds, rocks, and potatoes spilled up the rackety conveyor.

*The Steele family: Sherry, David, and their children, David, Kristin, and Kyle.*

# TWENTY-TWO

# Steele, Digging, and the Grader

THERE HAD BEEN a birthday party in late July for Kyle Steele, David's son, and John and Jeanne were there. When the workday was over, everyone went to David's mother's house in Mattituck for cake and ice cream. To keep the candles lit until Kyle was ready, John bent over the table and wrapped his arms around the cake.

"There aren't a lot of people around anymore like John Tuthill," David once told me.

In his quiet way, John had the characteristics of an older generation of New England men.

This was also true for John Wickham, as well as the other farmers whose roots went back to the boat that came from Connecticut and discharged its passengers onto the sandy beach just seven miles from where John Tuthill now lives.

These North Fork farms had survived for more than three hundred years because there was always someone in a family who kept the farm going. In the Tuthill family, there had been generations when there were many who farmed; at other times, just one or two. Now there is John.

Speaking about the death of his young son, John told me he could not guess what kind of future Edward might have had, or whether he would have been interested in farming. "I can't say, honestly," he said. "But I think it's likely he would have left the area to seek other opportunities. There's just no way to know. I suppose I am the last to do this. The Oregon Road Tuthills, they kind of petered out over the years. And the other Tuthills who were farming in years past in Cutchogue, they left it, too."

Hallock does not believe his son would have wanted to farm. William Ernest Tuthill was contemplating a career in marine law at the time of his death in a shipboard accident.

"Bill, as it turned out, loved the sea, and I don't think he would have been interested in the farming life," Hallock told me. "I think it really does end with my brother John and I."

When Parker Wickham died on the road east of the farmhouse, John Wickham could run the farm, and his brother Henry promised to do it if something ever happened to John. It went on with them, and it goes on today with Tom and Jonathan.

Bill Wickham wanted to be a lawyer, like his grandfather. He and his daughter Gail, who is also an attorney, share an office in Mattituck. Because of his son's death, the male line ends with Bill.

Ziggy Kurkoski has no children.

This summer, David Steele kept Tuthill land and Kurkoski land in production. And he hoped for decent potato prices, so he could pay bills and have money for the winter.

Even as McBride was eagerly digging his early varieties, David was holding back a bit. He had six acres of early potatoes, but unloading them right now did not seem prudent. Last year, the summer of 1993, he had started digging on August 8, on land south of John Tuthill's house, the land that this summer was in hay. He did not see the point of starting right now, for he knew that volume and tonnage a bit later in the season would be better for him in the long run.

Toward the middle of the summer, I stopped by the grader and found Carl Beamon's crew was back in camp. A few days earlier, McBride's grading crew had arrived from North Carolina and taken over the bagging of his early potatoes. Back at the grader at the railroad tracks, in the still of the summer, Carl's crew waited for potatoes to be brought in. Soon Walt Zilnicki would hit the start button on the machinery and six months of work would begin.

Inside the camp building, the air was stifling. Carl, who did most of the cooking on an old stove, was sitting in a chair, shirtless, his face and chest covered with sweat. His right hand was curled up, his fingers wrapped in a tight knot, the arm limp.

*Looking north and east over the cab of David Steele's fertilizer truck. "Once the old guys die off, what happens to this farmland?" David Steele said.*

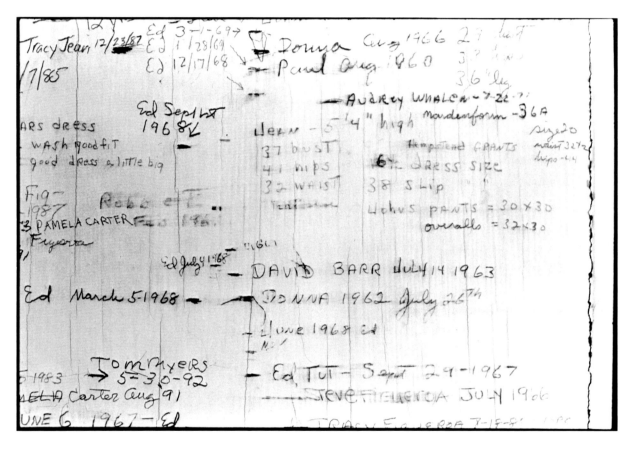

*The doorjamb in Jeanne and John Tuthill's kitchen, where she recorded family data such as dress sizes and the heights of their son, Edward. Marks for Edward's height crawl up the wall: from "Ed Tut—Sept. 29, 1967," through to September 1968, followed by, in Jeanne's handwriting, 12/17/68, 1/28/69, and 3/1/69. Edward, the couple's only child, died in 1973.*

*On the right, Richie McBride, Frank McBride's son, to the left is Richie's brother-in-law, Charlie Tyler.*

*Richie's son, Frank, riding in the pickup along Oregon Road near the family farm.*

*Mist over the land.*

*Chris Sidor drives the tractor on his family's farm.*

*Keep up: the Sidors planting cabbage.*

*Ziggy Kurkoski's land, where David Steele raised potatoes.*

*Eddie Clark cutting potato seed in Bill Wickham's barn.*

*A cold, wet spring: Eddie Clark riding on the potato planter.*

*Eddie Clark kicking out the last potato seeds.*

*Aerial view of a section of the North Fork, plowed land running nearly to the high bluffs overlooking Long Island Sound.*

*Marty Sidor walking an irrigation sprinkler system across a section of field.*

*The harvest: Chris Sidor.*

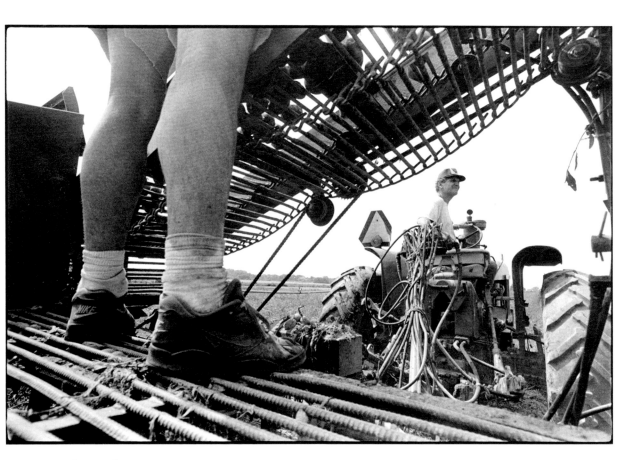

*Marty Sidor on the tractor.*

*Stuffed to the rafters: David Steele storing potatoes in Bill Wickham's barn.*

*Martin Sidor, Sr., in the family's potato grader.*

*Chris Sidor helping to load bags of potatoes onto a truck.*

*Filled to overflowing: David Steele drives his potatoes to the Cutchogue grader.*

*More and more houses: aerial view of a section of the North Fork.*

*Workers on the Sidor farm on the last day of the potato harvest.*

*David Valle and Angel Lopez, two of David Steele's workers, coming back from food shopping.*

*A farm worker who was struck by a car in Jamesport. He was treated by a local doctor and released.*

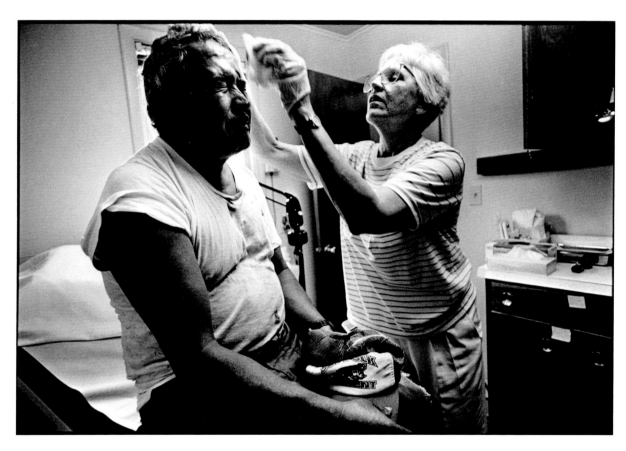

*Priscilla Steele treats Tony Almodoval, one of her son's farm workers.*

*Shrinking farmland.*

*Walt Zilnicki, a genius at repairing old equipment, in the Cutchogue potato grader. "We're the last of the Mohicans," he says of the few remaining potato growers on the North Fork. "Man, sometimes I just can't believe how much has changed out here."*

*Inside the Cutchogue farm camp, Carl Beamon on the right.*

*Bagging potatoes inside the Cutchogue grader.*

*A cold morning: one of the workers at the Cutchogue grader as potatoes pass up a conveyor.*

*At work in the grader.*

*Frank Bryant, born in Alabama and one of the workers at the Cutchogue grader, takes a break from loading potato bags.*

*Aerial view of the North Fork, looking north toward Long Island Sound.*

Carl had once owned his own trucking business and hauled produce, but had lost it all. Most days when the grader was down, he jumped in his heap and drove to Riverhead to spend a few hours losing money at the government-run OTB office. The same government that harassed the farmers also ran a betting parlor.

He limply waved at me with his left hand, too hot to get up. "Hey, how you doin?" he asked. Another shirtless man was sitting at a picnic bench in the kitchen, his head dangling from his shoulders as if the neck bone had come unhinged. In a back room, a group of men were listlessly watching *Star Trek* reruns on a black-and-white television with bad reception. The one white man in the group was curled up on a mattress that might have spent the last few years in someone's backyard. He was breathing hard, his toothless mouth agape, noisily sucking in air and pushing it out through his nose. The summer air was dead and the room reeked of sweat and burned food.

Inside the big grader, Walt was cleaning up, getting ready for operations to begin. Everything looked different from last winter when I had watched the crew grading in the cold morning air. Walt had cleaned out the junk in an effort to reclaim the inside. "I've got maybe a week or less to get ready," he said. "Pretty soon, the trucks will be lined up."

Walt has family in the potato business in Riverhead, and I asked him about the drought. He said, "The drought's been good to us. Drought is always good for us. Prices are up from last year— right now, ten dollars a hundredweight. Last year, it was seven-fifty, eight bucks. North Carolina is in. Delaware is in. They're way down in terms of quantity. They can't water like we can. Maine'll start up in September, and that'll dump a huge amount on the market. That could hurt us.

"And Canada. Shit! That's a whole other story. Their potatoes is subsidized. They don't care about prices. They can go on the market at nine bucks. Prices don't mean a thing to them because they're getting paid by the government. On the other hand, we're just a few left, and a drop in the price can kill us off. My argument is Long Island produce ought to have a premium on it. Our stuff is good, but we get killed by some other part of the country where it's not so good."

He mentioned Carl's crew working for McBride for a few days and said it hadn't worked out. "Carl's been doing this a good long time. He thinks everyone works for him."

His eyes flashed when he showed me the repaired weighing equipment. "I want this to stay working this year. I'm gonna have a real discussion with them guys about this stuff. Stuff's real old. We gotta fix everything and keep fixin it."

At the Horton barn later in the morning, Eddie and the two Puerto Ricans, Angel and David, unloaded straw from the Tuthill truck into the barn. They were stacking bales floor to ceiling, back to front. This was the straw Eddie had cut earlier across the road on the Baxter property. They cut the straw on the Wickham farm, which John stacked in his barn and, needing extra room, in Hallock's barn on Alvah's Lane.

I told Eddie I had been to the camp by the tracks, and he scoffed. Eddie did not like the camp;

he believed it was a hole for black men to fall into and never come out. You went to a labor camp when you wanted to give up and be run around by a crew boss.

"What's Carl got in there now? A bunch of nothing! He cooks for them, cleans up after them. When he needs somebody, what's he do? He goes to Riverhead and picks someone off the street. Go to the Bowery in New York City's what they used to do. Carl's sixty now if he's a day. I know him way back when he used to have his own trucks. That's all crap in there."

David drove up in the white pickup, his face red as a beet, his shirt on the front seat. There were more bales to load, and he wanted to get going. In one part of the Horton barn, he stored his hay; in the other, his chemicals for killing potato bugs. He sprayed up to eight times a season, and it was costly. The more he sprayed, the less profit at the end. Considering all his potato acreage and the high cost of spraying, it was no wonder Frank McBride began digging in July.

"The bugs are a constant problem," David said. "We've tried burning them up, even vacuuming them up. That got popular a few years back. Everyone went out and bought expensive equipment."

To the north, John Tuthill was riding a tractor and pulling the hay cutter. We could hear the throaty roar of the engine in the distance. After cutting on the Wickham farm, David would plant a cover crop for the winter; next spring, this land would be in potatoes.

We left and a few minutes later pulled up by Ziggy's pond. "I came down here the other day and saw a turtle the size of a fifty-five-gallon drum," David said. "It had a head like a damn football."

We followed the dirt road that snaked through to the Tuthill farm and found John was back. He was hot and burned. "Do you want me to go back to Wickham's after lunch?" he asked.

David said, "I gotta jump Horton's first." He had to move pipe on the Horton farm; another long section had to be watered. There was more hay to be cut on Wickham land, but the baler was jammed up. John tipped his cap as he headed out of the barn.

At night, black clouds passed overhead and lightning danced across the sky, but only a few drops fell to earth.

In the morning, the sky was still overcast, but a morning breeze was sweeping the clouds out over Long Island Sound. Always the clouds left the dance before the music started. At first light, David, Eddie, Angel, and David were loading bales on the Wickham farm, just north of the Main Road. From a distance they looked like tiny soldiers on a scorched battlefield. Far to the north, I could see the figure of Bill Wickham walking his dog along the tree line.

David slowed up when the thirty-year-old International began having engine problems. He did not need this. One of his trucks recently had the driver's side door ripped off, and driving it around the farms was a challenge. It would be a few weeks before he got that repaired. He popped the hood on the International and pulled off the air filter to look into the carburetor.

*Jimmy Wilson, born in Georgia and a longtime worker at the Cutchogue potato grader, with his son, Jason.*

"It's wet," he said. "Leaking." He started up the engine and gas squished out from under a gasket.

"Maybe I'll give Eddie a fire extinguisher and tell 'em to keep loading," he said. "If it burns up, the fire department will have to deal with it. I ever tell you about this truck? It was sitting outside a house with a FOR SALE sign on it—fifteen hundred bucks. I'd seen it; it looked all right. I stopped to look and heard a woman saying, 'I want that truck off my yard.' So her husband come out and I said, 'I'll give you two fifty for it.' He looked at me and said, 'Sold.'"

In the early evening, it grew cool and a southwest breeze brought in smells from the bay. I drove to the little bungalow Jimmy Wilson lived in on the Middle Road, west of the grader. A small, compact man with a gentle face, Wilson always went about his work at the grader with a minimum of conversation. He had run the grader for years, but now he was only helping out with the bagging operation. He has an air of self-confidence, unlike many of the other men who worked at the grader.

When I arrived, he was sitting outside under the protective boughs of a huge maple tree with a boy. "This is my son Jason," he said, and the boy jumped up to say hello. Jason said he was fifteen and went to private school in New Jersey. When I looked surprised, Wilson said, "Sure that's my son! My gosh. That sure is my son. The baby in my family."

A red pickup pulled up, and Wilson walked over to talk to Leslie Bates, who lived next door. "We'll be gradin any day now," Wilson told him, and when he came back he said the man was his oldest friend in Cutchogue. "I don't have no better friend. He has been a member of our little church up by the dump for fifty years. And you can take that to the bank."

The digging for David Steele began early on the morning of August 2. This was six days ahead of when he began to dig in the summer of 1993. Then, he began south of the Tuthill house; on this day, he started just north of Ziggy's big barn. When they moved onto this farm, the Kurkoskis found initials carved in the beams of the barn, left by a previous owner. What separated the Tuthill ground from the Kurkoski ground was a thick section of trees. Standing near Ziggy's barns, looking west, you could not see the Tuthill house this morning, just the green of the woods.

The sky was overcast. It felt like rain. David had been up since 5:15. He knew what he always knew: His future was in the ground he was about to dig up. Prices remained good, at around ten dollars a hundredweight. But that was now. Tomorrow, next month, later in the fall—who knew what to expect? Suddenly, a huge amount of potatoes could come on the market from somewhere and the price could plummet, and then David would have barns groaning with stored potatoes that would not bring him a profit.

While there were still faint stars flickering in the sky, he met Eddie, Angel, and David. Soon, young David Steele would come out of the house, too. The equipment—the tractor, the digger, the potato truck—would be driven to Ziggy's over the connecting dirt roads. They would line up by Ziggy's barn, facing north, all the way north—over the railroad tracks, the Middle Road, over more potato ground, all the way to Oregon Road and the wooded bluffs overlooking Long Island Sound. This expanse was Cutchogue, the vast middle breadbasket of the North Fork. This was the region with the most fertile and productive farms in the state of New York. This was Corchaug, the land William Wells coveted in the 1660s, and today another farmer, after so many generations of farmers, was here to extract his crops.

When everything was lined up, John Tuthill arrived in his little pickup. This had been his task for so long, and he did not want to miss the first pass of the digger across this brown soil. Today, seven decades after he had first walked behind his father, Ernest Tuthill, digging up potatoes, he came as a spectator. All wrapped up in this man on this morning was the legacy of his family—his father, his grandfather, and his great-grandfather, Elijah Tuthill, all the way back to Jesse, the first Tuthill in Cutchogue, and John, the first Tuthill on the North Fork. He was their history, all of it, and today he stood by himself and smiled and said nothing as the men got ready to dig. Today, David Steele, half John's age, was his legs and his future. David was a Tuthill today.

"Okay," David said. "We're about to begin." The sun was low, beneath the eastern tree line, the sky above it pale yellow. Far to the west, the sky jealously held on to the darkness.

John Tuthill walked behind the digger, leaning against it, smiling. Young David Steele climbed onto the digger to help separate rocks and weeds before they were heaved up into the truck. David took his seat on the tractor; to his right, there was a rack of levers used to control the hydraulic lines that operated the digger.

The engine kicked on, Eddie climbed into the potato truck, and Angel and David mounted a platform at one side of the digger, where their job would be to pull out dirt clods. Suddenly, the digger lurched forward, and John Tuthill, his legs a bit wobbly, held on until the last moment and then pulled his arms up and let it go.

They went up, turned around at the railroad tracks, and came back down again. By the third pass, the potato truck was filled with potatoes, heaving from side to side as Eddie guided it through the field. As they worked, Angel and David pulled out the big potatoes and tossed them into a bucket perched next to them. David Steele wanted to save them for his mother and friends. They were bigger than softballs. Looking at the potato truck, a pyramid of spuds reaching out of it, David knew he could not make another pass—it was filled enough. He jumped in the truck and drove it the half mile east to the grader, then parked it behind another truck waiting to be unloaded.

We went inside, and I heard Carl yelling at someone. "You gotta get off your ass, man! You gotta pick that up and take it over there!"

It was 8:30 in the morning and the conveyors were not up and running. Walt ran around with a wrench and a screwdriver, doing his best to ignore the workers.

Tempers were high, and several men seemed more than a little hungover. "It's day one and some of these guys are still in the bag," someone muttered.

David left the truck and we drove back to Ziggy's in his pickup. We were standing by the tractor when David spotted Ziggy's car coming down the lane toward the house, a cloud of dust following it.

"Here comes the king of Poland," David said.

Ziggy pulled himself out of the car to watch the proceedings, and I said, "So you're the king of Poland?"

He laughed. "My parents named me after a king—Sigmund."

Beaming, David held up the bucket with the big potatoes. "That's Ziggy's good ground."

"They look like pumpkins," Ziggy said. "You're satisfied with the crop, that's all that counts."

"I'm more than satisfied with the crop," David said, getting ready for another pass down the field. "It's prices a month or two from now that I'm worried about. You know about that kind of worry, don't you, Ziggy?"

"Oh," he said, smiling at his neighbor, "I know about that." He turned back toward his house. "If you need some help, give a shout."

*Chris Sidor, months after the accident that nearly killed him, with his sister, Maureen, on their Mattituck farm. "That boy is special," one farmer said. "I hope God always shines on him."*

TWENTY-THREE

# Fall and
# Chris Sidor

IN EARLY AUGUST, it began to rain hard. The hardest rain in months started late one afternoon

and continued into the evening. The ground sponged it up, pulling the water down. It rained hard

again toward the middle of the month. Potato digging stopped; the ground was too wet.

By the third week of the month, the ground was dry again and the pumps began to hum nearly

around the clock on the Wickham farm. I stopped by the farm stand on a hot afternoon and found

Jonathan and Stephen dumping buckets of water over their heads.

"We're irrigating everywhere we can," Stephen said. "This is all we're doing. The irony with the lack of rain is the cherries and peaches have never been better."

Jonathan suggested Stephen take a crew to a field the family called Freddy's South, where the peach trees were dry. Peaches need a lot of water, and Jonathan suggested they keep the pump going for the next six hours.

In the course of the summer, I had asked Jonathan to make a map of the farm for me. I knew from his grandfather that there were places on the farm that had long-standing family designations, like Freddy's North, Freddy's South (both named after Fred Tuthill), Shell Bank, Dam Meadow. His map showed that a knob of land on the eastern edge of the farm, near where Parker Wickham had built his house in the late 1920s soon after his marriage, was "the place where the dead horses were buried."

South of it on the map was a place along the west side of Wickham Creek called "the screwed-up orchard." I asked about that location, and Jonathan laughed. "That's down by Shell Bank. We put in the trees and they didn't line up very well. It's always been called the screwed-up orchard."

This was the first summer without John. His absence left a void in the landscape, an emptiness. It felt as if he should be there—at the stand, by the barns, inside at the kitchen table.

"One thing about my grandfather," he said, "was that he was very self-confident and didn't get worn down worrying about problems. It's very interesting how people in families can be so different. There's the engineer side, the side that wants everything to work out and fit together; and there's the artsy, musical side. The Wickham side is mechanical; the Lupton side is more musical. I think my grandfather learned over the years that farming was not something you can do to perfection. You can't be a perfectionist and be a farmer, because you'll drive yourself crazy. You have to roll with the problems."

By the third week of September, the potato harvest still under way, a friend phoned me and said Chris Sidor, Marty and Carol's son, had been in a horrible car wreck near their home.

"He's close to death; only a miracle will save him," my friend said.

I called Marty Sidor, Sr.'s house, and he sounded too upset to talk. "Chris and a friend had been at the grader and they were taking a truck back up to the farm. The car slipped forward or something, through a stop sign, and they broadsided another car. The woman driver of the car they hit was killed, and her baby was very badly injured. Oh my God. Oh dear God. My God, I can't accept it. It's killing me. You know, Marty took over for me. Chris was supposed to take over for Marty. That's how we all saw it. That was the way our land would stay in farming."

It seemed too incredible, too horrible an event to accept. I had seen Chris a few days before up on Oregon Road, and he seemed very much in control of the day-to-day operations. Marty seemed so proud of him, like his long wait for Chris to make up his mind about his future had suddenly ended. And it ended with Chris wanting to farm, to keep it going.

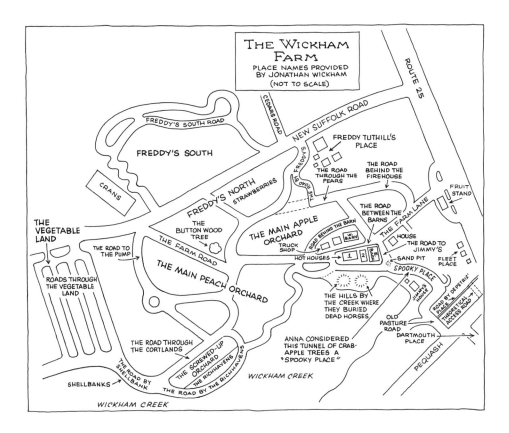

THE WICKHAM FARM
PLACE NAMES PROVIDED
BY JONATHAN WICKHAM
(NOT TO SCALE)

ROUTE 25

FREDDY'S SOUTH ROAD

FREDDY'S SOUTH

CEDARS ROAD

NEW SUFFOLK ROAD

FREDDY TUTHILL'S PLACE

THE ROAD THROUGH THE PEARS

THE ROAD BEHIND THE FIREHOUSE

CRANS

FREDDY'S NORTH

STRAWBERRIES

FRUIT STAND

THE VEGETABLE LAND

THE BUTTON WOOD TREE

THE MAIN APPLE ORCHARD

ROAD BEHIND THE BARN

THE ROAD BETWEEN THE BARNS

THE FARM LANE

HOUSE

THE ROAD TO THE PUMP

THE FARM ROAD

TRUCK SHOP

W. BARN

THE ROAD TO JIMMY'S

THE MAIN PEACH ORCHARD

HOT HOUSES

1  2

E BARN

SAND PIT

FLEET PLACE

ROADS THROUGH THE VEGETABLE LAND

SPOOKY PLACE

THE HILLS BY THE CREEK WHERE THEY BURIED DEAD HORSES

JIMMY'S HOUSE

ROAD BY DE PETRIS' PLACE

THEORETICAL ACCESS ROAD

OLD PASTURE ROAD

DARTMOUTH PLACE

THE ROAD THROUGH THE CORTLANDS

ANNA CONSIDERED THIS TUNNEL OF CRAB-APPLE TREES A "SPOOKY PLACE"

THE SCREWED-UP ORCHARD

THE RICHHAVENS

PEQUASH

THE ROAD BY SHELLBANK

SHELLBANKS

THE ROAD BY THE RICHHAVENS

WICKHAM CREEK

WICKHAM CREEK

"Chris, he was so handy on the farm," his grandfather said. "He could fix anything. He had his future now. We were going to pick up another truck. I was behind him. It's so terrible; it's just so awful terrible. We sat with Marty and Caroline this morning at the house and we all just cried and cried. Only a big miracle can save him—that's what the doctor said. Only the biggest miracle. Marty said this morning when we were crying, 'Life'll never be the same again. Life in our family will never be the same.'"

A few days later, I stopped by the farmhouse. Marty and Carol were in the kitchen. They had been at the hospital all day, sitting with their son, looking at him, praying to God that he would wake up and get better and come home.

"He's hard to recognize," Marty said. He looked exhausted, as if his life had drained out of his body. "His face has been destroyed."

"If he recovers, they'll need photographs to rebuild his face," Carol said.

"You know, I really feel Chris and I were connecting these last few months," Marty said. "He was enjoying the work. Farmers were coming around to talk to him. We've been to the hospital every day. We've just about stopped working. Our potatoes are still in the ground. I don't know what we're going to do."

As the weather turned cooler, David Steele, as busy as he was, let it be known to Marty that he could harvest his potatoes if he needed the help. Marty, desperate not to lose his crop, stayed home in the mornings and he and his father worked as much as they could, moving from field to field, running the grader the family kept by the A&P in Mattituck. I saw them there on several mornings, and Marty looked wasted. He was working, but he wasn't seeing what he was doing. He talked about getting done and getting to the hospital.

"We've got several weeks more to dig," he said. "I'd like to get everything in and stored and get it behind me. There's too much else on my mind."

By the middle of October, a month after the accident, the Sidors were feverishly trying to get all their potatoes dug up and stored. I saw Marty on several occasions, and he seemed too distracted to stop and talk. Early on the morning of the fourteenth, I saw a tractor working in a field west of Stan and Les Tuthill's farmhouse on the Middle Road. The air was cool, the warm sun burning off the moisture in the air.

I stopped and could see that Martin Sidor, Sr., was digging, an overflowing potato truck heaving back and forth alongside him as they moved east to west along a sloping field. Straight north of this field is the Sidor home farm; this land was the tract Martin's Polish father bought from Buster Tuthill. It is a rolling piece of land, although I never knew that until I stood in the middle of it and could not see fifty yards to the east. The land on the east side rises and then drops sharply into a shallow ravine left by a meltwater stream. I watched the tractor go up and over the hill and disappear from sight. A few minutes later, I saw the exhaust fuming up and then the tractor came back in sight.

When he saw me, Martin senior stopped at the end of the row, waiting until the potato truck turned around to go back the other way.

"I saw him, you know," he said. "I was behind him, a few minutes after the accident. I will never forget it. I will never forget that. I didn't even recognize my own grandson. I can't believe it anymore. You know Marty's got a lot of off-farm interests that keep him busy, too. Chris was helping him so much. What can we do but pray, pray, pray? Everybody's praying for us; we know that."

As we spoke, Marty drove up in the pickup. He was here to drive the loaded potato truck back to the grader. Over the past few weeks, I had come to admire Marty and Carol for their strength, but today Marty looked ready to break down.

"The doctor says Chris is in a vegetative state. I hear that and I think, Oh my God. They tell me it's a state above a coma. It's horrible, but it could be worse. He's not moving his left side. So they say—and I can believe this—maybe he had a stroke. His right hand twitches. We don't know anything at all. The parameters that were in effect from day one are still in effect—nothing's changed."

He wanted to get all the digging out of the way, to clear his mind so that he would have nothing but his son to think about. These were the last few acres in their last field. He jumped in the truck, overflowing with potatoes, and drove back to the grader.

When his son was gone, Martin senior whipped the tractor around and began moving toward the east. In three more passes, the truck was groaning with potatoes. It amazed me how much food these fields could produce, and how many potatoes were left in the field when the digger had passed. It seemed on this morning that Marty, David Steele, the McBrides, and the others could feed 100,000 people out of their fields. The bounty seemed unlimited. While I waited for the tractor, I walked north, toward Oregon Road. The land gradually slopes up, then levels off. From the plateau, I could see the tree line on Oregon Road and the roofs of the barns.

When the tractor came back again, Martin senior stopped and said, "After my father bought this tract, we had to clear it. We cut the trees down, cut up all the wood. We'd dig a hole under the stump and stick two sticks of dynamite down there, then run like hell."

As we spoke, his wife drove up with coffee and boxed doughnuts and everyone jumped down for a break. "We're all really pushing ourselves," she said. "Marty just wants to get it done before the frost does any damage. Frost can hurt potatoes. We had one the other morning."

The potatoes from this field were being stored at the grader near the A&P; potatoes from their other fields were at the home farm and next to David Steele's potatoes in the Horton barns.

"It's been cooler, but that's okay for potatoes. You need cooler ground to cool the potatoes so when you store them they don't give off heat. They can break down. But if you wait until the heavy frost, the potatoes can turn black. When we got Indian summers, those years, we could go into November. Now we like to finish in October."

She looked across the field and softly said, "This year, it's the fourteenth. All we're doing is praying for Chris. We'll take him any way we can get him. As I was driving up here, I was thinking about him and the family. I remembered that Marty grew up in a house just to the west of here. My husband's brother, Frank, used to live near here, too. Frank and Stella Sidor. Frank died when he was twenty-eight. We bought our house from Annie Tuthill, Nat Tuthill's widow. They had a crippled son.

"We got married in November. You waited in those years until the farmwork was done. That was forty-five years ago this year. Marty was the firstborn. He liked to sleep. Isn't it funny that I still remember that? During the cold season, he'd skate at Wolf Pit Pond, across from our house. Three of my kids went to Sacred Heart. Monsignor Brennan used to say, 'I need the Polish children and the Irish children to keep the school going.'"

She stopped for a moment and looked down the long row of freshly turned ground. The tractor disappeared over the little ridge.

"I don't blame anybody. We're just all praying for Chris, that's all. It's just so changed our lives. This has brought us together as a family." She paused and looked at me. "Chris is not the only child something awful happened to; he won't be the last."

Martin senior came back to the west again and turned around in a cloud of dust. The potato truck, half-filled, jockeyed for position. He pressed forward again, and one more back-and-forth and the truck was brimming with potatoes. Another empty truck was brought up, and by midafternoon, Martin had only four rows to go and the season would be over.

As if he knew how close his father was to finishing the field, Marty drove up. It was four in the afternoon, and the light was soft, beginning to fade. He watched as his father made his last run and stopped the tractor. Another year had ended, another harvest completed.

"I gotta hurry up," Martin senior said. "I want to wash up and go see Chris."

"Ordinarily," Marty said, "you'd see me skipping along like a twenty-year-old. It's mellow today; it's just very mellow."

*Leslie Tuthill on his farm in Tuthill Town. Leslie and his brother, Stanley, both bachelors, are cousins of John Tuthill. A friend who saw Les in the fall of '94 said he was uncharacteristically bitter. "Why did everything have to change so much?" he told the friend.*

TWENTY-FOUR

# Upon This Rock

In early November, the skies were clear, the nights cool and dry. The summer drought was

forgotten. Potatoes were in storage everywhere, and on the Wickham farm the heavy fall apple-

picking season had stripped every tree of its fruit. On weekends, the stand was quiet.

On a cool afternoon, I went by the grader and found Carl in the back, by the camp. The Bap-

tist church by the town landfill was soon to celebrate its seventieth anniversary, and I asked Carl if

he knew any of the older members.

"All I know is it was started by people comin up from the South, that's all I know'd," he said. I asked if he went there, or if any of the other residents of the camp did, and he said, "I can speak for myself, and the answer is no."

The smell of beans wafted out the door of the camp building, and soon a man floated out with it, his face covered with some sort of red sauce. He sat on a cinder-block wall.

"Place better be clean. Yes sir, it better be clean!" Carl yelled at the man.

I asked Carl again about the church, and he said, "I know'd people who went there. It was a goin place when I come up here from North Carolina. But I never heard of anyone at the old labor camp behind the dump goin there. Folks went there worked in the fields all right, but they was different. Not your everyday Joe livin at the camp went there."

A half century ago, the southerners who bagged potatoes in Cutchogue walked to this church, or borrowed farm trucks. They wore their best Sunday clothes and stayed after services for a midday meal, then prayer services. Their preachers were southern men, too. Some had worked in fields; others had left the fields and sought out better lives and taken to the pulpits of small country churches. Inside this tiny white church surrounded by potato ground, the worshipers were together, and it felt good to be together, and for a long morning and afternoon they were a people with the same goals, the same lives, the same concerns, worshiping a Savior who spoke to their hearts.

Carl arrived on Long Island in the summer of 1950 to dig potatoes. His father worked in Norfolk, his mother in a tobacco factory. ("My mother workin in a 'bacca factory is what put food on our plates," he told me.) His life was a model of the migrant farmworker's existence—from North Carolina to Virginia to dig potatoes, then north to Long Island to finish out the season.

"My sister know'd this man who had people workin for him. His name was Zite. My sister asked me to sit with him in his truck and talk. He asked me what I'm doin. He says he come up the road in June—Virginia first, then round July Fourth to Long Island. He says, 'You interested?' And I says yes. We come up in the back of a truck, probably thirty of us.

"That first year we came, we went to the Cutchogue labor camp up on Cox, behind the dump a ways. There was Porto Reecans there, and black people. Wasn't no Mes'cans. Zite's wife was the cook. She make collard greens, taters every meal. Hamburger. Pig ears. Hog feet. Oh, they was good. We stayed till November, then went back to Norfolk. We was always back here by July Fourth. After a while, I had a camp in Riv'head. I was the crew boss. I had sixty people at one time. You could have that many then. Now you can't have no more than twenty in one place.

"At Cutchogue, there be three, four hundred in one place. There'd be fights, stuff like that. I don't know them bad peoples. I been round drunks all my life, but I don't drink. My brother drink. My daddy, he drink. I was shinin shoes once in a place and a drunk, he gave me a five-dollar bill instead of a dollar. I put it right into my pocket. I thought, Hell, that's what you get when youse drinkin. You don't know the dif'rence between a five-dollar bill and a one-dollar bill."

The one white man in the camp came out the door and slammed it behind him. "You know where I found him? I was drivin along with my friend Willie. Willie was from the same place in North Carolina. Willie know'd him. He say, 'Hey, there's Fuzzie.' I stopped and asked him if he wanted work. He been here ever since."

A few days later, I stopped by the Baptist church to see Pastor Cornelius Fulford. He had erected a sign out front proclaiming that funds were being raised to buy land and build a new church. On the sign was a quote from Luke, chapter ten, verse two:

> Therefore said he unto them,
> "The harvest truly is great,
> but the laborers are few; pray ye
> therefore the Lord of the harvest,
> that he would send forth laborers
> into his harvest."

Seventy years had passed since the church was built. Frank McBride, Sr., had sold them the land they built on; this summer, the senior McBride's son harvested his early potatoes on some high ground across the street from the church.

The church founders' names were known to just a few people; they were not recorded in any history books, yet their contribution to Cutchogue was as great as that of anyone. They were Christian people far from home, and they found new homes here while bagging potatoes by hand.

After a succession of pastors, Fulford, who was born in the South and came north as a singer, took over the church leadership in 1989. He has seen the church membership grow dramatically, and to celebrate the seventieth anniversary he had planned a party for a Sunday morning later in the month. He thought it was no small miracle that the church had already been able to buy a tract of land nearby and was now raising building funds.

In speaking with Fulford, I had learned that many of the oldest members of the church, who were there when it was first started, were dead or had moved away. Sister Hubbard, a woman in her nineties and a founding member, was in a senior citizens' home in nearby Greenport, but her memory was a problem. One older couple had moved back to Virginia. I had mentioned to Fulford that I was talking to the farmworkers, and he said he wanted more of the ones who were here now to come to his church.

"I've been where they are," he said, sitting in the small office in the basement of the church. "I know what it's like to be down-and-out and living poorly. I've been there. The people who started this church was just poor country people up from the South to dig potatoes by hand. There was work here and they came, and they were glad for the work.

"Hard work every day, yet on Sundays they would get dressed up in their very best clothes and come to this little church and hear the word of God, hear that Jesus Christ loves them no matter where they lived or how they lived or whether they had money in their pockets or clothes on their backs. They were glad to hear the word of God. We were so poor when I was a child that my mother used to send us out to the fields to dig up corn that had been plowed under. In the dirt! In the dirt! Yes sir, that's what we ate, and we were thankful for it. We were always thankful for it. My momma taught us to be thankful to God for everything we had."

He told me about being a singer and making good money and then reaching a point in his life when he did not want it anymore.

"I have been down and I have been out. I can tell that to the men who live in that camp today. You come here, I would tell them, and you are coming back to your history. Your history is right inside this church. I know what it is like to be lost and aimless and not have two cents in your pocket. I know that. I lived that. But the word of God saved me, and I am here to tell them that. The word of God saved me, yes it did. Listen to me."

Over the summer and into the fall, two longtime church members, Frances Wilson and Leslie Bates, Jimmy Wilson's friend, had died. When I saw Jimmy Wilson on an afternoon in November, he seemed as if he was having a hard time getting used to his friend's death.

"I knew he was sick; everybody knew he was sick," he said. Wilson loaded fifty-pound bags of potatoes and big heads of cauliflower onto a table by the road near his house. His friend's empty home stood next door, as dark as a tomb. "He couldn't bend over. It's not his heart. It's like his lungs was filled up or something. He'd been to the hospital for tests. But there was nothin you could see. He's dead, that's the truth of it.

"The funeral was up at the church. Everyone come. Pastor Fulford, he asked me to say somethin, and I just couldn't do it. We been like brothers so long. He and his family used to live behind the church before they moved here. I know'd his children since they was born. He was my son's godfather. I'd of got up there and I'd have broke down. The good Lord knows best."

A car pulled up to the stand and he sold a woman a bag of potatoes and some turnips. "Oh, they look so good," the woman said.

"Course they look good," he said, smiling.

Walking back toward his kitchen door, I asked him if he knew Bates from the South. No, he said, they had met at a fertilizer factory in Riverhead. Wilson said he knew very little of his own history, and did not much care, either.

His chickens were in crates, waiting to be killed and frozen for the winter. The last of the summer's tomatoes sat on a table outside the kitchen door. The late-afternoon light bent over the treetops, and under the boughs of a maple tree outside the kitchen door, the shadows grew longer. There was a chill in the air.

He went inside looking for a knife to cut the green off a head of cauliflower.

"I was born in Georgia; my grandmother told me that. A little place outside of somewhere. I left when I was four or five. We went to Florida. There was work there cleanin places out. I went with my aunt. My mother was dead. I guess my dad was dead, too. I don't know. I have never thought about it much.

"My grandmother's name was Julia. I lived with her. There was no money in Georgia. Everyplace in Georgia is poor, as far as I'm concerned. In Florida, a man could make twelve dollars a day. I was grubbin, cleanin out land, diggin up roots. I worked all my life even when I was making two dollars a week. No one took care of me since I am nine years old.

"I come up to Jersey to work on farms and I was makin sixty dollars a week. That farm, the people who had it, they was all right. You know everybody got their problems. I'm just glad to be alive, if you want to know the truth. All I'm doin now is trying to make a dollar I can hold on to."

I spoke with Marty Sidor the week before Thanksgiving. The week before that, Chris, still unconscious, had been moved to a rehab center in Connecticut. As soon as he arrived, he spiked a high fever and had to be moved to a hospital. Now he was back on Long Island.

"His fever went to a hundred and five and it looked very bad. We don't know whether the ride up there was too much for him or what. I guess he wasn't ready to be taken anywhere. The hope was that with therapy we could wake him up and see what kind of damage he has. We still don't really know what we have, after all these months.

"Today his fever's back down, which is good. But this means something is still very wrong. I hoped we were further along. After the first of the year, after we get through Christmas, which is going to be tough, we'll make some kind of decision about what the next move is."

He said he was working most mornings at the grader. "Prices are somewhat down, but I guess you can't have everything," he added as we said good-bye.

A few days before Thanksgiving, I drove to Bill Wickham's barn and found Eddie standing at the bottom of the driveway, clutching a small bag and waiting for the bus. The morning was warm; a thick ground fog swirled around the sunken hollows in the land north of Fort Neck.

"I'm all messed up. My chemistry's off. I can't catch my breath. I gotta go for dialysis. I'll be at the hospital all day."

I mentioned Bates's death, and he said, "My God, when was it, two weeks or so, I saw him up at the store, sitting on the bench. He told me when he laid down at night you could hear that rattling sound in his throat. I meant to go to the funeral at his church up there. I should have gone."

David arrived on his tractor, and presently John Tuthill pulled up in his pickup. David was now without his two Puerto Rican helpers, Angel and David. On Saturday, they had flown back home for the winter, each with a few thousand dollars.

John did not get out of his car. I asked David why, and he said, "He's in a lot of pain. He's got to get some kind of back operation, probably in December."

David had decided to sell the contents of this barn and to hold the potatoes in Ziggy's barn for sale over the long winter. "These are from up north," he said as we walked down into the barn, a wall of potatoes in front of us. "Up over the Middle Road. That was the last field. The best ones came from Ziggy's land. They were planted early. I gave them plenty of water, and it's all good ground. They always said the potatoes on Stan and Les Tuthill's were the best, but I think Ziggy's are just as good."

I had heard from a friend who had spoken to the bachelor Tuthill brothers a few days before that Les had seemed uncharacteristically bitter. "He misses his chickens and he said, 'Why did everything have to change so much?'" the friend told me.

It was nearly nine o'clock, and John backed up the pickup to head for Stan and Les's for morning coffee. The three elderly men were the last residents of Tuthill Town, the end of a long family dynasty, and on this morning they would sit around the kitchen table and say a few words and nod good-bye when John left for his truck. Nod good-bye as if there would be more morning coffees, when, as far as anyone knew, Tuthill Town any day now might be shut down forever.

I mentioned I'd seen Eddie waiting for a bus, and David said, "I'm out a lot of people now." I sensed that David was impatient with Eddie, who he believed was not taking care of himself properly. "He's no good if he's sick," David said. "I just hope he can get out of this mess and keep working. I need him."

Using a bucket loader, he filled one potato truck until it was so topped with potatoes that they began to roll off the pyramid onto the ground. We drove to the grader, and David said prices per hundredweight were still in the seven-dollar range, but he feared over the next month they would fall to six-fifty, or even six dollars. A drop to six dollars would mean thousands of dollars in lost income on the potatoes he had stored in Ziggy's barn. All he could do was hope prices would stay up.

When we arrived, we found the workers standing around a small fire burning in a pit alongside the old building. They wore old coats and holey sweatshirts. David's would be their first load of the day, and they walked inside to get to work.

Back at the barn, David said he didn't know what was ahead for him. John seemed to be doing poorly, although he'd been through tough times before and had always gotten out of them. David loved farming, but some days his own future seemed hard to grasp. I sensed that David would do this if he was blind and needed a dog to get around.

"Once the old guys die off, what happens to this farmland?" he asked as he climbed back onto the bucket loader.

At the mouth of the big storage barn, the air smelled like damp earth and dusty potatoes. The morning sun had burned off the last of the ground fog and, standing behind the barn on that big expanse of Bill Wickham's farm, I could see south toward the bay and all the way north to Oregon Road. Bill Wickham's grandfather's grandfather bought this land 210 years ago, and Bill said he would never let it go.

HEAVEN AND EARTH

# Endnotes

## Preface

*only two families have held title to this Wickham land, the Hortons and the Wickhams:* Beginning in the 1660s, when the land was first divided into large tracts, three or four generations of the Horton family farmed a large tract of land in the area that is today west of the hamlet of Cutchogue. The farm ran from the road to Long Island Sound. In 1784, this tract was bought by a John Wickham. The Wickham family genealogy shows that John, who was born in Cutchogue in 1734, was the son of Joseph. John, who died in 1808, passed the land on to his son William, who was one of six children. William was born in 1773 and died in 1859. He passed the land on to his son William, who was born in 1819 and died in 1881. This William was the grandfather of the current William Wickham, who today lives on this same land.

*Frank McBride, grandson of an Irishman who came to Cutchogue a few days after the Battle of Gettysburg:* It is McBride family tradition that Owen McBride arrived on Long Island in the early 1860s and in July 1863 came to Cutchogue, where he bought the farm on which his grandson raises potatoes today.

*Wickham can trace his history back to the Englishmen who arrived in the fall of 1640:* The first Wickham on the North Fork was Joseph, who bought land in Cutchogue in 1698. A descendant of that Joseph married into the Reeve family, and it is acknowledged that members of the Reeve family arrived with the first group of English settlers or, perhaps, even two or three years earlier.

*Where the minister's group landed on the North Fork:* It is accepted that the Reverend John Youngs landed on the bay side, near where a creek emptied into the bay. But there is no solid history that anchors Youngs's landing to a particular spot.

*the English called it the Isle of Wight before Gardiner, now the lord of his own manor, blessed it with his family name:* Gardiners Island, which sits in the bay of the same name north of East Hampton, is today still in the Gardiner family. It is the oldest intact estate of its kind in the United States.

*They also found the native population low:* It is believed by many historians that the diseases that had largely wiped out coastal Algonquin communities farther north spread south into what is now New York State. But exactly what condition the North Fork Indians were in when the English arrived is not known for certain. Diseases hit the Long Island native populations hard in the 1650s, according to the letters of John Davenport.

*The native people, whom the English, in their fumbling attempts to understand Algonquin, called Corchaugs:* The name Corchaug, spelled many different ways, appears in the oldest town records. It may be that the English thought the natives were referring to themselves when they used this word.

# 1. Contact

*In the late fifteenth century, English fishermen began pushing farther and farther west:* David Beers Quinn, an English historian, argues that Bristol fishermen, in need of new fishing grounds, arrived at what is now the coast of North America as early as the 1480s. If this is true, they beat out Columbus by several years.

Quinn includes in his book *England and the Discovery of America, 1481–1620* (Alfred A. Knopf, 1974) the remarkable passage from *The History of the Reign of King Henrie the Seventh*. This brief passage would seem to indicate that the voyage of Columbus was inspired by the exploits of Bristol fishermen.

*The Indians, whom the English regarded as poor users of the land and therefore not its legal owners:* It is well established that Native Americans did not believe land could be *owned*. The English, on the other hand, believed in land ownership and the rights that went with private property. But while the English were quick to argue that the Indians were not the legal owners of the land, they still went through the motions of asking the Indians to sell them the land. This conflicting view—that the Indians did not own the land but could still sell it—did not prevent the English from collecting deeds. Quinn argues that the English, unlike the French, who tried to get along with and understand the Indians, came to despise them as a people and to loathe their customs. The English had an attitude of superiority, Quinn writes, and in re-creating their social order in a new land, they saw the Indians as being in the way.

*By the late 1590s and early 1600s, kidnapped Algonquins began appearing in London:* In his book, Quinn offers considerable evidence that Native Americans were in London as sideshow attractions. Other historians have offered additional evidence. Historian David Cressy has argued that William Shakespeare may have met a group of native Americans in England and based a character in his play *The Tempest* on one of them. In Quinn's account of the canoe demonstration on the Thames, he writes that the Indians were brought to a servant of Lord Cecil, who was later the Earl of Salisbury, and generously paid the sum of four shillings for their performance. The Indians also evidently met a collector named Sir Walter Cope, who in 1588 acquired a long Indian canoe of the kind used by coastal North American Algonquins. What happened to these kidnapped Native Americans? Some were probably turned into servants or entertainers, some may have been allowed to return to America on English vessels, and others may have died when, during the summer of 1603, the plague raged through London and surrounding rural areas.

*One of his men, John Coleman, went ashore and was killed by Indians:* Coleman was not the first European killed by Indians in North America. Five years earlier, a party led by Bartholomew Gilbert, exploring a river north of Chesapeake Bay, was set upon by Indians; there were numerous casualties. The bloodshed between Indians and whites did not end until a cold day in December 1890, when soldiers from the Seventh Calvary, hungry for revenge for the Indian victory at the Little Bighorn fourteen years before, slaughtered a large group of destitute Sioux Indians at Wounded Knee, South Dakota.

## 2. The Migration

*Who was this blond man?:* Historian James Axtell says this man was most likely a Frenchman who survived a shipwreck that occurred in the Plymouth area in approximately 1616, four years before the arrival of the Pilgrims. It is also possible the blond man was an Englishman from a group that landed at what is today Provincetown in June 1603, erected a trading post, and began uprooting sassafras, which was sold in England as a high-priced panacea. The group left for home in August.

*One of these ministers may have been John Youngs:* An account of the Youngs family in England prior to the great migration is contained in a book entitled *Youngs Family—A History and Genealogy,* by Selah Youngs, Jr., published in 1907. The book is part of the local-history collection at the Mattituck Free Library.

*for records show he was refused permission to leave the country:* Some historians believe Youngs was initially refused passage but then was quickly permitted to leave on the same boat. Youngs was said to be a follower of the Reverend William Perkins, who taught Calvinist doctrine. It would seem obvious that Youngs left when the *Mary Anne* did—in May 1637—because three months later, in mid-August, he was living in Salem. It appears Youngs stayed in Salem for three years. In May 1640—four or five months before his supposed arrival on the North Fork—Youngs's servant, a man named Robert, was whipped for stealing on the Lord's day.

## 3. God's Will

*What he knew of this incident, he picked up from old Cutchogue residents: A History of the Cutchogue Presbyterian Church to 1976* was written by Ralph Tuthill and self-published. He was a member of the church for eighty years. The church was built in 1732 and remodeled in 1852.

*except those who traveled to the seacoast to collect shells from which to make wampum:* Wampum was made from the lips of clam shells and the interior column of conch shells. The bluer the shell, the more valuable the wampum. Indians used to drill out the center column of the conch and cut the cylinder into small pieces. The pieces would then have tiny holes drilled through them so they could be strung together. The waters of eastern Long Island were rich in shells and were perhaps the most valuable wampum grounds anywhere on the East Coast. A unit of wampum was called a fathom. A fathom of wampum, strung together on either a hemp or skin cord, was measured from the end of the little finger to the elbow. One fathom was worth five shillings in English Colonial money.

*the journal of Governor John Winthrop:* The journal, published in the mid-1630s, is a valuable look at early English life in Connecticut. It is part of the collection of the library of the State University of New York at Stony Brook. Winthrop's comment in the journal that the eastern Long Island Indians were "very treacherous people" goes unexplained; there is nothing in the earliest records of the towns of the East End that would back this statement up. His comment about "canoes so great as one will carry eighty men" suggests these Indians moved up and down the New England coast in open water. Interestingly, the remains of such a large canoe have never been found.

*a lengthy manuscript published in London in 1638:* This manuscript is part of the history collection at the Queens Borough Public Library. It is perhaps the earliest document of its kind illustrating the tragic relationship between Europeans and Native Americans. It shows that Underhill and his backers were responsible for the deaths of more than one thousand Pequots—the largest mass slaughter of Indians in American history.

*Near the Pequots' main encampment, a log fort had been built:* A fort almost identical to this one was found beside a creek in Cutchogue by the English soon after their arrival on the North Fork. Historians and archaeologists believe similar forts were also built on a hillside in Southampton, near Montauk Point, and on Shelter Island.

*Some escaped to the North Fork to live among the Corchaug people:* Clues that the few survivors of the Pequots' slaughter came to the North Fork were found by archaeologist Ralph Solecki. Later work by archaeologist Lorraine Williams led her to believe that remnants of the Pequot found refuge on the North Fork. Ceramics found at a site in Cutchogue showed a close relationship between Indians on the North and South Forks, as well as a relationship to groups in southern New England, Williams said. There is additional evidence in the arrests, in 1649, of two Pequots for the murder of a Southampton woman. The English demanded the Montauks arrest those responsible for the crime. The two Pequots were located somewhere in the town and then were taken to Harford, where they were promptly executed.

## 4. Water Like Milk

*noting their whereabouts on maps with small x's:* One such map was drawn by Thomas Moore in 1797. It shows the locations of windmills, schoolhouses, and meeting halls. It is filed in the New York State Library, Albany, New York.

## 5. The Dead People

*C. B. Moore, a Southold historian:* Moore, perhaps, had a personal reason to have such an exalted view of the founding families. He was a direct descendant of Thomas and Martha Moore, both of Southwold, England. Martha was a daughter of the Reverend John Youngs, the minister who founded Southold. In some ways, Moore's study of history amounts to little more than ancestor worship.

*he had helped a historian named Peter Ross research a history of Long Island:* Ross's *A History of Long Island—From the Earliest Settlement to the Present Time* was published by the Lewis Publishing Company (New York and Chicago) in 1903. Ross appears to be the first historian of this region to use the word *extermination* in describing the fate of the Indians who lived where the English first settled.

He is also supremely contemptuous of the land transactions between the English and the Indians, arguing that historians had lied about them in order to make the English sound like saints. Of one Brooklyn transaction, he wrote that the natives were given tools and trinkets and then were supposed to be glad "as a matter of charity to be permitted to live on and cultivate a few of the poorest acres. . . ."

In his book, Ross writes of a burial in Canarsie, in Queens County, at which a Mrs. Ramsen made the funeral clothes for the the "last Indian" of that part of Long Island. He says all but a few of the Canarsie Indians were killed by upstate Mohawk Indians during raids.

*It is believed by some that Youngs's group, before their arrival in 1640, had made arrangements to buy the land:* It is also believed that a group of English explorers may have arrived on the North Fork, using as a base the land along a deep creek at the eastern part of the peninsula, two or three years before Youngs's arrival. Their purpose may have been to cut trees or make turpentine. Records show that one Richard Jackson, a carpenter, secured a deed to North Fork land from James Farrett, the agent authorized by the Earl of Stirling to sell real estate on Long Island, in August 1640, a date that precedes Youngs's arrival.

Jackson bought "meadow and upland lying and being upon the north of the river called Mahansuck on Long Island, to the eastward of a place commonly called the Five Wigwams." Because of his occupation, his arrival before Youngs would seem to indicate he was on the North Fork to build homes for future settlers. But Jackson does not seem to have stayed long after Youngs's arrival in the fall of 1640. That October, he sold his house to a sailor named Thomas Weatherly for fifteen pounds.

During the summer of 1639, the year before Jackson bought his land, Farrett took possession of what is today called Shelter Island, the island to the west of the one bought by Gardiner. Important to the debate of who was the first Englishman on the East End of Long Island is the fact that David Gardiner, in a letter to Governor Dongan in 1683, said his father was the first Englishman to settle in the colony of New York.

*The deed describes Mamawetough as the "sachem of Corchaug":* While there were most likely leadership structures within native groups, some historians believe that these sachem titles were invented by the English so that they could have someone with whom to negotiate the selling of native land. I would guess the English found someone they liked and who was pliable to their demands, appointed him the representative of the seller, and then sat down and drafted elaborate deeds only the English could understand. "The English went to a lot of trouble to draw up papers," said archaeologist Lorraine Williams. "They wanted the 'right' people to sign the deeds."

Mamawetough's (spelled Momometou in other documents) name appears on the April 1648 title to thirty thousand acres in East Hampton bought by a group of colonists. In this document, he is described as "the sachem of the Chorchake." In return for signing the deed, the sachems were given twenty coats, twenty-four hatchets, twenty-four knives, and twenty looking glasses. By the time of this sale, the South Fork Indians were under heavy pressure from the Narragansetts, their bitter enemies. They no doubt saw the English as their protectors, which would have given them greater motivation to sell off the land.

The items given the Indians by the English for the thirty thousand acres represents a huge departure from the items given them by Lion Gardiner a decade earlier. For his island, Gardiner gave the Indians a large black dog, which might have been a dinner item, a gun with some ammunition, several blankets, and a quantity of rum—probably used to wash down the dog.

The 1659 deed given to Lion Gardiner by Wyandanch, the sachem of the Montauks, for ten square miles of what today comprises the town of Smithtown, reads as if it were written by Gardiner himself in a moment of extreme self-promotion.

> . . . we had great comfort and reliefe from the most honorable of the English nation heare about us; so that seinge we yet live, and both of us being now olde, and not that wee at any time have given him any thing to gratifie his fatherly love, care and charge, we havinge nothing left that is worth his acceptance but a small tract of land . . .

Referring to this language, Kevin McBride, from the University of Connecticut, said, "They were not Wyandanch's words. He didn't write that."

# 6. Corchaug and Tuthill Town

*were keenly interested in the English living at the far eastern end of Long Island:* By their own writings, the Dutch viewed Long Island, nuzzled up to the island on which they first settled, as a land of enormous promise. A Dutch traveler in 1640 wrote that Long Island was "the crown of the Netherlands." The Dutch were particularly interested in the bays between the North and South Forks because of the enormous quantities of shells used to make wampum, which was as good as cash in trading with the northern Indians for beaver skins. One writer noted that "wampum was the magnet that drew the beaver out of interior forests."

Cornelius Van Tienhoven, an official on Manhattan Island, wrote in 1650 that the waters between the eastern forks were "adorned with divers fair havens and bays fit for all sorts of craft." He said the area was "very convenient for cod fishing, which is most successfully followed by the natives during the season." By grabbing the land along the bay, he wrote that the Dutch could "secure the trade of the natives in wampum, since in and about the above mentioned sea and the island therein lie the cockles whereof wampum is made, from which great profit could be realized by those who would plant a colonie or hamlet. . . ."

*a count done by the Dutch in 1650 shows there were thirty homes in Southold:* The Youngs family genealogy relates this fact; it is confirmed in state records. (Work by a genealogist named Wesley Baker shows thirty-six heads of households in Southold in 1658.) There is no way to determine who these homeowners were, but contained in the Youngs genealogy is this dubious observation: "Among the first to arrive were Matthias Corwin, John Tuthill, Thomas Stevenson, Robert Akerly, Barnabas Horton, John Budd, Abraham Whithear, Thomas and Richard Terry; and later came William Wells, James Haynes, William Salmon, Capt. John Underhill, Thomas Moore, and others."

As for Youngs, the family historian also noted: "It is not questioned that he was the first settler and founder of Southold, Long Island, and next to him in point of time is believed to be Matthias Corwin."

Whoever the homeowners were, it is clear they had to have been like-minded on all matters of religion. There was to be no religious dissent within the plantation controlled by the New Haven Colony. Notwithstanding their own troubles in England, where the drive to religious conformity was said to be so severe that it pushed thousands of people across the ocean, there was to be total conformity in New England and Southold.

In 1643, the general court in New Haven adopted a constitution stating that everyone living within the plantation, including Southold, had to be a member of the approved church and that no one could participate in government who was not a church member.

Quakers were singled out for punishment, and one prominent Southold resident, John Budd, was fined for harboring Quakers. A Southold Quaker named Humphrey Norton was shipped in chains to New Haven for punishment for the crime of "slandering" the Reverend John Youngs. He was fined, "severely whipped," branded with the letter *H* on his hand, and "banished the jurisdiction."

That the English intended to build a Kingdom of God in Southold, as well as in their other southern New England colonies, is evident in the letters of John Davenport. An Englishman born in Coventry, he later lived in Connecticut. See *Letters of John Davenport, Puritan Divine,* ed. Isabel Calder (Yale University Press, 1937).

Davenport favored a strict view of church affairs. Believing the colonies in Massachusetts had become corrupted, he favored moving south into Connecticut with a group of true believers. He learned of the good soil and harbors of the southern New England coastline from soldiers returning from the slaughter of the Pequots.

In the spring of 1638, a group of disillusioned Puritans moved south to set up new, stricter plantations. There, the New Haven Colony was created, which sent its believers to new lands such as Southold. Davenport believed the new towns should be run by a religious elect, men who would administer all town matters and punish all transgressors.

Perhaps better than any Puritan in New England, Davenport articulated the reasons they were there: ". . . namely to advance the kingdom of our lord Jesus Christ, and to enjoy the liberties of the gospel in purity with peace for which we left our dear native Country, and were willing to undergoe the difficulties we have since met with in this wilderness."

*Twenty-one residents were given forty-four lots in Corchaug:* The twenty-one are listed as follows in William S. Pelletreau's history of Southold: William Wells, Barnabas Horton, Wm. Purrier, Barnabas Wines Sr., Barnabas Wines Jr., John Elton, Jeremiah Vale, Richard Terry, Thomas Reeves, Robert Smyth, Mr. Booth, John Corwin, Samuel King, Joseph Youngs Jr., Rich. Benjamin, Thomas Mapes, Thomas Brush, Philemon Dickerson, Benjamin Horton, Wid. Cooper, Tho. Terry.

*"to earn the name we call 'Cutchogue,' meaning 'The principal place'":* Linguists such as Wally Chafe at the University of California at Santa Barbara say there is no way to re-create the meaning of names such as Cutchogue. In the nineteenth century, Long Island historians made long lists of Indian place names and their English translations. For example, Aquebogue was translated as "the end of the water place"; Cutchogue was "the greatest, or principal, place"; Mattituck was "no tree."

Chafe and other experts, including Ives Goddard at the Smithsonian Institution, say the Algonquin dialect spoken on the North Fork—part of the larger Algonquian language family—has been extinct for centuries, so the translations that appeared in the nineteenth century are suspect. These experts also say the native languages were "hyped" by the English in their favor—such words as *tribute* and *gift*—and inserted in land documents, when in all likelihood no such words were spoken.

James Axtell at the College of William and Mary said he doubted Thomas Jefferson was correct when, in his post-Revolution study of Long Island Indian languages, he said that the Indians spoke different languages, to the point where a North Fork Indian could not understand a South Fork Indian. Archaeologist Lorraine Williams agreed: "They all spoke different dialects. But they could talk to one another."

These experts say the East End natives probably spoke a dialect similar to Mohegan-Pequot, which was spoken by the Indians on the Connecticut coast. Therefore, a Montauk could understand a Pequot, but whether native people on the North Fork could fully understand natives on the South Fork is not known for certain.

Lists of native words were drawn up in the late 1700s by a descendant of Lion Gardiner, and ministers such as Azariah Horton, who was born in Southold, are also believed to have drawn up vocabularies. Much of Horton's personal records have never been found.

The parts of Horton's diary that have been found show that in the mid-1740s he traveled all along Long Island's south shore, from what is today Queens to Montauk. While his observations are sparse, it would seem the natives he encountered were destitute and dependent on the white man. This is a sample from his diary:

June 18th. Arrived in Montauk. The Indians gladly received me. Many among them are now sick.

June 19th. Spent most of the day in visiting from wigwam to wigwam, both sick and well.

June 20th. Preached.

June 23rd. Spent most of the day in visiting. Conversed with an Indian and three squaws, who, by the accounts they gave, and their conduct and conversation consequent thereupon, are hopefully converted. And these conversions were wrought, according to their accounts, while I was upon my journey to the western Indians upon Long Island.

*In the forests, the English found spruce trees twenty feet around:* In *Changes in the Land—Indians, Colonists, and the Ecology of New England,* William Cronon points out that in their first shipment back to England, in 1621, the Pilgrims packed only two barrels of furs aboard the fifty-five-ton *Fortune.* The rest of the ship's hold was, as William Bradford reported, "laden with good clapboard as full as she could stow."

White oak, Cronon writes, was used for the timber and planking of ships. It was ideal for barrel staves, as well. Black oak was used for the underwater portions of ships. Pitch pine produced a range of products, including pitch, turpentine, and rosin. The most dramatic tree in the New England forest was the white pine, which was the favored tree for a ship's mast.

From 1630 on, Cronon writes, the largest concentration of commercial lumbering for export was located in the Maine and New Hampshire woods. In these old forests stood tracts of white pine; these tracts contained trees six feet in diameter and two hundred feet in height. Trees of this size and straightness were unknown in Europe.

Prior to the cutting of these magnificent trees in New England—trees so tall, they could be turned into masts without several being spliced together—the English received pieced-together masts of fir from Baltic forests. During the Dutch war of 1654, however, the Baltic trade ended, Cronon writes, and the Royal Navy turned to New England for its wood.

*Once the English had planted their crops and built their homes, they appear to have done well for themselves:* After establishing their farms, the English did what any homeowner would have done in order to ensure he had crops to sell in the fall: He demanded trespassers stay out. Throughout the New Haven Colony, Indians were told to stay away from their new neighbors' cows and other animals. Groups of Indians living in their own villages were held liable for damages to English crops or other property.

Cronon points out that fences defined English property rights, and the construction of fences further reduced the amount of territory on which Indians could roam in search of food. Thus, the dividing up of the land, as well as the enforcement of trespass ordinances, increased English wealth while further reducing the Indians to the level of subsistence farmers. In 1653, authorities in New Haven suggested the Indians fence in their tiny tracts of land to keep English animals out of their crops.

# 7. The Hollow by the Road

*Born in Wethersfield, Connecticut, of English parents, Joseph moved:* Historical records in Wethersfield show that Wickham was also spelled Wikeham, Wickam, Wecam, Wicam, and Wickum. A pamphlet entitled *The History of Ancient Wethersfield,* published in 1904, states that the name "is of Puritan stock dating back to the earliest settlements of New England."

This Joseph Wickham was the son of Thomas Wickham, who had come to Connecticut with the company of the Reverend Ezekiel Rogers, which first settled in New Haven in 1638. Within a year or two, Thomas was established at Wethersfield. Rogers's company had its origins in the vicinity of Yorkshire, England. The Wickhams of Yorkshire can trace their lineage back to the time of the Norman Conquest. Among its earliest members was William of Wykcham, the founder of Winchester College and of New College, Oxford. A William Wickham, a bishop, preached the funeral sermon of Mary, Queen of Scots. Thomas died in 1688. His children were: Thomas, who died as an infant, a second Thomas, Sarah, William, Samuel, Joseph, and John. In 1686 or 1687, both Joseph and John moved to Southampton, on the South Fork. Joseph stayed there until he moved to Cutchogue in 1698; there are no records of what happened to John, although a man named John Wick was living at this time in Bridgehampton.

*Funerals were a weekly occurrence:* Salmon is an old name in Southold. One William Salmon, age twenty-five, left England in 1635. On board the boat with him were Thomas Terrill, age eighteen, and Thomas Reeve, age twenty-four. All three men would come to the North Fork. William's brother, Daniel Salmon, was a soldier in the Pequot War.

*Years later, a writer would find this home overgrown with weeds:* The writer was Dwight Holbrook. The home was later bought and moved to a lot near the ocean in East Hampton.

*They were either bought at the slave market in New York or, more likely, from other farmers on the North Fork:* One Southold historian, Wayland Jefferson, wrote that in 1700 there were forty-one black slaves in Southold and that they all came from the island of Madagascar. It should be noted that Jefferson was not adverse to making up information and passing it off as the fruits of his research.

A list called "Early Settlers of Southold, Suffolk County, Long Island," included in a book entitled *Long Island Source Records* (New York Genealogical and Biographical Record), shows that in the year 1686 there were twenty-seven slaves in the town. This same list shows there were 113 heads of households.

*The British, intent on knowing who opposed them, collected the names of those they called "refugees":* The names of the North Fork refugees were collected in Gregory Mather's *The Refugees of 1776 from Long Island to Connecticut* (J. B. Lyon Co. Printers, Albany, 1913). The book is part of the local history collection at the Cutchogue Free Library.

*Since British troops occupied the North Fork, Wickham Neck was out of the reach of the commissioners:* British officers made the grander homes in Cutchogue and Mattituck their personal headquarters. Troops were camped in open areas near creeks. British troops also converted the Cutchogue Presbyterian Church, founded in 1732 and built on a plot of land a hundred yards north of where Parker Wickham's family lived, into a stable. With the abundance of barns in the area, it would seem the British were making a statement about the church and the people who went there.

*Mary Wickham, his wife, died on March 25, 1780:* There are conflicting dates given for her death. One account says she died in April 1783. Parker and Mary's daughter Mary died in Cutchogue on December 13, 1763. Mary was buried near her daughter on the rounded knob of land to the east of their home, an area that had earlier been designated the Cutchogue cemetery.

*The buyer of the neck farm at an auction was Jared Landon:* Jared Landon bought the house and 240 magnificent acres of farmland, woods, and salt creeks from the commissioners of forfeiture for a total of nine hundred pounds. The owners of the old house that was the centerpiece of the neck farm were as follows: John Budd, then his daughter, Anna, when she married Benjamin Horton; Joseph Horton; Joseph Wickham, who passed it to his son Joseph, who in turn passed it to his son Parker; Jared Landon, who passed it to his son, Henry; Mary Horton, who was Henry Landon's niece; Elijah Horton; William Harrison Case.

# 8. Uncle James

*in Cutchogue, the very land originally bought by William Wells:* One Rensselaer Fleet, of Huntington, Long Island, married Sarah Wells, a fifth-generation descendant of William Wells. Sarah and Rensselaer's grandson was Henry L. Fleet, who for a time was one of the largest farmers in Southold. His 1881 potato crop, on seventeen acres, was said to be worth the tidy sum of five thousand dollars. He was also a breeder of fine horses. Part of the Henry Fleet farm was later bought by John Wickham, whose land bordered the Fleet farm. John liked to say this tract of land had only had two white owners before he bought it, the Wellses and Fleets. There are no Fleets farming in Cutchogue today.

*Perhaps the wealthiest of these Wickhams did not live here:* John Wickham's home in Richmond is today a museum. He was a prominent attorney who, after the Revolution, grew rich representing British businessmen seeking payment of debts in America. He was Aaron Burr's lawyer during Burr's 1807 trial in Richmond for treason. John Marshall was the presiding judge. Burr was found not guilty. The writer Washington Irving, who was a guest at Wickham's home, covered the trial for a New York newspaper.

*In late October, Behan was convicted:* Behan's public hanging in Riverhead was hardly a model for future executions, which may explain why it was the last one held before the public in Suffolk County. The *New York Daily Times* account of his hanging reads as follows:

> At ten minutes past 12 o'clock the Priest signified to the sheriff that "all was ready" and the officer of the law immediately severed the rope, with a heavy blow of the broad axe, the weights fell to the ground, and the wretched man was suddenly elevated into the air. The jerk was not of sufficient

force to dislocate his neck, consequently he struggled very hard, and his life was prolonged in great suffering.

At twelve minutes past 12 o'clock the examining physicians felt the pulse of the dying man. They counted sixty pulsations to the minute. There was but little motion of the body. A minute subsequently the body exhibited considerable spasmodic actions of the muscles with the pulse of "84."

Fourteen and a half minutes past 12 o'clock the doctors ascertained the pulse had been reduced to "64"—the spasmodic action of the muscles still being visible.

At twenty-two minutes past 12 o'clock the body had been suspended for twelve minutes. The medical gentlemen then made their final examination, and finding all pulsations had ceased, he was pronounced to be dead. . . .

After the body had hung forty minutes it was cut down, placed in a common pine coffin, and was conveyed for interment to the middle of a Pine woods belonging to Mr. VINLIN, about a mile distant from the village.

## 9. "Truly, He Was a Good Man"

*William's wife, Sarah Elizabeth Havens:* Havens is an old name on the South Fork. One branch of the family, as told in Peter Matthiessen's extraordinary nonfiction work *Men's Lives*, were baymen in East Hampton. Matthiessen writes: "The first William Havens came from Rhode Island to Shelter Island in the seventeenth century, and his clan would acquire considerable property in North Haven and Sag Harbor. On Shelter Island, the James Havens house (1743) is now a historical monument, and on North Haven (where the family had a British land grant), the beautiful northwest region of the island, called the Stock Farm, was once Havens farmland. The Sag Harbor Havenses were shipbuilders and whalers, and Benny [Havens] says that in the Revolutionary War a Havens whaleboat helped sink a British battleship in Long Island Sound."

## 10. Ernest Tuthill

*"That was the area called Tustin, on the north side of Oregon:* Tustin is a name of mysterious origin. Old town records show a family named Tusten living on the North Fork; it's unclear who they were, where they lived, or whatever happened to them, for that matter. I have gone with the spelling of Tustin with an *i* because the old-timers say it was spelled that way. None of these men or women know how Tustin got its name; it was just always Tustin, for as long as they can remember.

## 11. Workers

*In the late teens and early 1920s, there was a Ku Klux Klan chapter on the North Fork:* At that time in the United States, the Klan was at its most popular, able to boast of a million or more members. Huge parades of men in white sheets and pointy hats were a feature in Washington, D.C. In many communities, the Klan enjoyed a kind of respectability, and it even gave out local awards to firemen and other groups. As a sign of the Klan's limited activity here, no black men I interviewed who lived on the North Fork in the twenties said they knew the Klan was there. The older Irish, on the other hand, say they knew who the "Klukers" were.

*Photographs of the camp show bungalows set close to one another:* The photographs are the property of John McDonald, a *Newsday* reporter. John says they were taken by an employee of a now-closed Suffolk County agency that monitored conditions in the camps.

# 12. Spring of 1987: Transition

*So he took a minister, a Reverend Sinclair:* The church lasted from approximately 1861 until the early part of the twentieth century. John Wickham and his two brothers, Parker and Henry, were among the last members. Today, this church is part of the Cutchogue Free Library. It sits on what is now called the village green. On the green are two old Wickham houses, including the one bought in 1698 by Joseph Wickham, plus an old schoolhouse. A historical marker says the former Joseph Wickham house is the oldest English-built home in New York State. It was John Wickham's mother, Cora, and John's aunt Julia who were the driving forces behind the creation of the village green.

*"But he had broken his neck and died immediately":* There are a few people in Cutchogue who remembered Parker's death on the road east of the Wickham farmhouse. One, an eyewitness, lived in a home almost exactly where the accident took place. This man said he looked out when the fire engine passed and saw the Wickham car speeding down the road, John behind the wheel. Parker was standing on the running board the way a fireman might stand on the side of the fire truck. "He was standing there, I remember that," the man said, "just flying along. Then there was the sudden braking, and I think he just got thrown."

# 13. The Wheel of History and Indian Summer

*Along with a small number of public figures, John had helped create the county's innovative farmland preservation program:* Among the most important of these public figures was former Suffolk County executive John V. N. Klein. This program resulted in thousands of fertile acres being set aside permanently.

*He was also the father of the North Fork's wine industry:* John Wickham's experiments with table grapes convinced Alex and Louisa Hargrave to plant the first wine-producing grapes on an old potato farm in Cutchogue. Today, there are approximately three thousand acres of vineyards on the East End.

*At a time when the German owner of Robins Island was talking about bulldozing its woods:* The German later sold the island to a wealthy New York investor. In the winter of 1995, the new owner worked to remodel an old home on the island as part of an effort to turn the island into a family retreat.

# 14. A Cold Winter

*I knew that Stephen Wickham, Parker's younger son, who was four months old at the time of his father's death, had died a few years later:* Stephen was enrolled in the elementary school across the street from the family's farm stand. Walking home from school in the mid-1930s, he was struck and killed by a car. The section of road on which he was killed is less than a quarter of a mile from where his father died. Parker's oldest son, Jimmy, would years later receive crippling injuries in a car wreck. He still lives in Cutchogue, in the home on Wickham Creek his father built when he was first married. Parker's widow, Margaret, years after her husband's and son's tragic deaths, took her own life.

# 15. A Wet Spring

*This is all open land on the south side:* After his election, Tom Wickham made it a priority to push for the public acquisition of this land. Several years before his election, a joint purchase by the town of Southold and Suffolk County had been successfully negotiated with the land's owner, but the county later reneged on the deal, trying to reduce the purchase price—a price that had already been agreed on. In the fall of 1994, a town effort also failed to budge the tract's owner into selling. In the winter of 1995, this wide tract of land lay open and beautiful, a gateway into the hamlet of Cutchogue.

*Proponents of the bridge labeled the North Fork the "dead end" of Long Island:* The loudest voice in support of the construction of a bridge from the eastern end of Long Island to Connecticut was *Newsday,* the daily newspaper. In pushing for this idea, the newspaper went so far as to find obscure and even out-of-office state politicians in Connecticut to support the construction. At one time, when Connecticut continued to laugh off the idea, the newspaper printed a story suggesting a bridge from Orient Point, at the extreme tip of the North Fork, to somewhere in Rhode Island was a sound idea.

# 17. Corchaug Pond

*The simple truth is that the "history" these historians pursued was, at best, incomplete:* It was, in one glaring example, fraudulent and dishonest. In the late 1930s, Southold's town historian, Wayland Jefferson, concocted out of thin air a document purporting to show that a group of English businessmen and adventurerers had arrived on the North Fork in 1636–1637—three years before the arrival of the Reverend John Youngs— to cut trees and make turpentine. While it had always been believed that such a group may have been in the town then, no definitive proof had ever been found—until Jefferson came up with a document called the Osman Deposition. At the time he said he found it, Southold was preparing to celebrate its tercentenary, as was the town of Southampton on the South Fork, and each town was saying it was the "first" English settlement on the East End.

To prove Southold was first, Jefferson invented a document listing the names of a group of men who were in the eastern part of the town in 1636–1637. He reprinted the document in the town's official tercentenary booklet. It seems as though the document was never seen by anyone but Jefferson, who later claimed he gave it to a historical society. Efforts by individuals years later to find the document show the society never received it. On top of that, the family of the man from whom Jefferson said he received this three-hundred-year-old piece of paper said later it was never in their possession.

*Or, perhaps, across the bay to the wide, open meadows at Montauk:* This area was the ancestral homeland of the Montauk people, and it is very possible that Corchaugs fled there to live among them. Hoping to live Indian lives, many Montauks were later to move to upstate New York; from there, some moved west to Wisconsin. What happened to the Montauks is yet another example of how native people were cheated out of their land. After the 1879 death of Stephen "Talkhouse" Pharoah, a whaler and one of the last members of his tribe, Montauk Point was purchased by a real estate promoter named Arthur Benson. A tiny group of Montauks sued, claiming he had no legal right to buy the land, but the courts ruled against them, saying there really was no Montauk people or culture left, which was not true at all. As recounted in Peter Matthiessen's *Men's Lives,* a Montauk named Wyandank Pharoah, in a 1916 letter to the East Hampton *Star,* said of the court rulings: "Plenty of law but very little justice."

Today, a tiny group of people who claim Montauk ancestry say they want to put together a list of their people.

*The letter shows the Corchaugs were still around on the eve of the Revolution:* I found this extraordinary letter in a collection at the Massachusetts Historical Society, in Boston. It is interesting to note that some of those who signed this letter have names more associated with the Montauk people. This letter refutes the widely held belief by some historians that the North Fork Indians were gone by the early 1700s.

Supporting documents, such as the correspondence of state officials and attorneys who sought to help the Corchaugs, were located at both the MHS and the New York Historical Society.

It seems a little more than curious that these documents were not found in Southold archives. To me, it suggests that early residents of the town, hoping to cover their tracks with regard to whatever agreements were made with the Indians, "lost" key documents.

## 21. John Tuthill and Early Digging

*The three men were related on two sides of their families, the Hallocks and the Tuthills:* The branch of the family tree where both lines join looks like this:

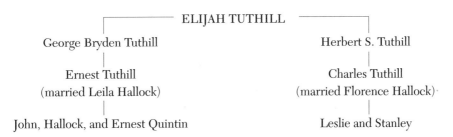

Leila Hallock and Florence Hallock were sisters.

## 23. Fall and Chris Sidor

*By the third week of September, the potato harvest still under way, a friend phoned me and said Chris Sidor, Marty and Carol's son, had been in a horrible car wreck near their home:* A friend of Chris Sidor's was driving the vehicle. Police say the driver struck a car driven by Janet Van Tuyl, killing her and injuring her infant daughter. Mrs. Van Tuyl was eulogized as a wonderful mother, wife, and daughter, as well as an active member of her church.

## 24. Upon This Rock

*I spoke with Marty Sidor the week before Thanksgiving:* By the middle of the winter of 1995, the horrible tragedy of Chris Sidor's accident had become fully evident. Although doctors believed Chris had not suffered permanent brain damage in the accident, they told the family he would, barring a miracle, never regain his eyesight. Throughout February and into March, Chris's therapists were teaching him such basic exercises as how to eat again.

His father, Marty, one of the best people in the tiny farming community of Mattituck and Cutchogue, was so dispirited he talked of not farming again when planting resumed in April.

*John did not get out of his car:* John Tuthill had major back surgery in December, and when he came home he rested on the couch in his living room as winter settled in. I saw him in the middle of February and he looked like he had lost a lot of weight. But the smile and dry sense of humor were still there.

All fall, I had wanted to ask him about the death of his son, Edward. On a cold Sunday afternoon, I sat at his living room table, he at his old desk. I mentioned Edward's death. He looked sad for a moment and said, "There's no way of knowing why some things happen." I said, "But his death leaves you as the end of the line, isn't that right? After three and a half centuries."

Yes, he said, that was right. "I guess you could say that's the way it worked out."

*We drove to the grader, and David Steele said prices per hundredweight were still in the seven-dollar range:* Prices did fall in late December, and one day David told me he figured he had lost twenty thousand dollars in profits just on the potatoes he had in storage in Ziggy Kurkoski's barn. "You can't make up a loss like that, no way," he said.

By February, the news was gloomier. The Cooperative Extension Association said that bacteria fed by the summer's intense heat had destroyed 10 percent of the East End's 6,500-acre potato crop. The association estimated that the area's potato farmers had lost more than $1 million.

In mid-March, a month before spring planting was to commence, David said, "We go on because that's what we do. But it's hard. It's always hard."

In late March, Noble Funn, a black man who came to Cutchogue when he was sixteen years old, died in his bungalow on the Glover farm. He was seventy-three years old, and had worked his entire life for one family.